THE QUALITY AUDIT FOR ISO 9001:2000

❖

THE QUALITY AUDIT FOR ISO 9001:2000

A practical guide

❖

David Wealleans

Gower

Published by
Gower Publishing Limited
Gower House
Croft Road
Aldershot
Hampshire GU11 3HR
England

Gower
Old Post Road
Brookfield
Vermont 05036
USA

David Wealleans has asserted his right under the Copyright, Designs and Patents Act 1988 to be identified as the author of this work.

British Library Cataloguing in Publication Data
Wealleans, David
    The quality audit for ISO 9001:2000 : a practical guide
    1. ISO 9001 Standard   2. Auditing   3. Quality control
    I. Title
    658.5'62

ISBN 0 566 08245 4

Library of Congress Cataloging-in-Publication Data
Wealleans, David.
    The quality audit for ISO 9001:2000 : a practical guide / David
Wealleans.
        p. cm.
    ISBN 0-566-08245-4 (hardback)
    1. ISO 9000 Series Standards–Auditing Handbooks, manuals, etc.
    2. Compliance auditing Handbooks, manuals, etc.   I. Title.
TS156.6.W44   2000
658.5'62–dc21   99-40394
                                                                                              CIP

Typeset in Garamond by IML Typographers, Chester and printed in Great Britain at the University Press, Cambridge.

CONTENTS

❖

FIGURES

❖

PREFACE

❖

I attended my first quality audit training course in 1980. It was a five-day event, centred mostly around the requirements of the UK defence quality standard 05-21, with a passing reference to the little known new publication BS 5750 (which is, today, commonly acknowledged as the primary antecedent of ISO 9001). I did not attend because I wanted to learn how to audit. I went to learn about what would be required of a quality management system capable of certification. As a young acting quality manager at a cable factory I had been asked to gain BS 5750 for the company and needed to understand what we had to do.

As far as I remember, the course lessons consisted mostly of discussing what was and was not acceptable within a formal quality management system. Auditors would have to make this judgement and therefore would have to know how to interpret requirements. I remember learning about the rules for checking soldering iron temperature, calibration record traceability and forklift truck driver certification but little about audit technique.

The audits, in my plan, were actually to be carried out by other members of the quality department, who would receive no other training than a brief explanation by myself and one other course graduate about how it should work. The audit programme was not seen as central to the project whose priorities were far more about the progress of document production.

Things have changed a lot since then. Interpretation of the requirements of standards is now seen as less important than good systems investigation, and quality auditing is taken far more seriously than it was. There is, though, still a long way to go. There remain many external auditors whose training took place in less enlightened times and internal auditors whose training is only just better than non-existent. The more that I both conduct audits and train others how to do it the more I see that the process has enormous potential which is only occasionally realized. I have also become conscious that many auditors graduating from a short training course feel barely equipped to go and do it on their own. They are certainly not ready to do it well and may find it hard to remember everything that they were taught whilst performing the juggling act that is the quality audit.

For these reasons, plus the fact that I never seem to have enough time in a training course to say everything that I think needs to be said, I decided to put my ideas into print. The fact that ISO 9001:2000 was also about to be released was an added bonus, as it gave me an opportunity to discuss quality auditing in the context of the re-invented update of the widely adopted standard.

I hope that those of you who are new to auditing find this book a useful reference tool, offering support and reinforcement of what you learnt at initial training and more detailed exploration of some of the elements of auditing than could be covered in your course of study. I also hope that more experienced auditors may find it of benefit, updating your thoughts on the subject, looking at how different auditors will approach the subject and gaining some understanding of the philosophy and requirements of ISO 9001:2000.

ACKNOWLEDGEMENTS

❖

My thanks to the British Standards Institution for permission to reproduce the process model diagram from ISO 9001:2000 and to refer to some of the text of ISO 9001:2000.

ABBREVIATIONS

❖

AQAP	Allied Quality Assurance Publication
ASQ	American Society for Quality
BSI	British Standards Institution
CPD	Continuing professional development
CQA	Certified Quality Auditor
IRCA	International Register of Certificated Auditors
ISO	International Standards Organization
PDCA	Plan-do-check-act
TQM	Total quality management

PART ONE

PUTTING THE AUDIT IN CONTEXT

❖

1

INTRODUCTION TO AUDITING

❖

BACKGROUND

Auditing is a long-established business discipline. It has certainly been around since long before I became involved in business management. Some have even argued that audits go back to the earliest recorded times, for example the device used by Gideon (Judges 7: 4–8) whereby he eliminated some of his army based upon the way that they drank from the river could be considered as an auditing technique followed by some decisive action.

If auditing has been around that long, it is surprising that so few organizations use quality auditing as a tool until it is demanded by ISO 9001 or similar standards. Yet quality auditing is one of the activities that is usually completely new to organizations introducing quality management for the first time.

FINANCIAL AUDIT

Other forms of auditing are more commonly accepted. The most obvious of these is the financial audit. Everybody understands that the financial statements of incorporated companies (both public and private) are subject to independent audit by qualified persons. This is intended to achieve a number of things. First, it is a safeguard against a company falsifying its financial position and thus cheating its shareholders, creditors, the tax office or other stakeholders. Second, it may help the company itself to identify weaknesses in its own financial processes. There is probably also a third purpose, which is generally stronger for public companies than it is for private, which is to provide an independently published, publicly available, statement of the company's financial status.

Statutory financial audit normally succeeds in the third objective, and quite often meets the first. Whether or not it achieves the second depends upon

3

whether one is speaking to the auditors or the company being audited. I often see things being done that management think are a waste of time but they are complying because their auditors have told them to. This often occurs because the auditors (not just financial ones, now, but all types) feel that they have a degree of power. They are thus reluctant to come away without feeling that they have added something, but may make recommendations without a detailed understanding of the precise nature of the operations involved. We will return to this theme later in the book.

Thinking about the financial audit does give us an initial idea of what auditing in general is all about. Readers should not, however, treat this as the sole model for understanding its nature. It differs from other types of audit in some important ways:

○   Statutory auditors spend far more time looking at records than do most other auditors, who place greater emphasis on study of operations and talking to people.
○   Most auditors rely on random samples, but the financial version typically ploughs through entire files, item by item and 'signs them off' at the end.
○   Financial auditing is a specialized discipline requiring difficult-to-obtain qualifications; most quality auditors need relatively simple qualifications together with a reliance on operational experience and a sprinkling of basic commercial common sense (quality auditor competence will be dealt with in some detail later in the book).

Indeed, some accountants attending training courses that I have run complained that their training took years, whilst the registration criteria for quality auditors involves simply attending a short course and gaining a few days' audit experience. The difference is that financial auditors need to be experts in finance but quality auditors are expected to be observant and analytical, not necessarily quality management experts.

HEALTH AND SAFETY AUDIT

In addition to the financial variety, we have historically seen a number of other types of audit. Probably the next most common of these is the health and safety audit. Most of us have experienced these, either from regulatory authorities, internal teams, or both. They are typically closer to the spirit of the quality audit than is the financial variety. They cannot, by definition, attest to the compliance of everything and are typically more concerned with the future than the past.

Health and safety audits have also been with us a long time. Ever since civilization has been concerned with the preservation of industrial life and limb, companies have been audited to ensure that they are adopting the right approach. These have evolved from the early days of simple observation to modern techniques which also take historical records into account to confirm legal compliance. They have thus grown close to the way that quality audits are conducted.

It is especially interesting to note that H&S audits have come from both external and internal teams of people taking time out of their main jobs. This shows a direct parallel with the quality audit.

THE QUALITY AUDIT

The quality audit undoubtedly began with the customer inspection. It has been a long-established practice for major companies to carry out on-site evaluations of their most important suppliers and sub-contractors. These have typically been intended to:

O   prove the 'technical' capability of the organization to provide the product or service;

O   check that the company has sufficient capacity and resources to cope with the customer demands;

O   confirm the commercial stability of the company;

O   assess the rigour of the organization's operational processes (e.g. will the work be looked after, or are they likely to misplace the paperwork);

O   form an opinion as to whether this is the type of organization that we would like to do business with (this is not usually formally acknowledged as an objective, but in fact is often the primary motive).

Customer audit teams have traditionally been led by a member of the procurement group, and would usually also contain a technical expert. The inclusion of a quality assurance professional is, by and large, a relatively recent innovation. Customer audits (often known as 'second party' audits) are typified by the following characteristics:

O   They are only interested in things which directly relate to that customer's business (in fact, confidentiality requirements may preclude the team having access to other data).

O   They are highly prescriptive, often insisting upon certain technical, operational or commercial procedures.

Customer audits are often conducted before permitting use of a new supplier, as part of a contract award process or to confirm continued suitability to supply. In the past, as these assessments became ever more popular tools, the recipients began to complain of their frequency. After all, each one requires preparation, is disruptive on the day and every customer has their own, sometimes conflicting, requirements. Their complaints were the main drivers behind the concept of independent ('third party') audits.

Customer audits are still as strong as they ever were. Companies still wish to prove that their own needs are being met and have strengthened the use of assessing their suppliers' systems as a key tool.

THIRD PARTY AUDITING

From the international similarity of quality management standards imposed by the various defence ministries was born the idea that a common standard could be applied to all commercial companies. This, it was reasoned, would allow organizations to create quality plans which would conform to a unitary standard and thus avoid the need to adopt differing approaches for each strong customer. This was closely followed by a logical extension: that there should only need to be a single audit which would confirm that the single standard was being followed. Ultimately the concept of independent, accredited, third party certification, which would be acceptable to every customer, was introduced. This would be the end of awkward and disruptive multiple customer audits. Unfortunately (for every supplier to major corporations) this did not work: each customer still felt that it had its own specific needs which were not met by a generic standard. Thus they continued to conduct their own audits. This is still the case. In fact what has happened is that these customers now expect both independent certification and satisfactory findings from their own audits. There appears to be no resolution to this in sight and it seems that we will simply have to accept it until some completely new approach is, one day, adopted.

WHAT IS AUDITING?

Auditing is simply checking the way that things are being done. It is a tool for making sure that activities are being carried out correctly, without relying on just asking people or waiting until it is too late.

To illustrate what I mean by this, let us look at the example of a customer seeking to award a major contract. If the procurement director simply asks, 'Do you always follow all the rules?' then the supplier would be unbelievably stupid to answer, 'No'. On the other hand, it is too late if you award the contract and only discover after some time that the supplier's disciplines are sloppy.

There is sometimes confusion between auditing and inspection. This is understandable; there is indeed some overlap. In fact the financial audit is certainly a form of inspection. For most types of audit, though, there is a difference. Inspection is intended to tell us whether something is okay to proceed. For example, to decide whether or not the widget that we have just made is acceptable for delivery to the customer. Inspection is mostly checking work that *has* been done. Auditing, alternatively, is about telling whether or not the processes used are likely to produce successful outcomes. For example, if a customer calls tomorrow and orders a widget, are they likely to be given the right item, on time and in good condition? Audits are about gaining some assurance of future good performance, based upon current observations. Sometimes, though, it is hard to distinguish between the two (e.g. if a supervisor carries out a monthly audit of the cleanliness of company vans). The answer to any confusion arising between the two is not to worry about it too much; as long as the desired level of checking and evaluation is carried out, what does it matter what we call them?

WHAT IS *QUALITY* AUDITING?

The quality audit is intended to ensure that our business processes are designed and operated in such a way that the customer's contract requirements (both stated and implied) are met. For those readers about to drop this book in dismay, saying that in their business they do not have formal contracts, it is worth pointing out that the laws of most nations consider that there is always a contract between buyer and seller, whether or not it is written down in a formal document.

Quality audits may be of an organization by itself (sometimes referred to as 'first party', but usually just 'internal'), by a customer assessing a supplier or subcontractor ('second party') or an independent assessor certifying against a recognized standard ('third party'). There are also audits carried out by consultants or other technical experts to identify problems or potential improvements; these have their own characteristics but for the purpose of definitions and formalities are usually thought of as a variation of the internal audit. These types of audit all have their own differing secondary purposes. Their main intent, though, is to give increased confidence that the organization is capable of meeting customer needs (note that audits do look, to some extent, at whether we *are* meeting customer requirements but concentrate more on whether we are *likely* to meet customer needs as and when they arise).

Thus quality audits are typically concerned with the business processes which form, agree and check the contract; plan and communicate how it will be delivered; how the contract itself is fulfilled (production, design, repair, etc.); how the success of fulfilment is evaluated and how the organization monitors performance and handles problems. This is a wide scope but some (not all) quality audit programmes include restrictions on which areas do directly contribute to contract performance, others being excluded from the audit regime. Some common exclusions from quality audit systems are listed below:

O   Many of the things designed to attract customers in the first place (promotion, marketing communication, front-end sales). The new version of ISO 9001 has strengthened the inclusion of marketing elements in the coverage of identifying customer expectations, but it still leaves out much of the marketing activity;

O   Most, or all, financial affairs;

O   Taxes and levies;

O   Strategy;

O   Health and safety (this is deliberate, since it is usually covered elsewhere);

O   Most personnel activities, other than training and development;

O   Employee social activities;

- O   Salaries and rewards;
- O   Works councils, trade unions and other employee representation;
- O   Security;
- O   Premises and building services (unless this is a direct part of the supply, such as in hotels);
- O   Catering;
- O   Travel, company cars and employee expenses;
- O   Environment; 'green' issues (since, like health and safety, this is covered elsewhere).

It is certainly likely that there are many people out there working in other areas, too, who can tell tales of their surprise at being ignored by quality auditors.

The one area not mentioned above (about whose deserved but often absent place in quality management systems I feel quite strongly) is information technology (IT). For many companies, IT is one of the single most, if not the most, influential function. It has an intimate relationship with every other activity in the organization and has a profound impact on many business processes, far more so than some dusty policy document sitting, forgotten, on a shelf. If a procedure manual tells me to do something in a certain way, and I do not particularly feel like it today, then I will not bother. But if the only way that I can do it is via the computer network, then it is usually pretty difficult to by-pass any of it. Yet so many auditors pay IT scant attention. If they do consider computer systems, they usually confine themselves to asking perfunctory questions about data back-up, virus control and (for a limited time) if the Y2K problem has been dealt with.

This approach is too narrow. What about the content, suitability, verification and control of that expensive company-wide SAP system? Or, even worse, the order processing and stock control program written by the corporate systems group? We should be applying design control and testing rules to such processes as well as basic configuration management.

To re-cap, then, a quality audit is about seeing whether the organization is capable of meeting customer needs (it also looks, to some extent, at whether it *has* met those but at a general level rather than the specifics which are more the realm of inspection). For some, this will include areas which do not directly impact upon customer satisfaction but exactly where the line is drawn is subject to variation.

WHO DOES IT?

The answer to the question of who carries out quality audits is the same as to that of who can carry out any other activity – somebody competent. 'Competence' is a well used, fashionable management word at the moment. Any HR professional with an ounce of oomph could probably draft a book longer than this one on the subject. The thrust of the message would most likely be that demonstrating an acceptable level of capability is more important than simple qualifications or experience (neither of which, it is true, are guarantees of performance).

This philosophy of competence applies well to quality auditors. For example, most auditors need to be trained, but do not require formal qualifications (with the exception of third party certification auditors, as discussed in more detail in Chapter 6).

Apart from capability in audit techniques, judgement of competence should also include some assessment of whether the auditor understands what he or she is auditing. There is no point, for example, sending somebody who knows nothing about engineering or manufacturing to audit a machine shop as they probably will not even understand half of the words used.

Third party certification auditors are usually quality professionals, exposed to quality management in industry for several years before taking up a job with a registered certification agency. Some of these agencies also use sub-contract auditors to help balance workload peaks and troughs, but effectively the same selection criteria are applied to these as for full-time assessors.

Where companies send auditors to their suppliers, they are usually subject specialists. This enables them directly to assess the capabilities of the potential sub-contractor. Indeed, in such visits technical skills are usually seen as more important than audit skills. Occasionally, companies may elect to use consultants rather than their own employees to do this on their behalf. A working example of this is the use of local specialists to assess potential overseas suppliers or agents, thus saving considerable costs (commercial sections of embassies and consulates, for example, will provide this service, within certain constraints).

Internal auditors (that is, those who monitor an organization's compliance with its own policies) are usually selected from amongst the organization's own employees. Anybody can be chosen. Members of the quality department often act as auditors, but they could just as easily come from the ranks of finance, operations, sales, development or personnel. It is important, though, to ensure that they possess the confidence and the interpersonal skills to carry it off. A school-leaver trainee who would not dare to ask a manager a detailed question, let alone point out errors or omissions, would not be a good choice.

INDEPENDENCE

When looking at the 'who' of auditing, one last consideration is independence. It is accepted that auditors should always be independent of the function being audited. This is emphasized more than once in the ISO quality standards. The most independent of auditors is the third party certification assessor, who is employed neither by the organization nor by its customer(s). Indeed, some certification bodies require assessors to sign a statement that they have no family, work or other connection with the organization before the job is finally allocated (one wonders, though, how they ever find anyone to audit organizations like British Telecom, or Marks and Spencer).

I suppose that we ought to acknowledge here that even third party auditors are not truly independent. After all, they are paid for what they do by the organization that they audit and they wish to continue being paid (worldwide there are hundreds of organizations, hungry for new contracts, who are qualified to do the job). This must, inevitably, introduce some element of commercial pressure. On balance, though, the commercial aspect intrudes little into such audits by accredited certifiers and the assessors can thus be thought of as truly independent.

Second party auditors are often the least independent, at least in terms of their outlook. They certainly *are* working on behalf of the customer and will have specific objectives from their employer, in whose best interests they are working. They must still, though, maintain their impartiality in that they should have no 'axe to grind' about the particular supplier being audited. They should not, for example, have a brother that works there, nor be 'out to get them' because their sister was sacked by the company two years ago.

On the face of it, internal auditors do not seem to be independent at all, since they are quite likely to work closely, every day, with the people that they are interviewing. In practice, though, most internal auditors adopt a fair and professional approach, doing their best to avoid expressing personal criticisms or trying to follow their own agenda. This is not to say that internal auditors should ignore prior knowledge. If, for example, the auditor knows of a possible problem, then it is quite right to investigate it. The benefit of this is that a known, or suspected, problem can be pinned down and formally allocated for action. There are some cautionary points to note:

○   The auditor should not be looking to punish a department for perceived personal reasons ('they make my life difficult every day, so I'm going to make them squirm during the audit').

○   There must be an investigation; an auditor who decides what problems to report even before the audit begins is not acting professionally.

HOW DOES IT WORK?

Quality audits tend to follow a fairly fixed format. First, the auditor collects information on requirements that have to be met, including laws and regulations, standards, customer requirements, objectives, plans, policies and standard operating procedures. The relevant activities are then sampled, at a detail level, to ensure that those requirements are being met, both on an individual and on a global basis. This is accomplished through a mixture of observation, interviewing and examination of records. Any instances of requirements not being met, or where the auditor believes improvements can be made, are included in verbal and written reports. A formal response to each point in the report is expected from the organization or area audited. The response should be aimed more at prevention of recurrence than at correcting the immediate discrepancy.

PRODUCING RESULTS

The answer to the question of whether quality audits really produce results depends enormously upon whom we ask and it is always difficult to guarantee objectivity. Certification assessors, for example, are impressively eager to tell of how independent auditing brings about valuable discipline. Most will even emphasize that they are able to 'add value' by judicious application of their skills and experience (a dubious concept in this case, as we will discuss later). Internal and second party auditors may well offer similar stories.

The real danger of all audits is that everybody involved may be there simply to go through the motions. This happens more often than many of those in the business would care to admit. It is especially common in routine, scheduled audits in a mature situation. The auditor has seen it all before and may raise one or two trivial comments, but otherwise devotes little effort to the process. In these cases, the answer has to be: no, the audit does not produce any useful results. If this is happening the organization needs to do something to inject more energy into the process.

Despite what many external assessors may believe, certification audits themselves rarely produce substantial business improvements. Indeed, since the purpose of these audits is to grant or maintain a certificate, then the emphasis is on 'passing'. Most organizations view the certification assessor's visit as something that has to be seen through with as little pain as possible. These audits are too shallow and too general to provide much more than a general confirmation of whether or not the organization meets the required standard. Probably the largest benefit of certification audits arises simply because they are happening. When staff know that the auditor is due, they will tidy up and complete their jobs list to ensure that they are not issued with too many 'parking tickets'. This aspect of auditing does work; systems are very likely to slip when not subject to this sort of regular examination.

Second party auditors are more likely to bring business benefits but this is still not the main thrust of the exercise. These teams are mostly looking to see whether their suppliers are meeting the specific needs of the individual customer. Since these needs could be idiosyncratic they are not necessarily good techniques for adoption across the board. Since the auditors are also looking at the actual satisfaction of particular needs, rather than the process by which needs are identified and then met, the main objective of those being audited, again, is to 'pass' and be eligible for further work. As, however, the rules for objectivity and impartiality are more flexible for second party auditors, they may be more likely than their certification cousins to put forward real suggestions for improvement. This can especially be true if the auditors are recognized technical experts who see their role as benefiting their own organization by helping their suppliers and sub-contractors to become more effective and efficient. Internal audits represent the biggest opportunity, from the standard set of audit types, to identify things that could be done better. They are conducted by people who understand the business and have the organization's best interests at heart. Done well, these audits can pick up opportunities for change which are hard to identify by any other means.

There is, I suppose, one more type of audit that we should mention: the consultancy audit. This is where a technical or business specialist is brought in to carry out a detailed investigation of one or more areas and recommend changes where appropriate. The only purpose of this type of audit is to identify business improvements. By definition these audits are the most likely to result in improved processes, although they are usually not so good at ensuring compliance or enforcing the tidy-up. Neither can they help with the PR or contract award criteria addressed by second and third party assessments. Of course, the benefits only arise if the right consultant is chosen and is given the time and resources to do the job properly, and if the recommendations are acted upon afterwards.

PROCESSES

We have already mentioned the idea of auditing a 'process'. It is probably a good idea, then, to explore what we mean by the term.

The diagram in Figure 1.1 provides a simple illustration of the concept. A process is a set of tasks or activities that transform one or more inputs into one or more outputs. This means that we can consider almost anything that we do, large or small, to be a process. Examples could be:

1.   Making a valve.
2.   Drilling bore-holes in a valve block (a sub-process of 1).
3.   Training somebody how to assemble a valve (a sub-process of 2).
4.   Setting up the classroom to train somebody how to assemble a valve.

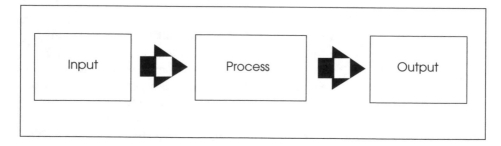

FIGURE 1.1   Process flows

We will look at the inputs and outputs for one example, but first we need to look at how those inputs are broken down.

One of the primary inputs to any process will be data, or information. This could be as simple as an instruction to begin, or could be something more complicated such as a contract or detailed command. In addition to this, there are six other considerations that may be taken into account as inputs, or sometimes as process support elements. We refer to these as '5 Ms and an E':

- O   Materials
- O   Machines (equipment and tools)
- O   Manpower (personnel involved in the process, but the pre-politically correct way of describing this has stayed with us since it begins with an 'M')
- O   Measurement (checking, monitoring and feedback)
- O   Methods
- O   Environment.

Note that this is an aid to defining those elements that support a process. We do not need to stick too rigidly to the definitions of which is which as long as it helps us to think of everything. To illustrate the point, we could consider that materials are anything transformed or consumed by the process. In catering, though, cutlery and crockery are essential items used as part of processes; we could call them materials even though they are not consumed, or could equally class them as machines since they are equipment even though they have no moving parts.

So, if we pick the example of training somebody how to assemble a valve, we have:

Data	the identified training need for one or more people
Materials	the valve, the component parts of a valve, course notes, overhead slides, test sheets
Machines	any equipment, machinery, fixtures and tools used in the assembly process; training equipment such as overhead projector, screen, video projector, tables and chairs
Manpower	the trainer(s), the trainees, a valve assembly expert
Measurement	success of trainees (final test), success of course (post-course critique sheet), business benefit (subsequent performance of operators)
Methods	valve assembly instructions and drawings, training principles (inform, demonstrate, practice, reinforce), course administration procedures
Environment	classroom, course timing/scheduling, venue.

The primary output of the process would be operators who are capable of assembling a valve. Other outputs might be test results and course critiques, plus feedback into future training events.

There are a number of reasons for thinking of processes, rather than functions, when we are auditing. It enables us to look at real activities with a start and a finish, rather than the artificial boundaries created by organizational functions. Processes are also easy to represent diagrammatically, from where we can readily explore the interfaces with other processes. There are other reasons, of course, why businesses use process models to manage their operations, and a number of books are available on the subject if readers wish to pursue it further. We will also visit the subject again in later chapters on preparation and process auditing.

VOCABULARY

Official definitions of terms used in quality management are given in the international standard ISO 9000 (until the recent version they were given in ISO 8402, which is now obsolete). I have made no attempt directly to reproduce those definitions here since they could be better read by looking at the standard itself. Another reason for this is that the definitions can seem rather dry and stuffy. There are, however, some words and phrases that are commonly used and which might benefit from some explanation here. I have avoided trying to give definitions of the words 'quality' and 'audit' since these are discussed at length throughout the book. Described below are some other key terms.

Auditee
I start with this term because it is commonly used but does not appear in many dictionaries. My guess is that it is not a 'real' word and has been invented by the quality fraternity on the basis that interviewers have interviewees, so auditors must have auditees. It means 'the person who is being audited' (another definition that I have heard is 'the victim of the audit' which represents a cynical, but nevertheless amusing, viewpoint). There is some confusion in the use of the word since sometimes it is used to mean the person actually being interviewed at the time, and on other occasions it can mean the person responsible for the area or organization being audited (i.e. the person who will have to address the required actions). Both are reasonable uses of the word; auditors will simply have to be careful that there is no confusion about who is being referred to when the word is employed in their audits.

Assessor
In theory this is synonymous with the word 'auditor', although in this book I use it to mean somebody carrying out audits on behalf of a third party certification body. The IRCA (the world's leading auditor registration organization) used to employ this word for the same purpose but changed it to 'auditor' to reflect the fact that auditing techniques are basically the same for all

types of audit. The five-day event which trains third party auditors is still unofficially referred to as the 'lead assessor course' by
many in the industry.

Procedure

This is a powerfully mis-used word. I see many audit findings
which report something like 'there are no procedures for this
activity', when what they really mean is that the standard practices are not defined in an official document. Statements such as
this make many a seasoned practitioner cringe. It represents a
common misunderstanding that a procedure is a few pages of
documentation defining standard operating methods. This is yet
another jargonistic abuse of the English language. A typical dictionary definition of the word is 'a standard method of carrying out
an activity'. It says nothing about documentation. Auditors should
be wary of confusing a standard way of doing things with a documented way of doing things. They must also understand that a
procedure can exist without documentation, provided that the
absence of such documentation does not adversely affect quality.
Unfortunately, ISO 9001 itself adds to the confusion by referring
to 'system procedures' when talking about documentation.

Non-conformity

What an inelegant word! It sounds wrong every time I hear it.
Personal foibles aside, this word means a failure to comply with
defined requirements. Thus if there is a rule of any sort which is
broken, this represents a non-conformity. 'Non-compliance' and
'non-conformance' are equivalent terms which mean exactly the
same thing (and may be gentler on the ear) and are in common
use although not usually included in official definitions of terms.
For no particular reason other than consistency, I have used
'non-compliance' in this book.

Observation

Like 'procedure' this is another word which is different in its true
meaning to its common usage amongst quality auditors. ISO
10011, the standard which outlines the basic requirements for
quality audits, uses the word 'observation' to mean any audit
finding which requires action. This is probably a valid interpretation: something that has been observed during the audit. Most
often, though, it is used by auditors to indicate something raised
where a non-compliance has not been proved but where the
auditor is of the opinion that some thought should be given to
the topic (assessors often define this as something which could
become a non-compliance if ignored, whereas other auditors
often consider it to represent an opportunity for improvement).
To be safe, I suggest that confusion is best avoided by using the
common interpretation rather than the 'official' one; a policy that
I have adhered to for the rest of this book.

Quality control	This is the set of activities which confirms that the individual product or service has met specified requirements. It covers all forms of checking, including inspection and testing at all stages of manufacture or service delivery. It is the function in the organization (not necessarily, though, a distinct organizational unit) which identifies product or service faults and refers them for correction. It is the historical heart of quality management and for some organizations still the way that they principally manage it, although the modern trend is for quality control to be seen as only one part of a good quality management system.
Quality management	This means everything that we do to ensure that we meet customer needs and pursue policies of continuous improvement. It is usually taken to indicate a formal, systematic approach (thus quality management is often achieved through a quality system, which is a planned, structured, coherent and documented approach to pulling all quality-related activities together).
Defect	It is worth discussing the meaning of this word since there is sometimes confusion between a defect and a non-compliance. A defect is something which will prevent the product or service being acceptable to the customer. This covers, of course, faults which stop the thing from working, but may also include cosmetic or similar faults where appropriate. Thus a blown cathode ray tube (CRT) on my computer video monitor is a defect because it no longer operates as a display screen. Similarly a scratched cover of the monitor is a defect since I probably would not want to put such a thing in my smart, tidy (ha! ha!) study. On the other hand, if the manufacturer supplies a black monitor cable instead of their usual grey one (perhaps because their usual cables are out of stock) then it does not represent a defect because it is perfectly usable and the customer may not even know the difference – it would, however, represent a non-compliance against our assembly procedures. A defect is always a non-compliance, but not every non-compliance represents a defect.
Quality plan	This is another area which is often misunderstood. We all accept that we have to plan to achieve something and are familiar with action plans and project plans. Although ISO 9001:2000 does place more emphasis on planning to achieve things than do previous versions, there is still a difference between most plans and a quality plan. A quality plan is usually thought of as one or more documents which define the specific quality system requirements for one set of circumstances such as a single project, customer, product, etc. The construction industry, for example,

makes extensive use of quality plans since every project is different. Other industries may have no need for such special sets of documents or practices since their 'standard' system is able to cover all cases and eventualities.

INTEGRATED AUDITING

It is impossible, today, to speak about quality auditing without mentioning integrated auditing. Indeed, aside from detailed interpretation of standards, it is probably the biggest topic of conversation amongst quality audit experts.

The idea is that it is neither efficient nor effective to have one team visit to conduct an audit for quality, then another for safety, another for environmental protection, yet another for data security, another for Investors in People, and so on. It should be possible to combine many of these so that the area or organization is visited only once by a team of wide competence who will examine the operations against all business requirements.

The chief advantages of this approach will be to keep the costs of carrying out audits to a minimum and to reduce the disruption caused by a constant stream of visiting auditors. There will also be management and system advantages, in that people will no longer, for example, think of this as 'something we do for ISO 9001'. The systems will be integrated, not simply arising from one requirement, and will just become 'the way we do things'. It may also make audits more effective since auditors will be looking at what goes on from all points of view, not blinkered by the restrictions of any one standard or policy.

Much work has to be done before this integrated approach is widely adopted, although there are early moves in this direction for both internal and third party audits. For example, the ISO 9001 auditor's guidelines, ISO 10011, will not be revised to coincide with the release of the latest 2000 version of the quality standard, since it is considered preferable to combine them with ISO 14010, the environmental auditing standard, to create an integrated set of requirements. This will take some time and for the moment we have two distinct guideline documents.

A large stumbling block, as the integration progresses, will be the range of expertise that we can expect a single individual to possess. Many certification and other audits are carried out by a lone auditor. Is it reasonable to expect that one person to be expert in the interpretation of quality, environmental issues, health and safety, personal development and whatever else the audit is intended to cover? Probably not. An answer may be to move towards team audits, where the team contains both generalists and experts, but that is always harder to manage and may defeat some of the potential advantages.

The idea does, though, have much in its favour. Certainly the management and progression of most audits is extremely similar, and even the investigation techniques have huge overlaps, with only differences of emphasis between the various types. Thus once a person has learnt the basics, transition to being able to conduct other types of audit simply requires an understanding of the issues involved, with little relearning of audit techniques needed.

Integrated auditing still requires detailed knowledge of the specific topics, some of which alone can be the subject of entire academic volumes. It is beyond the scope of this book, therefore, to deal with this subject in detail, although we will speak a little about it when we discuss future trends and improvements. Having the basics of quality auditing under your belt, however, will make it easier to make the transition towards other types, provided that sufficient technical capability in the other fields can be developed.

LEARNING FROM THIS BOOK

The intention of this book is to act as 'everything you ever needed to know about quality auditing'. Thus it is envisaged that some readers, especially those new to auditing, will study it from beginning to end. It can, though, be used in other ways. For experienced auditors, it can be used as an ideas generator or refresher by simply 'dipping in' to the appropriate chapter or paragraph as required. Others may see it as a way of enhancing knowledge in just one or two areas, such as the requirements of the 2000 version of ISO 9001 or how to cope with the new need to identify customer requirements.

It ought to be said that this book is not intended to be a direct replacement for formal training. Although its contents represent a comprehensive set of reference materials, equivalent to the handout binder provided in many courses, simply reading a book is never as good as participating in a proper training course with the attendant interactive, expert personal guidance and reinforcing group exercises. It could, of course, be suitable preparation for a training regime, or reference materials for those newly trained but feeling that a short course did not satisfy all their needs.

SUMMARY

○   Quality auditing has some things in common with other types of auditing, but there are also differences.

○   The practice only really became popular with the introduction of BS 5750 and ISO 9000 standards.

○   Auditing is about confirming a capability to do things, as opposed to inspection which checks whether or not we *have* done it correctly.

○   Quality auditing is a sampling exercise, not a 100 per cent verification.

○   Audits do not always cover every element of the business.

○   Auditors must be suitably trained and be reasonably independent of what they are examining, but in most cases do not require formal quali-fications.

○　Quality auditing has proved to be a tool which does meet its objectives, although effort has to be applied to make sure that this happens and that the benefits are maintained.

○　Thinking of business processes has always been a useful auditing tool and fits closely with the flavour of ISO 9001:2000.

○　There is a variety of jargon and special applications of phrases used in quality auditing, for which definitions are given in ISO 9000:2000.

○　Future developments include moves towards integrated audit teams which examine various topics concurrently, such as quality, environment, and health and safety.

○　This book is a complete guide to the ins and outs of quality auditing in all its forms.

2

PURPOSE, BENEFITS AND TYPES

❖

BASIC TYPES

B efore we can explore what audits are for and what they achieve, we need
to appreciate the different types of audit. The purposes of the different
types are related but do have slight differences.

We have already, in the introductory chapter, looked at the most common
categorization of audits into first, second and third party. There is probably no
need to explain these any further here; the different approaches to them for
particular audit elements are well explored below and in subsequent chapters.
We do, however, need to look at the other differences in types of audit.

HORIZONTAL AND VERTICAL AUDITS

Audits can cover either the customers, projects and products in an organization,
or an individual project or product. These two approaches are often known as
horizontal and vertical audits. Exactly which is which has caused some debate in
the past but ISO 9001:2000 has now come to our rescue. It defines the horizontal
loop as everything satisfying the customer need from identification to completion.
A vertical loop is a functional or organizational approach incorporating policy,
planning, resourcing, processing and evaluation. Although this represents the
converse of the definition that I and many others have traditionally used, at least it
defines a reference standard and I have adhered to this new convention in this
book.

Vertical audits are the most common. In this type auditors will typically examine one function, for example purchasing, personnel, sales and so on, and will
permit themselves to look at anything done in that area, no matter what product

or project is involved. These are relatively easy to manage since they will usually take place within a single area with a limited group of interviewees. Unless the organization is heavily project-based, it also means that there are a limited number of documents and manuals involved.

Horizontal audits involve selecting a single project, customer, product, etc. and following the entire cycle from the start (e.g. project inception, customer enquiry) to its completion (e.g. project closure, product delivery). This is usually far more difficult to administer. It is likely, in most cases, to involve visits to many different departments and interviews with a very wide range of people. It also requires a lot of digging to pursue the links between one function and the next. Timetabling is a nightmare too; it is virtually impossible to say when, or even if, the team will visit each area. It can be a powerful tool to test the interfaces between different parts of an organization but definitely requires more work. Horizontal audits are sometimes used, for reasons of necessity, by second party auditors since confidentiality requirements often limit them to looking only at things which directly relate to their own contracts. Even there, or in project type organizations like the construction industry, it is often preferred to carry out a series of small vertical audits than attempt the complication of the true horizontal approach.

Internal audits are nearly always vertical, unless the examined activities are heavily project-oriented, although some 'advanced' programmes are beginning to place more emphasis on horizontal audits. Third party audits are sometimes thought of as a combination of the two types since the assessors sometimes try to follow an audit trail as they progress through the organization. They rarely, however, stick strictly to the trail, or are restricted by it, so in reality these assessments are probably more like a series of vertical audits held back-to-back.

REVERSE TERMINOLOGY

As discussed, this terminology can be used the other way around. This is especially confusing for new auditors or those who need to work with several organizations. It is always best to clarify terminology if people with whom you do not work regularly begin discussing horizontal and vertical audits.

In most cases, it does not really matter since certification audits and internal audits (the two most common of the three main types) have nearly always been done in a single, standard way so that ambiguous terminology has not been an issue. With the advent of the year 2000 version of the ISO 9000 family, however, a possible source of misunderstanding has crept into being. The first is that ISO 9001 suggests that the company should identify the need for process and product audits. The implication is that, although functional audits may be the norm, process and technical audits may sometimes be required (it is unlikely that the answer will be 'no' every time you ask yourself if they are needed). This means that a commonly understood way of describing the various types is required.

MANAGEMENT AND TECHNICAL AUDITS

Most quality audits in the past, at least those directly related to ISO 9001 pro-grammes such as internal and third party audits, have been of the management type. That is, they look at the way things are planned, monitored and recorded rather than, usually, the activity itself. Thus a management auditor would confirm that the calibration of test equipment is planned, done according to defined and documented practices, recorded, analysed and carried out by trained personnel. The auditor would not, though, observe the calibration process itself to see that it is being done correctly and efficiently. This approach has a number of advantages:

○   The auditors do not need detailed technical knowledge of the process.

○   Many operations can be covered by browsing through the records file, whereas observing the operation itself can be very time-consuming.

○   It is easy to plan since you can look through a records file at any time, regardless of exactly when the operation is carried out.

○   They do not incur the Einsteinian penalty that the observer affects the results (i.e. we all perform differently when watched).

The main disadvantage is that management auditors rely heavily on basic records of activity which may not present a full, or even accurate, picture of events.

A technical audit (sometimes called a process or product audit) does look closely at the actual operation. It is intended to determine whether operations are being carried out in line with both policy/procedures and current best practice. An example of this type of audit is the regular course audit carried out by a lead-ing IT training provider of my acquaintance. This involves one of the company managers, an experienced trainer herself, attending courses and picking up tips which could be used by other trainers and points which could be improved. This type of audit has often been used by second party auditors who may be more interested in proving the technical capability of their suppliers and sub-contractors than checking their management systems.

WHAT ARE AUDITS FOR?

One of the constant questions encountered in any audit system is why bother con-ducting audits at all. Sadly, the most common answer given is that we have to. We have to submit to certification audits because we need an ISO 9001 certificate to be eligible to bid for contracts. We have to allow customers to audit us to remain on, or be admitted to, their approved supplier list. We have to carry out internal audits because the assessor will expect it. These arguments are thin and difficult to support. If the only reason that we do something is because the assessor expects it then it represents inefficiency and a waste of time.

However, this argument varies in strength. For certification audits it is accepted that the only reason we have them is to obtain and keep a certificate. We could adopt the ISO 9001 framework far more cheaply and flexibly without third party certification, as long as our customers did not demand it. The reality of life is that many customers do insist upon a recognized certificate so that we do, in fact, submit ourselves to an assessment just to satisfy their requirements. This means that all we require from an external assessor is the certificate; if it had no commercial or marketing benefit then we could control our quality just as well without it. Assessors working for certification bodies should remember this and appreciate their role. Managers may smile politely when assessors give their opinions about how things could be run better, but they are probably not really interested. After all, if they wanted business advice they would seek a contract with a recognized consultancy firm, not with an ISO 9001 auditor.

This is a difficult message for certifiers to swallow. Many of them are keen to emphasize that they will 'add value' to the audit as part of the need to distinguish themselves from their many competitors The basic purpose of the independent certification process, though, means that adding value by identifying improvements is neither what customers want nor the intention of the regime.

Whilst we can accept, reluctantly and with some limitations, arguments from certification auditors that we must do something in order to obtain the certificate, this is less acceptable from internal auditors. If internal auditors insist that something is done simply because 'the assessor will expect it' then it is unlikely to be well received by managers.

So, what are audits really for? ISO 9000, the standard defining quality vocabulary, says that they are to confirm compliance with planned arrangements and to confirm that the systems are implemented effectively; other definitions also mention that they should look to see that the systems are suitable to achieve corporate objectives. Some of this is more difficult to achieve than the rest. It is difficult for any auditor to tell, from a short examination, whether or not a manager is running an area in a way suitable to achieve overall corporate objectives (which probably have a lot to do with growth and profitability). In reality most audits clearly distinguish between findings which represent straight compliance issues and those which suggest ways of improving effectiveness.

The real results expected vary from audit to audit as discussed below.

PURPOSE OF THIRD PARTY AUDITS

The only purpose of a third party certification audit is to grant (for an initial audit) or to confirm continuation of (for ongoing surveillance audits) ISO 9001 or other certification such as product marks. Some organizations (a minority, but still a significant number) avow that they have followed the ISO 9001 model because they are looking for internal benefits. This may be true; the quality system model does represent good business practice. The reason that they subject themselves to accredited certification, however, is to obtain a recognized certificate.

We could equate this to learning to drive. We all like to feel that we are good drivers and usually are willing to pay for professional training to achieve this. The only reason that we take the test, though, is to obtain a licence. Similarly, we can possess superior driving skills without taking the advanced motoring test but we do it because we want the badge.

Certification bodies may like to think that they have a wider role but they must learn to stick to their remit. Driving examiners do not attempt to give pointers for minor improvement and neither should certification assessors.

The reason that I emphasize this is that a misguided approach from assessors can actually be harmful. In order to be of value to their employers, assessors have to be 'qualified' in as wide a range as possible, thus ensuring that they can audit a decently broad client base. This means that they are probably not focused experts in the industry that they are auditing and therefore know less about the real issues than the auditees. Even where they previously have direct industry experience of the type of organization that they are visiting, their in-depth knowledge will quickly fade and/or become stale. Additionally, they spend only a very short time with each client, far too short a time to make sound judgements about the nature of the business. Despite this logic, organizations often feel obliged to listen to the advice of assessors. This is because we know that we need to keep assessors feeling warm and happy; if we do not we are in danger of upsetting them so that they give us a hard time and our certification is thus endangered. As a result we may act upon poorly informed advice because we are scared not to.

All of this leads me to repeat the message: certification assessors must stick to noting pure compliance with the assessment standard. Anything else is unprofessional and can be dangerous.

SECOND PARTY AUDITS

A second party audit is conducted by a company on its sub-contractors or suppliers. Perhaps it is appropriate here to explore a little terminology before we go any further. The term 'sub-contractors' often confuses people since they see sub-contractors as being the people who work for the contractor who works for the customer; exactly where our own organization fits into the chain is unclear. This is not helped by the fact that we normally think of contractors and sub-contractors as people who supply services, whilst those who provide us with goods are called 'suppliers'. In many ISO 9001-based systems, though, the term 'sub-contractors' is used to describe anybody who supplies us with anything. This is because previous versions of ISO 9001 (and ISO 9002) have had their own, unique, way of looking at this. The writers reasoned that since we were adopting ISO 9001 with the intention (supposedly) of ensuring that we met our customer's requirements then we were 'the supplier'. This name applied whether we provided goods or services, or both. We, then, were the prime contractor for our customer, so organizations that supplied us with goods or services were known as sub-contractors.

If this seems confusing then do not despair; it has tripped up even the most experienced quality professionals. Luckily the new standard sees the relationship more simply as shown in Figure 2.1.

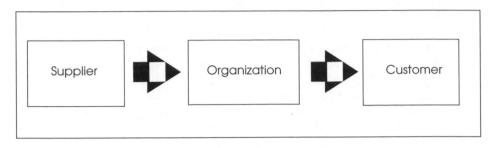

FIGURE 2.1   Supply chain terminology

So, when our customer audits us, or we audit our sub-contractors or suppliers, this is called a second party audit. It is typically carried out for one of two purposes:

O   to decide whether future contracts can, or will, be awarded; or

O   to determine whether existing contractual performance is satisfactory.

Either way, there are strong vested interests involved. Customers want perfect goods and services at minimum cost supplied with maximum flexibility (i.e. no minimum order quantities, zero lead time, same day delivery and exactly customized to our needs). Suppliers want to sell as much as possible of the standard offering at maximum price in a way that lets them securely plan for the future. These lists are not entirely mutually exclusive. 'Reasonable' requirements from both sides can usually be satisfied, provided that there is some willingness to negotiate and show a little flexibility.

The point of all this is that the two 'sides' involved in a second party audit are not directly interested in systems, more in the specific technical and commercial requirements of their relationship. This is the major reason why one of the original aims of the independent, third party certification process – to reduce the number of audits to which companies are subjected – has largely failed. Customers may indeed desire that their suppliers follow consistent practices and are aiming to achieve continuous improvement, but this is only part of a wider picture. In fact, they may both ask for independent certification and impose their own audit regime, relying on the certification to cover the systems side of things. This approach leads even more towards second party audits which place little emphasis on compliance with management standards and heavy bias towards specific technical and commercial competences.

The purpose of this type of audit, then, is for a customer to decide upon the merits, or otherwise, of its suppliers. Individual sub-contractor audits usually will have one of the following three objectives:

O   to decide whether a sub-contractor is worthy of being added to the approved supplier list, or the 'eligible to bid' list (this process is sometimes known as 'pre-qualification');

O   to update the sub-contractor qualification list and see if they continue to operate in the expected way (for example, if we approved them three years ago, how do we know that they are still okay today?); or

O   to help sub-contractors identify areas where they could improve quality and efficiency or reduce costs.

The first two are the simplest audits to explain. They tend to follow conventional audit practice with the exception that they are looking at what the individual customer expects, rather than basic standards compliance. Preparation of an initial checklist, for example, will still take place but will be against an agreed set of technical criteria rather than a universal standard, and findings will be largely based on the technical judgement of the audit team rather than the impartial compliance assessments made by third party auditors.

In fact, I have found it quite difficult to deliver the standard five-day audit training course to groups who are there largely because they want to audit their suppliers. They often find the ideas of checklist preparation and formal action requests quite useful, and may even appreciate the tips on observation and other techniques, but have difficulty coming to terms with the impartial and non-prescriptive approach that is taught for third party assessors. One area manager from a large management services company complained that he was being asked to 'turn his brain off' simply in order to pass the end-of-course examination. Since he would probably never, in practice, employ the impartial techniques looked for in the examination, I had to agree with him. Although such courses purport to give equal emphasis to all types of external audits, the only sub-contractor auditors who are truly likely to follow the practices taught are those working for government agencies such as defence ministry departments.

By the nature of things this is inevitable. Most audit practice and teaching has been built around those used as part of formal systems. By bearing this in mind, however, it is hoped that I have paid enough attention to the particular needs of second party auditors to provide equal value to them.

INTERNAL AUDITS

Although the formal training for internal auditors is usually less than for external assessors, they can often do it better than their certification counterparts. To justify this statement, we need to look at the accepted reasons for carrying out an audit:

O   To confirm compliance with 'the rules'.
O   To ensure that the rules are implemented in an effective manner.

O   To identify whether the 'system' is applicable to the overall objectives of the organization.

Third party certification audits satisfy the first of these as far as ISO 9001 is concerned, although often do a poor job of looking at anything else (since the assessors are very familiar with ISO 9001 but rarely have an in-depth knowledge of the business-specific requirements which also have to be followed in as much detail). They only partially cover the second reason since a short management audit cannot really identify whether we are effective in supplying the right goods and services (in theory we could be awarded a certificate if we currently receive a customer complaint for everything that we do, provided that we can show that we are attending to those complaints, even though our system would be clearly ineffective). They do not really address the third reason at all; third party auditors are forbidden from judging whether the system is the right one. No amount of non-compliances will enable an assessor to truly judge that the system we have is not capable of satisfying our customers.

Internal auditors are not bound by the same strictures. They are employed by the same people that they are auditing and thus have the same ultimate objectives. They also have a decent level of understanding about how the organization works, including a feeling for the internal 'culture'. They are thus well placed to see where effectiveness and customer service requirements are not being met. Indeed, many internal auditors quickly find that basic compliance issues fade into the background after the first few audits. Internal auditors can feel able to comment on anything that they see which they consider could be done differently to the benefit of the organization.

This does raise some questions about auditor training, experience and competence. Many companies have traditionally appointed internal auditors at a low level whose job is only to confirm compliance for the purpose of ISO 9001 certification (managers have far more interesting things to do with their time). The value judgements of such auditors are unlikely to be listened to very attentively by the rest of the organization. For auditors really to be able to identify and recommend improvements they need to have the skills and knowledge to make sensible recommendations and have sufficient respect in the organization for them to be listened to. This is likely to require a determined development programme for the people concerned. It is not enough simply to pick employees from halfway up the organization chart and send them on a two-day course. Internal auditors should be selected from amongst those who are respected (not necessarily for their position but for their expertise, intelligence or capability) and it should be seen as an honour to serve in that capacity. For some organizations this will require them to take internal quality auditing far more seriously than has been the norm. Still, this should not present a problem – if it is worth doing it is worth doing well and if it is not worth doing then it is not worth doing at all.

WHO WANTS AUDITS?

Initial certification audits are usually wanted, and initiated, by senior managers in the audited organization. This is done for no other reason than that they think it is useful for the organization. The first prompt for the audit can come from no other source. Of course, the reason that they seek the audit may be driven from outside: a common reason for inviting the auditors in is that customers want their suppliers to be independently assessed, thereby showing that they believe in and operate a good system of controls. In this case it could be argued that it is really the customer who 'wants' the audit; the managers may be just doing it to keep the customer happy.

Continuing certification audits are often prompted by the certification body. It could be argued that the certification body wants the audit to take place since it wishes to maintain its schedule and ensure that it is providing a professional certification service. It also wants them because it wants to retain the client and not lose them to another certification body, or worse, to the ranks of those who do not maintain their certificates. It is still really, though, the certified organization who wants the audits and, in the end, who decides whether it wishes the audit to happen or not.

Second party audits are definitely wanted by the customer. It is the customer who decides that an audit is necessary and who pushes the organization to accept it. Although some might argue that the organization itself wants the audit since it wishes to become a supplier, it is more a case of the organization accepting the audit as a prerequisite to the relationship (I have never heard of a company that has pleaded with a customer to audit it when the customer did not demand it).

Many say that internal audits are only wanted by ISO 9001 certifiers, and that organizations only conduct them for that reason. In fact, of course, it is the organization itself that wants the audits since it has decided that it wishes to have the certificate. Internal audits, though, have the most potential for improvement. In enlightened organizations, therefore, internal audits are eagerly anticipated by senior managers since they represent one way of identifying areas for potential improvement.

THE CLIENT

The person on whose behalf the audit is being carried out is usually referred to as the audit client. This is generally the same person as the one who 'wants' the audit.

I have heard it suggested that there is a danger of confusion since some consultants and certification bodies also use the term client to refer to the person who is paying them. In fact in all circumstances that I can think of the commercial client is the same person as the audit client. For example, a consultant assessing a supplier will be both paid and instructed by the supplier's customer. There is, then, little real chance of confusion and I have used the word client in both contexts at various places in this book.

VARIATIONS IN TECHNIQUE

Actually the variation between first, second and third party audits is relatively small. They all include the basic three activities of a quality audit:

- ○   interviewing
- ○   examining records
- ○   observation.

Interviewing is about talking to people and asking them to explain what they do. External auditors tend to ask more naïve questions than internal auditors, since they are less familiar with the processes. All of them, though, tend to ask general, open questions about the job and then follow up with more detailed probes.

Examining records is usually used to reinforce or confirm what has been discussed during interviews. This is done by all auditors with little real difference between the way that internal and third party audits work. Second party auditors also follow the same approach but may be restricted as to the records that they are allowed to see (since records relating to work for other customers are likely to be confidential).

Observation varies depending upon what is being audited. There is a great deal more opportunity for observation when auditing a manufacturing area, for example (when you can look at identification and protection of materials and products, handling techniques, communication displays, housekeeping and so on), than there is in an office or telephone call centre. There is almost no difference in the amount of observation that is used in first and second party and internal audits. It is possible that the 'flavour' of observation may vary, in that internal auditors will know where to look, but on the other hand external auditors may usefully look at something which internal auditors do not think to examine because they see it every day.

The above discussion of variation applies largely to management audits. There is certainly some intrinsic variation between how these are carried out and how technical audits are performed. The former look principally at management capability, whereas the latter are conducted to evaluate technical adequacy. Whilst we are principally addressing management audits in this book, Chapter 13, Product and Process Audits will explore the subject of technical audits and will clearly highlight the differences.

DRAWBACKS AND PITFALLS

Voluble auditors will always have a tale or two ready to tell about a disaster they have had, or a trap that their colleague (never themselves) fell into. Things that an individual may have to face and overcome are dealt with in Chapters 9 and 12. There are a few things worth mentioning here, though, that can go wrong with audit programmes as a whole:

○   The biggest danger is that audits are trivial or 'thin'. They find little apart from the odd wording or typing error in a document. This can happen after the initial enthusiasm when audits go 'stale' or can even be a problem right from the beginning if things are not done well. The solution is to train auditors well and make sure that you know what you want of them, setting clear objectives for the audits. Constantly finding new ways to inject life into an audit programme is also essential.

○   Another possible failing is that only certain things are covered. This happens when we forget one or more of the less obvious functions or processes in the organization, or we keep going back to the same thing (a colleague told me only recently that she knows that only one project team, the largest one, in her company even attempts to follow the design rules since that is the only one that the auditor ever visits). Audits must be planned to give a wide coverage over time and auditors will usually need the help of the audit programme manager to do this since individual auditors may well not really know what to ask for when they visit an area.

○   Sometimes an organization spends a disproportional effort gearing up for an audit. This is particularly true for customer or certification audits. Countless hours are spent double-checking and tidying up. Try to avoid this. It is wasteful and unnecessary. Some preparation will undoubtedly be useful but you should not go overboard. A purist might say that everything should have been checked and tidied away as part of normal operations, but the real answer lies somewhere to the left of this perfect solution. Yes, if things have slipped so badly that you are in danger of losing your contract or certificate then you will want to put in extra effort to avoid that. For most organizations, though, records and housekeeping are mostly okay with one or two holes. In this position we should need to do little more than flick a quick duster over the copy of the quality manual that the auditor reads; he or she is quite likely to raise some minor points and we cannot hide them all. Responding to a few minor discrepancies found in an audit is not arduous so there is no need to panic about it in advance.

○   One thing that all auditors experience but that internal auditors seem to find particularly distressing is the tendency of auditees to take the audit personally. They see auditor questions as subtle tricks, or even direct insinuations, and view any audit findings as personal criticism. This one feature of audit programmes alone can make them fail. Managers and other employees need to understand that it is, if the auditor is doing the job properly, a positive exercise. It can help managers and team leaders to identify where there are areas for improvement and can identify potential benefits which the people operating the tasks and processes have not seen because they are too close to them. The company must avoid reporting 'numbers of non-compliances' by department and then jumping on the manager who has the most. It should all be seen as a no-blame exercise and a positive culture promoted at all levels.

SUMMARY

○   Most audits follow the vertical loop, examining everything in an area or function.

○   Horizontal loop audits follow processes or projects from start to finish.

○   Horizontal loop audits are more difficult and therefore rarer, but can be quite powerful.

○   Quality audits usually look at management processes but technical audits can also be part of the overall programme.

○   Audits are conducted to keep us on our chosen track and identify improvements (internal), to make us eligible to do business with a customer (second party) or to grant a certificate or award (third party).

○   Audit teams need to understand why they are there and not overstep their remit.

○   The person who commissions the audit, for one of the above purposes, is known as the audit client.

○   The basic techniques employed by first, second and third party auditors are similar, with variations only in detail and intent.

○   Audit managers need to take steps to avoid programmes being superficial, personal or causing disproportionate amounts of work.

3

QUALITY AND QUALITY MANAGEMENT

❖

WHAT IS QUALITY?

In the early days of industrial development the meaning of this word was barely discussed. If it was thought of at all, 'quality' probably would have referred to items that the gentry would buy, with other items seen as being of inferior quality. A gentleman, for example, would have bought a finely tailored coat, whilst his manservant would have a durable but otherwise basic outer garment. Using more modern equivalents, this relates to the Bentley being described as 'quality' while the Morris 1000 was the more basic commodity.

Later developments gave rise to the concept of quality as an objective in its own right. Possibly the initiatives of the American gurus (Deming, Juran, *et al.*), whose ideas found such a receptive ear in Japan, led to the first stirrings of a movement which took quality seriously as a management discipline. Then industry began to clearly distinguish the idea of 'better' from 'acceptable quality'. This led to a very common concept of 'fitness for purpose' as a good definition of the word quality. 'Fit for purpose' implies that the good or service does the job for which it is intended but does not necessarily offer frills; the number and type of frills (or 'features') will purely depend upon the needs of the customer, the cost expectations and the purpose to which the item will be put. Thus in this example a Volkswagen is a quality car since it serves the purpose of taking someone from one point to another, permitting individual transport door-to-door. The Bentley has more features and thus is also a quality car but of a higher 'grade'. In theory, if Bentleys proved to be faulty and unreliable and Volkswagens extremely reliable and fault-free, then the VW would represent quality and the Bentley not.

The problem is that conceptions of quality have moved on. One of the reasons that Bentley and Rolls-Royce cars were so respected, for example, is that they could be purpose-built to one's own specifications and each customer was treated

33

as a special client. Rolls-Royce, for example, has records of everyone who has ever bought one of its cars and addresses letters to them personally. People are now beginning to expect this level of service from everything that they buy, not just when they place a luxury order. Thus any business must offer top class attention to the customer, whatever it is doing. For example, the very day that I was writing the start of this chapter, I took lunchtime off to go into town and buy a few things. One of the shops that I visited was a music store to buy a CD which my nephew had specified. I could not see it on the shelf and asked a passing employee. He not only indicated the right place on the display racks but also helped me to hunt, then when we could not find it straight away he went into the stock room to fetch one for me. For the margin which the shop made on the product this was probably exceptional service and I was impressed. If he had not taken the trouble, though, I am so used to customer care being a priority these days that I would probably have grumbled to my friends and family about it.

Thus our expectations have changed. We not only want what we buy to be fit for purpose but we do not expect to have to wait for it, we want it with a smile and courtesy and we want our every request dealt with instantly. Then, when I arrive at home with the product, I will be irritated at every minor imperfection. In a modern business environment, then, the old automotive idea of an item which meets the specification consistently is no longer an adequate definition of quality. In consumer and business transactions we all expect a lot more than that. And, even more, our expectations increase as the level of service improves.

This means that we cannot set a level of expected customer satisfaction and aim to meet it. We must continually strive to improve. World leading companies aim to do better than the rest, thereby exceeding standard customer expectations. This should always be our aim, as long as we remember that what exceeds today's expectations will only just meet tomorrow's.

Since we are principally concerned about auditing here, the auditor's lesson is that the organization needs to constantly consider and re-consider what the customer expects from it, and take action to ensure that practices are geared towards meeting those expectations. Thus in an audit we are looking for evidence of up-to-date practice which reflects today's business and customer needs. In this sense the exact definition of quality is an irrelevance, despite the fact that the typical standard audit training course syllabus includes discussion of its meaning. In fact, I was recently asked to present an audit course concentrating on improvement rather than simple ISO 9000 compliance, where it was agreed that the word 'quality' was not to be spoken throughout the event. It was refreshing to be able to talk about performance without becoming bogged down by debates over the interpretation of words.

LITTLE THINGS MATTER

Everybody (or anybody that is likely to survive in business) is becoming good at what they do. This means that whoever we buy our products or services from (unless it is a comic market trader from Peckham) we are likely to see basic quality requirements met. If we use the example of motor vehicles again, we find the old jokes about East European cars have virtually disappeared as their products have vastly improved in terms of reliability, appearance, economy and comfort.

When we are choosing to buy something these days, then, very few suppliers will be rejected because their offerings are simply not up to scratch. The chances are that every established organization in the field will be able to perform the job in a generally satisfactory manner. What makes us choose one supplier over another, apart from the price factor, is the small differences which make them special. Or, looking at it another way, it is small things which make us vow never to buy anything from them again. We can all probably quote anecdotal evidence for this latter viewpoint. These include the otherwise perfect holiday spoilt by the poor hotel check-in arrangements; the annoyance in our luxury car that the electric windows will not open when the ignition is off; the dream home with that inaccessible place behind the banisters where dust collects; the smart cooker whose automatic ignition makes tiny clicking noises, and so on. Now that we have come to expect good basic service everywhere we go, the little things can either thrill or irritate us sufficiently to influence our buying decisions. In particular, when we are annoyed we will not only avoid that supplier in future but will also tell all our colleagues and friends to do the same.

This means that auditors also need to concern themselves with the small things which impact upon the service given to customers. This does not necessarily mean trivia such as typographical errors on internal memoranda, but it could include things such as the way that the telephone is answered or how the reception desk is staffed.

PREVENTION VS. DETECTION

'Prevention is better than detection' is the classic phrase which we are constantly told is at the heart of quality assurance and quality management. Historically, craftsmen made sure that the work they produced was acceptable; their own pride and reputation was at stake if they got it wrong. As craftsmanship gave way to mass manufacture, other approaches were needed and the resultant classic quality control consisted of inspection: teams of laboratory-coated inspectors who would check final output and reject it if it failed to meet defined requirements. This was intended to ensure that customers never received anything substandard.

Today, we recognize that this has limitations. If inspection is the only quality tool then this is expensive; we have to return every rejected item for re-work or even the more costly horror of scrap. We also have to pay for employing the inspectors and the resources that they use. In fact there is an argument that such a system pays workers to make mistakes. After all, if we decide that we need to employ a given number of inspectors, then we must be making enough errors to keep them busy. This is a philosophy which sits uneasily and in which it is probably easy to pick holes, but it does reinforce the feeling that inspection alone is not enough. A final nail in the proverbial coffin of the old quality control approach is the understanding that inspection (including its more technical forms of measurement and test) does not always give the definite answer that is expected. To illustrate this, I'd like you, the reader, to carry out a simple inspection of the words in the section of this chapter entitled 'Little Things Matter'. Inspect the section for one characteristic, the number of times that the letter 'e' appears. When you have finished, check your total against my own count given at the end of the chapter. It is highly likely that the two answers will not be the same. I usually describe this as demonstrating that inspection is not totally reliable, although a statistician recently told me that it actually just shows that the results show a statistical distribution. Either way, it reveals that it is not precise, and that if we ask an inspector to check a value for us he or she will often get it wrong. The fact that people are never sure whether the instruction includes the heading and upper case letters just reflects the communication errors that can also occur.

This understanding that end-of-line checking is flawed has resulted in the development of quality management ideas which are intended to prevent faults rather than just detect them at the last minute. This means controlling processes, designs, inputs and support functions to guarantee successful outputs. This will not preclude all forms of output inspection, for which there will always be some need, but it diminishes its importance as the only tool. In fact there are organizations that have their concepts and processes so well organized that final inspection really is only a formality, knowing that the results will always be good. These are special cases whose circumstances lend themselves to tight control, but it proves the point that strong quality preventive techniques can work wonders.

Auditing is a prevention technique. It is about confirming that the management of business and operating processes is in accordance with policy and good practice. Thus it is an integral part of the prevention of quality and customer problems.

QUALITY MANAGEMENT

As we have discussed, managing quality is about more than just checking that the product shipped out of the door is okay. The word 'management' implies coordination of a wide, integrated range of activities which come together to ensure that the customer is pleased with what he or she has bought.

Certainly auditors should be trying to apply an integrated approach to their assessments. It is not enough to look at one activity intended to ensure quality and examine it in isolation from anything else. Since quality has to be managed and coordinated, it follows that the coordination of activities must be assessed by auditors.

The global view is something that comes out very strongly from the planning and preparation of audits. Later in this book we will discuss, for example, how looking at one small process or set of tasks reveals little about how well the organization is working. The scope of the audit is often set at the planning stage, so whoever plans and runs the audit programme must also be aware of the need to look at the whole picture.

The fact that quality has to be managed also tends to push audits towards examining management-level activities. This does often lead to the tendency for auditors to speak only to managers and supervisors. Whilst this is, to some extent, inevitable, it should be recognized that management disciplines are enacted via all levels of the organization, not only via those who have official managerial responsibilities.

As well as looking at all levels, we also need to examine interfaces between levels and processes. Many managers quickly learn that interfaces between different functional or process areas are as important as the activities which are bounded within their own bailiwick. This is a lesson which must not be ignored in auditing. Process consultants are fond of telling us that interfaces and communication boundaries are the primary cause of process errors. Thus any auditor must take account of interfaces between functions when auditing. If an auditee tells us that information arrives from outside, auditors must ask:

○   In what form does it come?
○   How do we review it for accuracy and completeness?
○   Are there any feedback loops?
○   What do we do if there are omissions and errors?
○   Whom else do we have to keep informed?

Quality management information flows, both internal and across boundaries, can be formal or informal. A good auditor should be able to identify what those interfaces are, how the information passes from one place to another and what the consequences are. These issues are just as important as how the controls for the process operate within a functional area.

TOTAL QUALITY MANAGEMENT

The words 'total quality management' (TQM) present us all with a problem. They have been around since the 1950s; they represent, probably, the most persistent (and thus most likely the most valid) management philosophy of this century and are universally recognized as a good thing. They do, however, have some disadvantages:

○   TQM is not the same as ISO 9000.
○   TQM has a better public image than ISO 9000, even though they are not necessarily in competition.
○   Each one of us has encountered somebody who has told us (in a superior tone) 'Oh, we haven't bothered with ISO 9000; we've gone straight for TQM.'

There seems to be a curious phenomenon that has caused the words 'quality management' to be heavily associated with ISO 9000, while putting the word 'total' in front conjures an entirely different mind-set. In the context of auditing it makes life unnecessarily complicated in that auditing is not, traditionally, a standard feature of TQM programmes.

Both TQM and systems based on the ISO 9000 model have been aimed at achieving the dual objectives of customer satisfaction and internal effectiveness. In a sense, though, they have made the lives of some of us more complex because they both rely on the word 'quality'. Complex, because until recently TQM was seen very much as about continuous incremental improvement and ISO 9000 was about consistency and control; two approaches to the same objective. There was no question of one approach being 'better' or 'wider' than the other; they were just different.

The new version of ISO 9000 has removed this clear division of styles. It has a strong communication and continuous improvement flavour and is, thus, trying to move closer to the TQM approach, whilst seeking to retain its traditional flavour of control and consistency. Of course, certification of an improvement culture is an interesting concept and it remains to be seen whether ISO 9000 certified companies will truly have TQM-like systems or whether the standard compliance and consistency feel will remain.

For auditors, much of this debate is irrelevant. Whether or not the main concentration in an organization is towards regular improvement or towards control and stability, we can still look for compliance with specific requirements and for factors affecting efficiency and effectiveness. In all cases, certification auditors must continue to place their emphasis on compliance, and internal auditors will look for best practice, with some inevitable overlap between the two styles.

PROCESS MANAGEMENT

We have already looked at the concept of processes. In audit terms, though, there is some confusion over what we mean by process auditing. I was once asked by a service supplier to the pharmaceutical industry to devise an 'advanced' training course to steer its internal quality auditors away from simply looking at document control and other basic compliance issues. 'Aha!' I said. 'You must be looking at process auditing.' At that point I believe my client almost decided to go elsewhere as she carefully explained that they were already auditing processes; this was too narrow a scope and they wanted to audit by function. I later discovered that the processes audited were small, self-contained sets of activities within a single department, typically covered by a single standard operating procedure, whereas I had envisaged large cross-functional processes. Both are valid interpretations but we had misunderstood each other.

Much of the modern move towards process management and process thinking is intended to shift people away from traditional functional or specialist boundaries. Process thinking, done well, can push us towards seeing how what we do fits into the whole organizational jigsaw, rather than seeing our work as an end in itself. It is this end which is most important. If we can create a situation where we see everything we do as being part of the looped chain which forms the entire operation of our organization (the ideas of internal customers and suppliers apply here) then we are able to manage our processes without becoming too embroiled in the debate over exactly what a process is.

For management auditing, it is probably best to avoid the discussion as to whether we are auditing functions, but ensure that we are looking at areas which are not too narrow, which are coherent and which have clearly defined interfaces. This is not to say that process management has no use in the field of quality management. There are many process management initiatives which have brought great benefit to their respective organizations. Just do not become too worried about whether it is a process or not when conducting quality audits.

QUALITY MANAGEMENT SYSTEMS

Just as we have said that quality management is about coordinating all the activities that go towards achieving customer satisfaction, so a quality management system is a defined set of rules and disciplines which cover how we are going to manage quality. Since the word 'system' is used, this implies that it has been consciously designed and forms an integrated whole. Thus while organizations who have gradually grown up with a range of individual disciplines and standard approaches can achieve ISO 9001 certification, this would still not be classed as a quality management system by purists.

In practice, a quality management system is usually what organizations create when they are seeking ISO 9001 certification. The typical process is to pool together what we already have and fill in any gaps by documenting a few more standard disciplines such as an audit programme. A quality manual is then produced, ostensibly to pull everything together and provide a central focus, but normally it is a boring document to read and attended to by nobody other than the certification assessor and the occasional quality manager of large customers (who must have copious quantities of time to spare to want to read these documents).

From an auditor's point of view, this 'getting by' approach to defining the system for certification purposes is not necessarily a problem. This is because what is thought of as the quality management system in an organization does not necessarily reflect the real and complete system. For a start, managers often think of the quality system as comprising only elements which have an impact on their ISO 9000 certification. This is clearly not true; there are other factors which impact upon the customer which tend to lie outside the scope of the standard (image, speed of response, advertising, cost, payment terms and procedures and so on).

There is also the problem that written quality management systems are often seen as something different to the real operation of the company. We will often hear managers talking about 'Following the ISO 9000', when what they mean is following the rules for working set down in their area. This leads to many tasks and activities which are clearly aimed at maintaining or improving quality which nobody considers to be part of the quality management system.

I prefer not to use this term. I would rather tell the auditees that I am looking at 'the way we do things' rather than auditing the quality management system. That way I am more likely to be told about everything that they do and not just 'the ISO 9000 procedures'.

QUALITY DOCUMENTATION

This is one of the areas which has, traditionally, been the most annoying and tedious, and least beneficial element of ISO 9000 and quality management systems. This is partly due to a misunderstanding of what ISO 9000 is all about. I have heard many experts, consultants and trainers tell their audiences that the 'quality system' requirements of all versions of ISO 9000 standards mean that we have to write down the way we do things. In fact the spirit of the standard asks organizations to think about and agree upon the way that they would like to do things. Writing it down is secondary to this and is only done in the same way that we write other things in business: to make sure that we all have a common understanding of what we agreed and so we can remember. That is why we create minutes of meetings and written contracts. So the first problem that we encounter is that writing things down is not the main aim: it is about making conscious decisions about what we do.

The second problem is the tedious way in which the documentation of quality management systems is created and structured. This is usually described via a diagram similar to that shown in Figure 3.1.

QUALITY MANUAL

At the top of the pyramid is a document universally entitled the 'quality manual'. This has become a standard document of between 10 and 40 pages, depending upon exact style, which sets out the organization's general approach to meeting ISO 9001 requirements. It will have the following contents list:

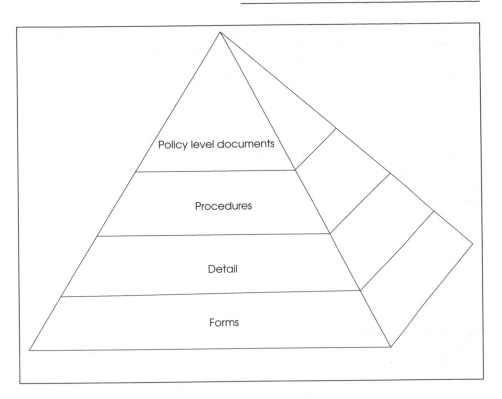

FIGURE 3.1   The documentation pyramid

○   An introduction to the organization and what it does
○   The exact scope of activities covered by the quality management system
○   A quality policy statement
○   A broad description of the organization structure and senior level responsibilities
○   A statement against each requirement of ISO 9001 explaining how it is interpreted for this organization
○   A cross-reference to the remainder of the quality management system documentation.

Although people have experimented with different formats and contents, in most cases they run foul of assessors who expect to see the standard approach. This has resulted in the vast majority of quality manuals being standard, boring, meaningless documents which are written by taking a manual which worked somewhere else and changing a few words. This, plus the fact that the document is only ever intended to express general intent, means that the quality manual is of little direct interest to most auditors. Certification assessors are obliged to review it to see that every requirement of the standard has somehow been addressed, but second and first party auditors usually pay it little heed. The only exception to this is in very small organizations which may elect to put some detail procedures in the quality manual to avoid making a general statement in that document and then having to repeat it in a lower level publication (examples are management review and records policies, which can often be easily covered within a quality manual format).

The approach to the creation of quality manuals may become more practical with the issue of ISO 9001:2000 which specifically states that system documentation does not have to be structured to fit the format of the standard. As, however, most organizations will continue to adapt their old manuals or models borrowed from elsewhere, the current practice is likely to be prevalent for the foreseeable future.

OPERATING PROCEDURES

It is the next level down of the pyramid which is of particular interest to most auditors. This level, normally known as 'procedures' or something similar, is the level which describes the main operational and management control practices in the organization. These are directly auditable since they cover how things are planned, controlled and recorded so that the entire cycle can be examined. There are usually one or more procedure documents to cover each significant activity. In order to understand what goes on in the area to be audited, it is usual practice to review the procedure documents in advance (see Chapter 8 on preparation) and basic auditing looks to see that actual practice follows the described preferred way of doing things.

Although procedure documents may be quite specific in terms of describing how things are managed, they typically will not cover very detailed instructions such as sequence of key presses on a computer program, or how to operate a machine, or intricate data lists; these are left to the next level down.

Unlike quality manuals, there is no real standard format for procedure documents. They are found written in all styles from flow charts or other diagrams, bullet points, directive or descriptive text and so on. Auditors typically have no right to comment upon style (unless the organization has an official policy on what the style should be and someone appears to have deviated from it) but should accept that they are written for the people in the area to use. If an auditor finds these documents difficult to follow this certainly represents an area to investigate, but it may transpire that they are perfectly clear to the specialists in the workplace.

These documents will also vary greatly in length. Some organizations keep them to a page or less, while others comprise 50 pages of small, close text. My own experience is that two to four pages seems to be a good length, but of course every organization and function has its own needs and auditors will have to be prepared to deal with all lengths, as well as with all styles.

DETAIL LEVEL DOCUMENTS

Quality professionals are fond of calling the third pyramid layer 'work instructions'. Indeed, early versions of BS 5750 and ISO 9001 referred specifically to the use of work instructions and the terminology has been revived in ISO 9001 after disappearing in the 1994 version. Certainly in most organizations, some functional and process areas need to have documents which describe certain tasks in detail. For example, in a manufacturing organization with a range of products an instruction is probably required telling packers exactly what to put in the final box (product, cables, instruction manual, registration card, installation disc, promotional leaflet, packet of mounting screws, etc.) since this will vary from product to product. These detail documents, telling employees what to do in specific circumstances, can take a variety of forms. They can be called instructions and written as text or flow charts, they can be technical drawings, instruction manuals, training guides, checklists, leaflets, prompt cards and so on.

These detail documents are a firm part of the quality system and often provide some of the most important controls. For example, I knew a petrochemical company in the Middle East whose technicians used to perform routine checks and calibration of instruments from experience. When they were given one-page standard checklists for the job, the recall rate (i.e. the number of times that an instrument was returned to the line after servicing and was immediately found to be suspect) dropped overnight from about 10 per cent to under 4 per cent.

For auditors, however, these documents often present a problem in that they are too detailed to audit properly. There are four main reasons for this:

1. The well-known fact that observation affects the results – if the auditor is watching me and I think they are trying to catch me out, I shall make sure that I do the job to the letter of the instruction. (Old work study research has shown that being studied often improved work rate more than adjustment of local work conditions such as lighting or space.)

2. Auditors will often not know what they are looking at. Unless they are experts in the precise task that is being carried out they will not be sure that what is being done is correct unless the work is performed like a tutorial, which defeats the object.

3. The specific task may not need to be carried out at the time that the auditor wants to audit, and records will usually only show that the task was done and the results recorded (procedure-level information) and not whether the operator pressed the green button before the blue one.

4. If the auditor decides to watch the task being performed, he or she could spend the entire allotted audit time watching that one task and see nothing else.

Thus auditors are usually less interested in detail level documents than in second level procedural types, although the nature of the paperwork needs to be assessed on a case-by-case basis so that something important and highly strategic is not missed just because its title suggests that it represents low-level detail.

FORMS

Blank forms will often be seen as included in the third, 'detail' level of the document pyramid. I like to describe them separately since they need their own explanation. First, they are different to other quality documents in that they are created in order to be written upon; whereas writing on other standard documents is specifically discouraged. The other main difference is that forms are usually available in large numbers, to be taken as required, where other documents typically have a restricted formal circulation list. Third, blank forms are, actually, part of the quality documentation. After all, we could ask everybody just to submit their information on blank sheets of paper. We do not because we wish to let them know exactly what information we require and in what format. Thus a form is a type of instruction and is therefore a quality document.

PROCEDURE OR WORK INSTRUCTION?

One of the biggest difficulties with this traditional pyramid approach is understanding where the boundaries lie. In practice the title 'procedure' is sometimes given to detail level documents and there is often confusion between the two. Occasionally writers will insert a piece of pure detail instruction into a second level document simply to avoid the complication of creating a separate document just to house the small specific instructions. Similarly checklists can sometimes be called work instructions and sometimes forms (because we write on them).

Practical systems have blurred boundaries between the levels of documents. Frankly, this does not really matter. After all, what does it matter what we call this document as long as it says the right things, it gives useful guidance and it is followed? Auditors should not worry too much but concentrate more on what is written down and how well it is being applied. Auditors who spend their time arguing over what a document should be called or whether this paragraph should be split out into a separate document have missed the point.

WHY HAVE FORMAL DOCUMENTATION?

It is an interesting feature of ISO 9000-based quality management systems that managers appear to dislike the formal procedural and instructional documentation, finding it a chore to keep them updated. Yet those same managers will often happily write a detailed memorandum to their staff telling them about how things will work from now on.

The formal instruction is intended to do the same job as that memo. The difference is that memos can lead to confusion. I once met a technician who was following completely the wrong practices because years ago his manager had sent him a memo telling him to do it that way (and he still had it, grey and crumpled by now) and nobody had ever sent him a memo specifically telling him to do it any differently. If the instruction had been in an official, controlled instruction, then it would have been easy to tell which document superseded another. So document control is about making sure that we are following the latest instruction.

If it is the sometimes formal and difficult way that documents are written that upsets us that can be easily corrected without upsetting the operation of a management system or the requirements of ISO 9001 (by this I mean that if you have written your documents badly then it is your own fault and you should do something about it).

THIS IS NOT THE COMPLETE PICTURE

The real problems with the idea of quality documentation is that people see the pyramid (or whatever model they prefer) as representing all documentation that makes up the quality system. Internal auditors have used the procedure documents as their sole guide in preparing for an audit and external auditors have ignored general policy documents which are described as 'nothing to do with ISO 9000'. In fact there is a far wider set of documents which has an impact on the quality of products and services and which affects customer service. This set includes contracts, the quality policy statement, value statements, corporate objectives, business plans, service targets (e.g. mean running hours between required service interventions), performance targets (fault rates, failure rates, etc.), service level agreements, departmental objectives, cost analyses (e.g. looking at whether one area has normalized costs or profits higher or lower than other areas) and so on.

Auditors can then not only check for basic procedural compliance but also help to identify which areas are not performing as well as they could, maybe even helping to find out why. All of this requires an acknowledgement that the documentation which affects quality does not merely consist of what was written to pass the ISO 9001 assessment, but everything which has an impact on efficiency, effectiveness and both internal and external levels of service.

QUALITY COSTS

As we will see in the next chapter, the ISO 9001 standard requires an organization to monitor and measure its quality performance. Since the objective of any business is to make money (and even those organizations whose objective is not profit-related have to make best use of monetary resources) then it is sensible that at least some of the measurements employed should be related to costs. Most major quality initiatives include some element of quality costs. It is beyond the scope of this book to explore the concepts of quality costs in detail; indeed this could probably warrant a full publication in its own right. There are, though, some thoughts that an auditor needs to bear in mind.

Quality costs are traditionally classed as 'failure costs' and 'preventive costs'. Failure costs are the costs of quality errors and can include:

○   scrap
○   rework
○   repair
○   warranty
○   service
○   repeating actions (e.g. remaking a product, a second service call, reprinting a report)
○   delayed payments from customers
○   contract penalties
○   reduced prices for regraded items.

There may also be fewer direct costs of getting things wrong. These can include lost future business through customer dissatisfaction, management time dealing with complaints and problems, overheads associated with employing staff who deal with failure and lost opportunities. Lost business through quality failure can be enormous. If customers are not dealt with effectively, then the obvious failure cost is the cost of the refund or other remedial action, yet there is also the potentially much larger cost of lost future business from that customer. Even worse, dissatisfied customers are likely to moan to everyone that they meet about their poor impression and thus dissuade others from doing business with the organization. The lost business (and therefore the costs of failure) is unlimited. Prevention costs are those things which the organization does to reduce or eliminate the risk of failure.

Obviously the desire of any quality-conscious organization should be to drive quality costs towards a minimum. There are two schools of thought on this. The 'zero defect' point of view is that failure costs must constantly be driven lower since any one failure can have wider implications than we simply cost it for. To do anything else, the argument goes, is to accept a certain level of poor performance as 'good enough'. The other approach is to consider that there is a certain level beyond which it is not reasonable to delve, since further work trying to reduce failure costs will result in soaring prevention costs. It is usual in this case to assume a logarithmically decreasing failure cost curve and an exponentially increasing prevention cost curve, which gives us a diagram such as the one in Figure 3.2. If we add the costs of the two curves together, this gives us a minimum cost beyond which it is not economic to improve further (note: this minimum may occur at the point where the two curves cross, but not necessarily, depending upon the relative slopes of the two curves).

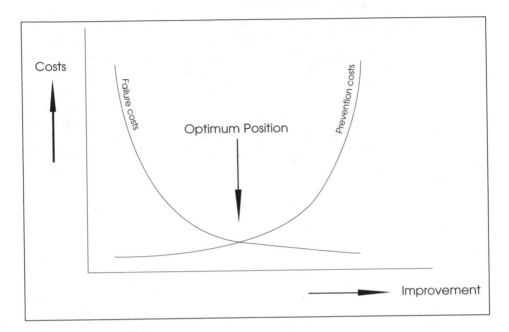

FIGURE 3.2   Prevention and failure costs

For auditors, then, it is first important to determine whether quality costs lie within the scope of the audit (for certification auditors they probably will not, unless that is the way the organization has chosen to measure its performance), then to discover how the client sees quality costs (it must be the client, not the auditee, since it is the client's requirements that we are there to satisfy). From that we can look at what the quality costs are, how they are measured and reported and what action is taken as a result. In some audits, especially internal audits aimed at identifying areas for improvement, calculation of quality costs may even be part of the audit itself, although we would normally see this as the job of either the people who incur and control the costs, or perhaps the finance function who are more familiar with the task of analysing monetary measures.

SUMMARY

○   Quality means different things to different people.
○   A reasonable way of looking at quality is whether or not we are constantly making our customer pleased with what we do.
○   Most organizations can perform a basically competent job; it is the little things which make a difference and really produce quality.

○   Managing quality is about prevention rather than detection.
○   Managing quality requires a comprehensive approach.
○   ISO 9001 and total quality management have historically taken different approaches to achieving the same goal but are beginning to move closer.
○   Looking at processes can be a good way of controlling the management of quality but we should not agonize too much about their definitions.
○   The quality management system is the overall set of rules and plans which aim to manage customer satisfaction.
○   The system is written down in a tiered series of documents.
○   Costs are an important factor in any quality programme and for all performance measurements.

In the section 'Little Things Matter', there are 218 occurrences of the letter 'e' in both upper and lower case.

4

ISO 9000 QUALITY STANDARDS

❖

HISTORY AND DEVELOPMENT OF QUALITY STANDARDS

Written standards for product quality have been around for as long as there has been business, certainly since the days of the Industrial Revolution when specifications began to be written for mass-produced goods. These days we do not think twice about creating a specification for business-to-business sales. Indeed, we hardly think of this as a 'quality' standard.

During the twentieth century, acceptance gradually grew that defining the technical specification alone was not enough. Those buying goods from others, especially complex equipment, recognized that the methods of control, test and inspection had to be defined as well as a set of final functional requirements. It is generally accepted that the first real quality practice standards emerged in the United States of America in the aftermath of the Second World War. The military establishment in those days, faced with the prospect of using hardware of ever-increasing complexity and sophistication, wished to ensure that its weapons would actually work when used in anger. This led to the production of a series of inspection standards. As their use and scope increased internationally, they began to include more 'management' activities until various standards were developed which bear some resemblance to the international quality standards with which we are now familiar.

The commercial standards institutions and promoters took note of what was happening and eventually came to the conclusion that a similar approach would be good for all industry, not just those manufacturers who supplied the various defence establishments. The first real commercial quality management standard was published in the UK by the British Standards Institution (BSI) which, after an initial experimental period, emerged as BS 5750 in 1979. It was based heavily on

49

the AQAP (Allied Quality Assurance Publication) standards in use at the time, approval to which was an essential prerequisite for approval as a supplier to most Nato armed forces. Its various parts equated exactly to the AQAP standards (BS 5750 Part 1 was the commercial translation of AQAP 1, BS 5750 Part 2 was the equivalent of AQAP 4 and so on). This initial standard was aimed solely at manufacturing companies (the clause which later became 'process control' in the 1987 and 1994 versions of ISO 9001 was called 'manufacturing' in the 1979 version of BS 5750).

The early BS 5750 standard was adopted with enthusiasm by some organizations, notably British Telecommunications, and almost ignored by others. I was a design engineer in a telecommunications cable factory when BT first started to apply pressure for us to adopt the standard, and acting quality manager responsible for its implementation by the time that we finally sought assessment of our company in 1981 (the certification process was also different in those days: major customers were allowed to grant 'independent' certificates). This was exclusively a British Standard and thus, strictly speaking, only applied to the UK. It remained so for quite a while, but eventually was picked up by the international community. Although there are a variety of stories about exactly how it was translated to an international standard, there are probably a number of reasons why it gained international recognition:

O   Since it had seemed a good idea to British standards writers, it is logical to conclude that similar thoughts had occurred to others.

O   The AQAP system was becoming difficult and expensive to police (the assessments were typically done by defence ministry staff, paid for by the military; as the number of approved suppliers grew so did the burden on the defence budget).

O   Leading UK corporations were applying common rules to all suppliers, so that some non-British manufacturers were being asked to adopt BS 5750 disciplines.

O   The nature of international standards making was changing, so that national standards bodies no longer were standards authors but were increasingly becoming providers of resource to international committees, turning themselves into local publishers of international standards.

As a result, BS 5750 was adopted, with a few changes to make it more widely applicable, as ISO 9000 in 1987. Again, the ISO 9000 standards equated exactly to the parts of BS 5750 and ultimately to the AQAP standards (ISO 9001 was the equivalent of BS 5750 Part 1, ISO 9002 was the equivalent of BS 5750 Part 2, etc.). For this reason, many will report that the entire quality standards certification movement began in the UK. This is only a half-truth, since BS 5750 itself grew out of military standards which already had international recognition.

When ISO 9000 was produced in 1987, the British Standard was updated to match the international content, but the name BS 5750 was retained.

The ISO 9000 series was updated in 1994, mostly with a few wording changes for clarification (although in one or two areas some argued that it caused further confusion) but with no real change in substance. At this time the name BS 5750 was dropped, although in the UK the British Standards Institution tried to keep some proprietary connotations by calling it 'BS EN ISO 9001' (the 'EN' stands for European Norm). Other national standards bodies have similar conventions, although the content of the standard behind the front page has always been identical. Translations from the official versions (the original is in French, but there are official versions in English and Russian, for example) are permitted as long as it is made clear that they are translations.

Officially, at the time of writing, the 1994 standard is the latest issued version. The new standard, ISO 9001:2000 and its sisters, is still only a draft and will not be fully issued for some time yet, although many organizations are already adopting the requirements and philosophies of the draft version to be ready for compliance when it is finally authorized.

The new standard is more than a simple wording update; it is a complete rewrite with the contents entirely restructured. The rewrite was prompted by the following:

O   The common trend for the use of process models in quality management.
O   Some confusion over the adoption and use of the different standards in the family and their application to organizations with different types and scopes of operation.
O   The difficulty that small firms have had in interpreting the requirements.
O   The debate as to the associated business benefits.
O   The desire to have a standard which is closely compatible with the recent (1996) environmental management system documents – the ISO 14000 series.

THE ISO 9000 FAMILY

The ISO 9000 family of standards has, for most of its life, been large, with a wide number of associated and supporting standards, many of which have had limited application and were not enforceable. In the 1987 and 1994 versions the three certification standards were ISO 9001, ISO 9002 and ISO 9003. Without going into detailed definitions of the three, the first of these was for companies who designed their own products or services, the second was for companies who did everything except design, and the third was for those whose products or services could be verified by inspection and test only.

Since modern quality fashion says that inspection and test alone is not enough, ISO 9003 had fallen into disuse. It is now seen as a hangover from the military days and no new certificates of this type have been issued by reputable certification companies for many years, with most of the old ones converted to ISO 9002.

Even with only two certification standards to choose from there was still confusion. There was always debate as to whether the audited organization or the assessor decided which standard to audit against, what exactly was meant by design, the perception that ISO 9001 was 'tougher' or 'better' than ISO 9002 and the sometimes disproportionate extra time that certification bodies required to audit ISO 9001 companies compared to their ISO 9002 counterparts, especially in the very small end of the range. In any event, there have always been organizations to which some elements of the standard have not applied, and they have simply ruled it out in their manuals. A common example is servicing. Post-sales service is something that many companies simply do not perform and so exclude its requirements from their systems. If that is possible for other requirements, why not for design? As a result the standards have been combined so that there is now only ISO 9001. Every company will be certified to the single standard and will simply exclude design if it does not apply to them (many already do this simply to keep the numbering in their manuals 'neat'). This should certainly make things simpler and less confusing in the future.

For companies already certified to ISO 9002 who are worried about this, it does not represent a real problem. Everyone will have to 'update' their systems to cope with the new requirements and will, after the next assessment after the standard has been issued, be given a replacement certification quoting ISO 9001:2000. This will apply to those previously registered to both ISO 9001 and ISO 9002.

In addition to rationalizing the certification standards, the total list of other standards has also been reduced. In fact the main family consists of just ISO 9000, ISO 9001 and ISO 9004.

ISO 9000 now becomes an introduction to the concepts involved and a repository for the vocabulary, replacing the old ISO 8402.

ISO 9004 remains a set of guidelines on the implementation of an all-encompassing quality system. It has also been completely rewritten so that it now directly relates, paragraph by paragraph, to ISO 9001. It is intended to be read and followed by those organizations who wish to adopt a system which goes beyond ISO 9001 certification requirements but still has ISO 9001 as a central framework. It is not a guide of how to create and maintain an ISO 9001 system.

The only other member of the family that remains of interest to us here is ISO 10011. This is the standard which describes how to conduct quality audits. It was originally intended that it would be revised for publication at the same time as the others, but its release is delayed to allow a common standard for both quality audits and environmental audits (currently ISO 14010) to be created. This shows an interesting move towards the view that management systems will, ultimately, have several integrated elements. This is reinforced by the fact that ISO 9001 and ISO 14001 are directly compatible and are written to have a consistent approach.

PURPOSE AND INTENTION OF THE ISO 9000 SERIES

The original purpose of having recognized quality management certification was twofold: it had intended benefits for both the organization and their customers. For the customers it would:

O   encourage their suppliers to adopt good practices;
O   make their requests and expectations seem more reasonable since the assessors would probably be looking for similar things;
O   provide an extra decision aid when choosing a short list of suppliers;
O   avoid having to audit every supplier to see whether or not they had a basic management system in place.

For organizations adopting the standard it would:

O   help to provide a standard framework for adopting good practice instead of having to invent their own;
O   provide a marketing tool ('choose us since we've shown that we take quality seriously');
O   offer escape from the burden of continual customer audits;
O   ideally, provide real internal benefits through introduction of the required systems and disciplines.

All of these benefits have probably been achieved to some extent, although some to a much lower level than might have been hoped. Certainly the ISO 9000 series has provided a standard framework and has been highly instrumental in increasing overall awareness of quality topics and how systems can be created. As a result it has also brought business benefits in many areas and every consultant has tales of their favourite customer who, through something identified while introducing ISO 9001, has saved significant costs and improved profitability.

Except perhaps in rare extreme cases, it has not, however, produced the complete business transformation that many evangelists had originally promised. This is for two reasons. The first is that the evangelists got it wrong. Despite what management experts will tell you as they coin their latest catch-phrase, no one business initiative can solve every problem and guarantee a rush of profitable orders. The ISO 9000 family is simply a tool to help to manage one part of the business. The second is that, even if the standard was the one panacea for every possible quality and customer care problem, it still would not be enough to be a success formula. As long ago as 1916 the French management writer Fayol told us that there are fourteen things that need to be attended to in order to create the successful organization:

1.   Division of work
2.   Authority
3.   Discipline
4.   Unity of command

5. Unity of direction
6. Subordination of individual interest to the general interest
7. Remuneration
8. Centralization
9. Scalar chain (line of authority)
10. Order
11. Equity
12. Stability of tenure of personnel
13. Initiative
14. *Esprit de corps*
> (H. Fayol, General Principles of Management from *Organization Theory,*
> *Selected Readings,* third edition, Penguin, 1990)

Notwithstanding any arguments about how well one or two of these principles apply in a modern business environment, we can see that few of them are really addressed by ISO 9001. Which shows us that ISO 9001 is important (since it helps to provide us with order, for example) but that it is only one element of a much wider management picture. Thus we could have a perfect quality management system praised by our certification assessor but if we do not show any initiative or *esprit de corps* then we are prone to fail.

The other aim that managers often complain has not been achieved is the elimination of customer audits. This is true but it would probably have been unrealistic to expect every audit to be replaced by that of an independent certifier. After all, each customer has things that they specifically want, above and beyond the requirements of a formal quality system, and they have the right to examine suppliers for those things. It is likely that independent certification has reduced the overall quantity and lengthiness of customer audits, but this is hard to measure and can only ever be a piece of imaginative guesswork.

Today, the aims have not really changed. There is perhaps more emphasis now on encouraging companies to adopt best practice and become more effective and efficient, but it is only a shift in viewpoint rather than a fundamental change.

THE NEW STANDARD

Since the year 2000 version of the ISO 9000 standard series is substantially different in appearance to previous versions, it is likely that the name 'the new standard' or something similar will stick until we begin to talk about its replacement, or at least until it has been with us for a few years.

It has been written to be more closely geared towards what a company does and with a heavy process-oriented flavour. The approach to the standard is summarized in Figure 4.1. This diagram provides the heart of many expert's explanations and, indeed, does provide a useful single picture to illustrate what the whole of the standard is about.

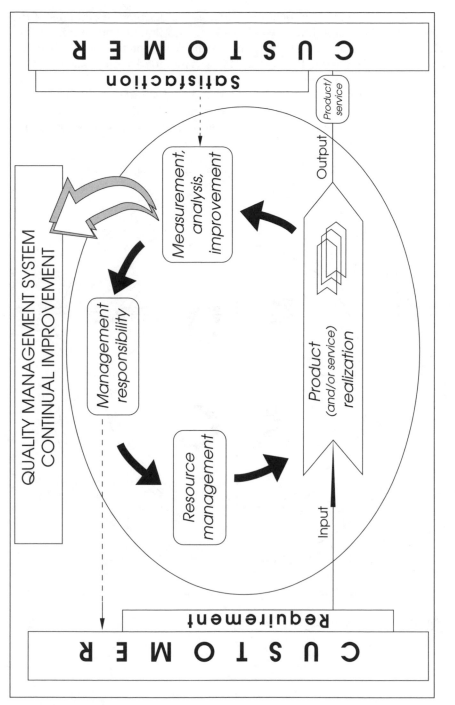

FIGURE 4.1 ISO 9001 quality management process model

The meaning of the diagram becomes clear as we discuss the contents of the standard later in this chapter. It may be worth mentioning that an earlier draft of the standard included a small PDCA (plan-do-check-act) picture in the diagram, similar to the model shown in Figure 4.2. This was intended to emphasize that the well-understood PDCA approach should be applied to everything; that is, to confirm the effectiveness of actions and act to correct shortfalls rather than do something and assume that it worked. I would guess that the PDCA picture was removed because it was not mentioned in the text and this caused people to ask what it meant.

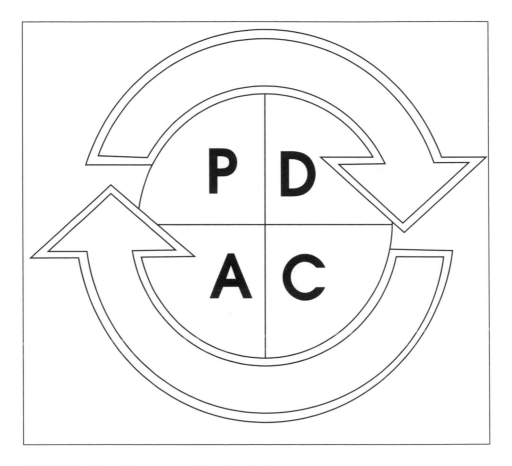

FIGURE 4.2   Plan-do-check-act

CONTENTS OF ISO 9001

Previous editions of ISO 9001 have had a few basic introductory statements but nothing of real interest to most auditors. The year 2000 version, though, has a few features which are worth discussing:

O   It contains the process diagram shown earlier. It discusses the idea of management of quality being looked at as both a vertical loop (through management, resources, processes and measurement) and a horizontal loop (from customer requirement, through the processes that deal with it, to the output which finally satisfies those requirements). This has shifted terminology towards calling a process or product audit a 'horizontal loop' audit and those looking at an organizational approach a 'vertical loop' audit.

O   It specifically states that uniformity of systems is not the objective and that each organization can create a system which fits its own needs. This has always been the enlightened view but it is good to see it now written into the standard.

O   It states that organizations do not need to change or create their systems to reflect the structure of the standard. Again, those with a good degree of business insight have always thought this but the statement in the standard will reinforce the message. It particularly means that nobody will have to rewrite their system based on the 1994 version to include new cross-references.

O   It requires a knowledge of, and adherence to, legal requirements.

Within the section entitled 'Scope' at the start of the document there is also a discussion of how to tailor the requirements for particular types of organization. It states that the standard can be tailored to fit circumstances where only certain parts of the business contribute towards meeting particular customer requirements, but that it only applies to the requirements under process management. This means that we are allowed to omit some product or service processes for which our customers do not require certification (for example if we are an aluminium smelter with a recycling facility, we could decide to omit the recycling function from the system) but we must include all management and support requirements (thus we cannot decide to leave out the procurement department or opt not to include inspection and test).

    I was at a meeting of assessors only recently where they all insisted that certification scope statements would have to be strongly worded to clearly differentiate between companies who design and those who do not, now that ISO 9002 no longer exists. I fail to see why. In fact I am pleased that the standard no longer explains in detail that design may be excluded from the scope if activities include no current or foreseen design work, as appeared in the first draft. This diminished the benefits of moving to a single certification standard where everything that does not apply to the organization is excluded, whatever it is.

The only terms and vocabulary defined are those of supplier, organization and customer, as we have already discussed. All other terminology is left to ISO 9000.

SYSTEM REQUIREMENTS – MANAGEMENT SYSTEM .

The requirements of the standard begin with a general statement (paragraph 4) that the organization should both identify, define and manage all those processes which together make sure that the customer requirements are being met. This sets the scene. This is what the standard is all about and tells us 'why' we are doing the rest of it. The standard goes on to say that a means of doing this is to create a quality management system which covers the requirements of ISO 9001 and which is both documented and permanently maintained. Again, this is fairly obvious, although this is the central requirement that causes an organization to document its major processes. This is where the instruction to 'write everything down' comes from and it thus gives an assessor apparent authority to complain that a system has not been adequately documented. There is also a reference to the tiered structure of documentation with a call for system level procedures, sequence and interface procedures and low level instructions.

A reference to making the system appropriate to the needs, type and scope of the organization appears again here, stating that the system should be appropriate to its application. The remainder of the requirements are then divided into the four main blocks shown in the diagram:

O   Management responsibility
O   Resource management
O   Product realization
O   Measurement, analysis, improvement.

MANAGEMENT RESPONSIBILITY

This section is a combination of specific things that the organization must do and a set of more general, non-specific, responsibilities for 'top management'. There is a strong emphasis on ensuring that 'top management' are committed to the entire quality system approach. Most of the requirements for commitment are reflected in more specific items under specific headings, but there is a requirement for top management to create an environment that allows people to be aware of and to implement systems for identifying and meeting customer needs. The problem with this is that it is difficult to audit. Whilst we all recognize that any business initiative needs senior level support for it to work, it is difficult to verify during an audit. Certification assessors will probably have to ask the most senior person with an operational role what his or her approach is to quality, but will find it hard to report anything as a result. Even if, for example, the managing director says that he believes ISO 9001 to be a load of rubbish, but recognizes that he has to do it, then this at least shows that he sees the need. Internal auditors may well be able to identify, from their prior experience, that the senior manager is not creating the right environment, but this will still be hard to raise during an audit since these concerns and impressions cannot easily be verified or traced. It may be better for this to be dealt with in other ways. The result is that few audits will lead to actions relating to senior management approach and commitment, so auditors should not spend too much time on it.

There are then a number of specific sub-headings:

Customer needs and requirements

This sub-section states that we should find out what customer needs are and define organizational requirements which will give the customer confidence in what we do. We also need to have ways of making sure that these requirements are understood by everybody and are met. Since customer requirements at order/contract stage are dealt with later, this is interpreted to mean that we have to look at what customers require generally and design our organization to meet their expectations. For example, we would be expected to have some sort of support organization or procedures if we sell the type of product for which customers are likely to call in with problems.

This sort of activity is traditionally seen as a marketing function. As a result some believe that the marketing activity of customer surveys and market surveys has now been brought into the scope of the standard (which may, if we do not watch out, result in a huge increase in the number of customer surveys and questionnaires which plop through our letter boxes). In reality, the requirement here is not terribly specific and one could easily argue that the whole way that the company is organized is based around the perceptions of what the customer wants in the first place. If an organization decides to write procedures for some form of regular market survey and suggests this as a way of meeting this requirement, then it should be audited. Otherwise there is nothing in the standard itself which is directly auditable and auditors should pay this item only limited attention. It should be emphasized that this sub-section does *not* require anybody to conduct market or customer surveys (although neither does it stop you if that fits your business needs).

Legal requirements

This is a completely new requirement which did not exist in earlier versions or even in the first draft of ISO 9001:2000. It requires an organization to have procedures for how it identifies and keeps track of legal requirements with which it has to comply. Auditors will now have to be familiar with the legal obligations (product marking, electrical testing, user documentation and notices, user rights, regulations, licences, qualification of personnel, regulator's guidelines, etc.) of the particular industry in order to be able to make valid assessments.

Policy

This is the now traditional requirement for a policy statement from the person at the top, as typified by the framed two or three paragraphs in the reception area (note that the word 'quality' has now disappeared from the requirement). The new standard emphasizes that the statement must relate to what customers want (which is not how many have been written), enable quality objectives to be set and reviewed, be widely communicated, implemented and understood, and must include a commitment to continuous improvement. This last requirement is new and will require most people certified to the 1994 version to rewrite their policy statements.

For an auditor, the basic approach is to see that the statement exists, that it is signed by the chief executive, that it has been communicated somehow, that it contains the improvement commitment, that employees understand it (that is they know that there is one and that it says that quality is important and that we must continually improve; they do not need to be able to recite it – indeed people who recite it make me nervous since I wonder if they really understand it) and that the operation and suitability of the statement are regularly reviewed (for example at management review meetings).

There are two further aspects that auditors will need to examine:

O   The policy statement should be compared to stated objectives and targets – can we see a pattern there? Are the objectives related directly to what the policy says?

O   For internal auditors, in particular, we need to ask whether what we are doing reflects our policy statement. To take a sensitive but common example: if our policy statement talks about individuality and empowerment but says nothing about appearance and image, yet we forbid employees to put their own posters and pictures up in their workspace, are we conforming to our policy statement? The new standard is likely to push internal auditing even further towards this kind of question rather than basic documentation compliance.

Objectives

Written quality objectives need to be established, which should be set at appropriate levels and functions in the organization and should be consistent with other system requirements, with the quality policy statement and with the need to improve.

This represents a change from the 1994 standard in that the objectives do not have to be in the policy statement, thus allowing them to be multi-level and to have objectives associated with specific parts of the business. Note that there is no need for these to be quantitative objectives. Thus it may still be difficult for third party auditors to do anything with this requirement other than to check that some objectives have, in fact, been documented and appear to be consistent within the system. Internal auditors, and possibly second party auditors too, can look closely at the objectives and ask questions about how we are trying to achieve them and whether or not we have.

Quality planning

The requirement for quality planning has, perhaps, caused the biggest confusion for those implementing quality systems. Some organizations have virtually ignored it while others, such as the construction industry, have come to terms with the fact that a quality plan is not really a plan in the way that we would think of a project plan, for example.

The requirements for planning have not changed a great deal in the new standard, in that they require the organization to decide how it will go about meeting customer needs by identifying resources, responsibilities, processes and procedures, verification, records and standards. For some organizations this just means setting up the basic quality system whereas others will need to create special quality plans to enhance the main system for special projects, customers or products. Indeed, a quality plan is normally thought of as a set of requirements specific to a particular situation. If all customers and products are basically dealt with in the same way, then no special quality plans are needed.

There are two differences, though, that are of interest to auditors. The first is that the list of things to be addressed by quality planning includes defining the processes involved and identifying their inputs and outputs. Although some will inevitably argue that their written procedures identify internal and external interfaces, often these procedures are not the same as the major business processes. It is likely that certification auditors will insist upon there being some identification of the key processes and their inputs and outputs. Flow charting will be a common way of doing this but is not essential, and simple descriptions will probably suffice. This is akin to the identification of process customers and suppliers prevalent in TQM and process improvement programmes. For other auditors, the fact that this information exists will be a great help since those interfaces are a prime candidate for error or inefficiency and a good target for investigation.

The second difference is that quality planning is to be aimed at achieving quality objectives. This could be interpreted to mean that a plan in the conventional sense is expected; that is, here is an objective so we have produced a plan of what we are going to do this year to meet it. Although there is no indication at the moment that certification assessors will take this view, it may be a good idea for those auditors looking at improvement to see whether managers have taken positive steps to do things which will lead towards achievement of objectives (and, of course, have they done those things, confirmed their efficacy and corrected any deficiencies).

Quality management system – general requirements

Again there is a general statement here, to the effect that a system should be established. It also says that the nature of the system should reflect the activities and size of the organization. Thus auditors will be quite within their rights to point out that the system in use, modelled on documentation borrowed from a much larger company, is inappropriate and cumbersome. This has a number of implications and will require some flexibility from those auditors who see many different types of organization. Communication is a topic that is in need of this adaptive approach. Many small companies believe that ISO 9001 systems require them to send each other formal memoranda and forms, when in fact the best method of communication is simply to lean over and speak to the person who is sitting only a few feet away from you. On the other hand, insisting on face-to-face verbal communication in an organization where the recipient is located several hundred yards away in another building and whom you have never met in the flesh is impractical and a more formal system is probably needed.

Responsibility and authority

This simply requires that roles, responsibilities and authorities are defined (documented) and communicated. This means that our system must say who does what and who is allowed to authorize what (e.g. who can sign things off). The best place that this happens is in the system procedures:

> Any person may raise a purchase request. This is passed to the head of their department for authorisation before sending to Procurement. From the purchase request, the Buyer prepares a purchase order, reviews it for completeness, then submits it to the Finance Director for authorisation before transmittal to the supplier.

This statement clearly sets out the roles and responsibilities. There may be other documents, such as financial sign-off limits and delegation lists, but the system procedure documents are the main source of information. Note that the standard does not require job descriptions or organization charts. These can be created if the organization believes they are useful, but they are not a requirement *per se*. Job descriptions, in particular, rarely contribute much to a quality system since they do not show a person's specific place within an activity nor define precise authorities (and most organizations are terrible at keeping them up to date). Organization charts can help an auditor to plan an audit and to understand what functions sit where, but for the most part job descriptions, where they exist, should be ignored.

Management representative

This requires the organization to appoint an individual who is responsible for maintaining the quality system, reporting on quality performance and proposed future developments/improvements, and for maintaining awareness of customer needs and requirements. This last point was introduced to the new version of the standard and it will be interesting to see how this develops. I am particularly worried that this requirement, in conjunction with one or two others, may lead to a dramatic increase in the number of surveys that are sent out.

The role is traditionally occupied by the 'Quality Manager' although it could actually be allocated to anybody. There are organizations that have a quality manager but appoint a board-level person as the management representative to speak for quality at the highest level. Management representatives do not need to actually manage the various quality processes, the role can be delegated, but in practice they often do. In smaller organizations the management representative (often given the courtesy title of 'Quality Manager' or something similar) is not a full-time role and is occupied by technical managers, administrators, and even accountants.

Third party auditors, on their initial assessment, will wish to see that such a person is appointed and is of a level sufficient to make his or her voice heard, but otherwise there is little to investigate (except perhaps when that person leaves or a new person is appointed to the role).

Internal communication

For the first time, reflecting a similar requirement to ISO 14001 and representing a change from the first draft, ISO 9001 requires procedures for internal communication. This requires an organization to define how functions and processes will communicate with each other and how all employees will be kept aware of developments.

Auditors have always sought to confirm that employees are aware of key quality issues. The new requirement for internal communication confirms that this is a valid avenue to explore.

The quality manual

There is a specific requirement to prepare a quality manual. This is the top level document which describes the organization's overall approach to the subject of quality management. There is nothing new in the year 2000 version of the standard and it is likely that quality manuals will remain the uniform ISO 9000 compliance document that they have always been. A quality manual typically includes:

○   the quality policy statement;
○   an introduction to the organization and how it is structured;
○   key responsibilities;
○   a definition of how the system is addressed in specific areas, typically written against the requirements of ISO 9001 (although this may happen less with the new emphasis on not having to write systems directly to reference the standard);
○   A cross-reference to the system procedures in place.

This type of document is of interest to third party auditors who wish to see that all of the key issues have been thought of and related to the needs of the organization, but has nothing to offer other auditors, especially those carrying out internal audits. Second party auditors will probably be more interested in the quality plan that relates to their contracts (if one exists) rather than the quality manual.

Control of documents

This is the traditional quality management system requirement with which most people are familiar (and to which, frankly, far too much attention is paid). The requirements are as follows:

○   Documents are approved for use, usually requiring a signature or some other verifiable means (which is not always easy in electronic systems). This should apply to standing orders, reminder instructions posted on the wall, etc. as well as to 'normal' documents such as system procedures.

○   Documents are regularly reviewed and revised as necessary. Some organizations take this to mean that they have to send every document around once per year to everybody with an interest in its contents and ask them to sign off that they have reviewed it, identifying any required changes. This method is slow and expensive, and often means that required changes are left until the next review, which could be several months away. A better way is to insist that managers and teams update their documents as soon as needed, keeping them under continual review. They can then demonstrate to auditors that this requirement has been met by the fact that there are frequent changes, throughout the year, to documents within the system.

○   Current versions of all documents are available to those who need them (or might need them). This does not mean that everyone has to have a copy on their desk or at their work station, but they must have 'reasonable' access to one. Thus it is reasonable to expect that a field service technician has his or her own copy of key documentation, whereas a group of administrators in an office may share a single copy between them. The necessary availability of documents will also depend upon their exact nature; management-level procedures will not need to be referred to very often, whereas a detailed circuit diagram will probably be needed every time that a fault on the circuit board needs to be traced.

○   Obsolete documents are removed, marked or destroyed. This basically means that auditors should try to ensure that nobody could mistakenly be working to an out-of-date document.

All of the above requires documentation to be suitably referenced and revision controlled. Although some of the specific revision control requirements such as a master index are no longer prescribed in the standard, the need for 'revision control' still calls for similar controls to be applied to those that we have always seen. Some tips for simpler document control are listed below:

○   Try to avoid systems which rely on updates of individual pages within a larger document. This makes indexing and referencing difficult, it is confusing for readers and copies are never kept up to date (recipients typically place the received pages in the front of the binder and promise themselves that they will go through the tedious chore of replacing the pages later). This practice originated in the days when whole documents had to be retyped to revise the whole text; those days are long gone and updating whole documents is now recognized as the best approach.

○   For similar reasons to the comments on individual page updating, try not to have documents which have two levels of revision control (e.g. an issue number and revision number). This again leads to confusion (in fact authors often are confused as to which number to increment, never mind the readers).

○   Dates can be a perfectly adequate indicator of revision status for some types of document.

○   Auditors should not spend too much time on this. Third party assessors, in particular, are often tempted to spend a disproportionate amount of time examining for this requirement; remember that this is only one of many parts of the standard and treat it accordingly. Those looking at improvement issues should also remember that although it may be important if we find a drawing or technical specification being used incorrectly there are very few ground-breaking business improvements that can be identified by studying document control.

○   If the organization is very large, or there are many workers based remotely (e.g. teleworkers) then it may be necessary to have some sort of confirmation of receipt of document copies but otherwise this practice is slow, cumbersome and expensive and it can bring its own problems.

○   Having the documentation web-based (or using a similar electronic storage and retrieval system) solves many of the control problems associated with paper systems.

Control of quality records

There has always been confusion over what is a document and what is a record. Essentially a record shows what has been done (a report, meeting minutes, a completed test sheet, etc.) and a document tells us what will be done (a specification, a drawing, a system procedure, a user manual, etc.). The confusion is understandable, though, because there is sometimes an overlap. For example, is a purchase order an instruction, because it tells the supplier what it has to do and references the associated requirements, or is it a record of purchasing activity? The answer is that it could be considered as either or both. Auditors have to take account of this and not be too strict when seeing how the requirements are applied in an organization and to which documents.

The requirements are that there must be established ways of identifying, indexing and accessing records. Thus the organization should always, within reason, be able to access key records, even when the person who looks after them is away. The rules for throwing records away (i.e. after what minimum retention period, and under whose authority, etc.) also need to be defined.

There is sometimes a misinterpretation of what is meant by quality records. Some organizations think that this only means records that would not be kept if the organization did not have an ISO 9001 system. In fact it means everything that affects quality or customer service. This includes purchase orders, training reviews, test sheets, production plans, monthly reports, visit reports, quotations and tenders, to name but a few.

Management review

At defined intervals (in practice at least once per year, typically more often than this), the most senior personnel of the organization must review performance in quality terms, and discuss whether the quality system is doing its job in the most effective way. Almost everybody conducts the review as a meeting with a strong representation of the senior management team present, but it need not be done like this; it could be written feedback to a detailed report or a series of individual discussions. The meeting tends to be easiest and most effective, though. It is a good idea, if possible, to make it a separate meeting; if it is included in the monthly management meeting, or tacked onto the end of another meeting the issues are in danger of being submerged or being paid insufficient attention to be meaningful.

The review must consider, as a minimum:

O   internal, certification and customer audit reports
O   customer complaints and satisfaction measurements
O   reports of process performance, including failure rates, reject rates, return rates, etc.
O   any improvement or problem correction or prevention actions taken, concluded or begun since the last meeting
O   new circumstances that will have an impact on the quality system.

Quite often this is achieved by consideration of a report circulated in advance by the quality manager or management representative. The meeting should allow discussion of all aspects with identification of any investigations or other actions that are needed as a result.

The review should be recorded (usually by minutes of the meeting) and should specifically describe any resultant actions relating to the overall system, the quality policy and related objectives, the needs for special product or process audits, or further allocation of resources. Actions from such meetings often also include areas where top management identify that improvement action should be taken, or at least investigated. As represents good practice with any action planning, actions should be allocated to an individual or team and given a target completion or report-back date. Auditors should examine this element by seeing that the review has happened and that it was organized appropriately. An important area for investigation will be the identified actions, looking at whether they were completed on time and whether they have been effective.

RESOURCES

Resource management – general

This part of the standard continues the requirement from the 1994 version to provide enough resources to establish the system, now with the added need to provide enough to also improve it. The necessary resources are not limited to those which support processes, but include resources for supporting the organization and special projects.

I have always thought that this aspect is one of the most difficult to audit. Most managers, if directly asked the question, will say that they could manage better if they had more people, or more computers, or a bigger budget, or all of these or more of anything. It is very difficult for most auditors to make a sensible judgement as to whether extra resources are needed or not. Even if the work is obviously behind or over-stressing the staff, is this because there are inadequate resources or is it because there is poor management and coordination? Usually within the time allowed for an audit it is difficult to tell, in which case it is better to report the symptoms rather than try to pin the problem down to resources.

Certainly third party auditors can almost never audit sufficiently to prove lack of resources. It is also difficult for internal auditors since the issue of resources is likely to be politically sensitive within the organization and closely tied with financial targets and budgets which may not allow room for current expansion of resources. It is perhaps only second party auditors, with the authority of the person who pays the bills behind them, who can suggest that allocated resources are less than they would consider acceptable to control a particular activity.

Assignment of personnel

People whose job affects how the product or service is produced and delivered should be competent. This is a fashionable business word which creates much debate as to its meaning and value. Luckily the standard helps us out, stating that competence is determined based upon applicable education, training and experience. Thus we are allowed to decide for ourselves what makes a potential appointee 'competent'. Since there is a general requirement for documented systems, rather than having the requirement repeated against each clause, it is possible that certification assessors will now interpret this as requiring documented procedures for recruitment and promotion/appointment. Having said that, many organizations have previously had documented recruitment procedures and, for those seeing the documented system as an aid to management, it is probably a good thing to define how the recruitment process should work.

Auditors should not treat examination of the recruitment (or internal appointment) process as an opportunity to criticize the placement of any individual in a role. Investigation should be based upon deciding whether an effective decision-making process exists and is followed. Such decision-making processes should, of course, take account of any employment law relating to fairness and discrimina-

tion. Ethical issues should also be considered, although auditors, especially certification assessors, must understand that these can be highly sensitive.

Competence, training, qualification and awareness

The topic of 'competence' arises again here, although the requirements have not
really substantially changed from the previous version of the standard. It is
required that training needs are identified (usually via some form of training
review or needs analysis, typically at performance appraisal time), that something
is done to address those needs and that the effectiveness of training is evaluated.
There is also a statement that the organization should qualify people to cope with
what is expected of them and that competence and qualification should be verifiable.

Auditors have to apply a lot of common sense in this area as they check:

○   that everyone has had their training needs reviewed within the last year
or so, according to the policies of the organization, and that there is some
record of what those training needs are – it will be acceptable if the training needs for some are recorded as 'none' but suspicious if there are no
training needs identified at all;

○   that the identified training has been provided (note that 'training' does
not only mean formal classroom events but can be self study, on-the-job,
distance learning, etc.) – if most of the training has happened but some is
outstanding, even a year later, the auditors have to decide what is 'reasonable' since often excessive training needs can be identified for
favoured or poorly performing employees which budget restrictions and
the constraints of the job will not allow, although again there is probably
a problem if none of the identified training has been conducted;

○   that there is some way of identifying whether the training has done the
job – this could be via the performance appraisal again but there could be
some other, more direct and more immediate means;

○   that all training, experience, education and specific qualifications are
recorded – the requirement for competence to be demonstrable reinforces the widely held belief that everything relevant should be recorded,
thus avoiding the occasional prior practice of only recording what training has been received since the employee joined the organization (or
perhaps since the system was first introduced).

We need to understand what we mean by 'qualified' and 'competent'. These terms
do not necessarily require formal qualifications or official competence verifications such as the UK NVQ (National Vocational Qualification) system. Mostly they
require an informal approach, although some organizations may have their own
qualification system, such as internal certification to operate particular machines
or perform certain technical tasks. There are a few jobs which do require official
qualifications that auditors can check for, examples include:

O   medical staff in a hospital
O   lawyers in practice (legal advisers in industry do not have to be formally
       qualified)
O   external financial auditors
O   heavy equipment operators
O   welders
O   vehicle drivers
O   ISO 9001 certification assessors (see Chapter 7 on auditor qualification
       and competence)
O   air pilots and vessel masters.

Remember, though, that although we might expect or anticipate a certain level of qualification for particular jobs (certified management accountant for finance director, chartered engineer for technical director, IPD member for personnel director) these are not essential and many people hold down such jobs quite successfully without formal qualifications, although they are undoubtedly 'qualified' in the ISO 9001 sense.

There is also a requirement to keep everybody in the organization aware of how important the system is, how this work impacts on the business, how improvement of personal performance can benefit everybody, what their place is in the overall picture and the consequences of getting things wrong. This will provide auditors with even greater opportunity than previously to investigate employee awareness.

Information

This is a completely new requirement. It considers information as a resource (again, following the current management fashion for the idea of the knowledge-based organization) which must be defined, maintained, readily accessed and protected from corruption or error.

This applies to two areas. The first is keeping a library of the necessary standards, specifications and regulations which apply to the processes and having methods of making sure that they are always current and relevant.

The second relates to information technology. The organization needs to ensure that its IT system has effective and disciplined system management, that programs and other software are suitably verified and controlled, and that data is subject to routine backup. Although these requirements already existed in the 1994 standard, under document and data control and control of quality records, this was often ignored. Now every organization will have to recognize that the impact of the IT system on quality management cannot be ignored.

Auditing this aspect should not present any particular technical difficulties. There will, however, be two barriers to overcome, the aversion that some people feel towards understanding the details of IT operation, and the almost universal feeling amongst IT personnel that ISO 9001 has nothing to do with them.

Infrastructure

Infrastructure is considered as yet another resource which must be identified and provided. This is an area for which there may or may not be defined procedural documentation, although it is unlikely in most organizations. As with other resources, there is little that auditors can specifically investigate or prove in this area.

Work environment

The standard says here that the physical and human elements of the work environment which affect quality must be defined and implemented. This can be interpreted as setting policies for, and maintaining, good housekeeping.

This aspect can best be audited via observation, permitting any auditor, internal customer or certifier, to raise comments on poor storage, poor cleanliness, untidiness leading to potential damage or identity confusion, work attire (e.g. in sterile or similar areas), temperature and humidity and so on, as appropriate to the circumstances.

PRODUCT AND/OR SERVICE REALIZATION

General requirements

Although many of the actual requirements of the standard have not changed since the previous version, the flavour now has a very strong process element. This section of the standard rewrites traditionally recognized quality system expectations in a process light. It also adds some new requirements specifically aimed at process thinking.

The general introduction to the realization section is quite lengthy and contains some specific requirements, some of which will be satisfied through other activities but some of which will need their own actions and systems.

The first is that the organization is expected to identify which processes begin at receiving customer instructions and end at customer satisfaction (which the standard calls a horizontal loop – Figure 4.1 (p. 55) helps to visualize this), with a cross-reference to the earlier quality planning section. Auditors should determine whether or not the area being audited has identified which activities are part of this horizontal loop and which are more aimed at support. They should also ensure that the people involved know what this means and how support activities contribute to quality.

There are requirements for process sequences and interactions to be determined and for responsibilities to be defined. This is normally adequately covered in system procedures. The only particular thing that auditors need to look for is to see that procedures do actually cover interfaces and describe responsibilities within the body of the text (headings entitled 'responsibilities' at the start of procedure documents may contribute but are rarely enough; full responsibilities are best described in the actual activity description/instruction).

A number of further items then call for all processes to be adequately planned, controlled, documented and resourced, all of which is probably adequately covered by addressing other sections. There is, though, a requirement for verification that processes can be operated to achieve a quality performance. It is likely that, in many cases, organizations will have to do nothing here except to show that they are, in fact, delivering conforming products or services, but some may wish to carry out process capability studies for new technical or complex processes. Certainly it is expected that new plant and technical capability should be trialled or commissioned before full integration into company processes. To examine this requirement, auditors can look at process design and determine whether it is arranged to meet the appropriate quality objectives. Of course, this does require some element of judgement and subjectivity, so may be difficult specifically to assess for certification auditors, although it may be an excellent target for internal auditors looking for potential improvements.

Customer-related processes

When dealing with customers we are expected to understand how much the customer specifies its requirements, which unspecified requirements are still necessary for us to meet (for example my local British electrical shop should supply goods to work at 240V 50Hz, even though I will probably not remind the sales assistants of this fact),what other requirements need to be met such as laws and regulations (e.g. informing the customer that our product contains nuts to avoid unnecessary allergic reactions) and to take account of all those secondary factors such as delivery time, post-sales support and so on which are often forgotten.

Then, when we receive a specific instruction from a customer (separately titled under 'review of customer requirements' and 'identification of customer requirements' but really an extension of the same theme) we must review what the customer wants to make sure that we have enough information, we understand what the customer wants, that any conflicts with prior quotations etc. are resolved and that we are able to meet the requirements. This last is particularly important where we formally acknowledge or accept orders, since we must not promise what we cannot achieve.

For auditors, there is a large scope here to investigate how the relationship with customers is established, how we define what we are going to supply to each customer and how each individual order or event is managed. This should all be done in such a way that the customer is protected from receiving the wrong thing or from our failing to meet its expectations. Auditors can look for evidence of consideration of customer requirements at every stage of the relationship, from enquiry and proposal through to delivery instruction. Decisions on what to do must be recorded somewhere. Some of the early parts may be covered, for example, at the design stage where we consider what are the general fitness for purpose and legal requirements. Others may be covered by some sort of recorded contract or order review at the time of receiving individual customer instructions.

Customer communication

There are expected to be defined system approaches to dealing with customer communication other than those directly relating to contract award or order placement. These include general information, general enquiries, complaints and other conformance/satisfaction information and recall processes.

Auditors will expect to see that defined procedures exist for all of these and that they are being followed. Where enquiries require action, it should be possible to follow up to see that the action was taken and has been effective (appropriate to the type of communication; we would expect to see more substantial records on what was done as a result of a customer complaint than when a brochure is requested).

There are some interesting new requirements here beyond those in previous versions. The largest is the recognition that sometimes customers will communicate about product or service conformity issues without making a formal complaint. This relates to simple batch rejections or warranty returns, which often are not classified as complaints but still need a suitable handling and communication procedure.

The other new aspect is the requirement to establish procedures for handling enquiries, which previously had often been considered outside the scope of the standard, unless they led directly to a quotation or proposal. Auditors should look particularly at the sales contact tracking systems here and be prepared for some resistance; sales staff are notoriously reluctant to adopt ISO 9001 or other systematic controls.

Design and development – general

This first part of the design and development requirements calls for conventional project management controls to be applied. That means that development plans should be prepared and documented which include or reference the stages involved, the points at which some form of evaluation (design review, testing, trials, commissioning, etc.) will happen, the responsibilities for the various activities and any other necessary controls. These plans have to be available as needed and updated when required (note: the standard makes no mention of 'baselining' original project plans to identify total deviation and slippage, although this is a sensible project management technique and would be a good idea for all development work). There is also a statement that the interfaces between various groups must be managed to ensure good communication and to avoid confusion of responsibilities. It should be borne in mind that this is especially important where some of the development work is to be carried out by sub-contractors, contract staff or teleworkers.

There is little to be gained here from auditing to see whether the project is on track according to the current plan. If the project leader is not doing that and keeping track of delays then there is something seriously wrong. It is worth, though, looking to see whether the plan is being updated as changes occur, since this is something which is occasionally forgotten.

More significant audit findings can be made through looking at interfaces and communication, actions and plan changes resulting from evaluations and verifications (early tests and reviews will inevitably show that the design does not yet meet requirements), and whether the planning process itself is sufficiently rigorous to make design success likely. For example, project plans which consist only of PERT or Gantt charts produced from a computer package are unlikely to be sufficient since they cannot adequately describe responsibilities, interfaces or any design rules and procedures specific to this project.

Design and development inputs

At the start of the design process, there must be some definition of what the design is intended to achieve. This is typified by the marketing requirements document, or similar, that is produced by organizations that conceive their own designs. These should reference all requirements that the design should achieve, including regulations, design philosophies, company standards, information from previous designs and resolution of any potential confusion.

Where customers provide a requirements specification (for example to contractors or design consultancies) then the organization itself may need to add requirements that are missing (design standards, regulations, etc.) from the original requirement.

Input requirements form the basis for eventual evaluation of the design. The only thing to audit here is that the input has been defined and that it appears to be complete and appropriate.

Design and development outputs

The output is the 'thing' (product, service, etc.) that the design programme was intended to achieve. This output must be defined by physical items and documentation in such a way that the auditor can confirm whether it has met input requirements.

The whole definition of the output must be reviewed before release to ensure that it has, in fact, met input requirements, that it contains or references safe and proper use criteria and definitions of application and general usage (i.e. user instructions, maintenance guides, interface specifications, data sheets, etc.).

Auditors should review output information and see how closely it has been verified against input requirements. They should check, for example, whether there are input requirements which have not, or cannot, be proved in the final design or if the verification and validation has been rather 'thin'.

In ISO 9001 terminology:

○   verification of designs usually means testing, inspection and checking of the design to see whether it meets input (e.g. laboratory test);

○   validation means evaluation of the design in circumstances similar to those in which it will be used in practice (e.g. field trial).

Design and development review

Design programmes must include at least one design review (if there is only one then it is often at the end).

A design review is not the same as a progress review. It is not about checking progress or chasing up information, but is a discussion of what has been designed so far and whether that design is suitable to achieve the input requirements. Design reviews are usually conducted as meetings, with participants from all involved functions. The design is discussed in detail, with each element reviewed by people who understand what is being discussed and can ask sensible questions.

For large projects, reviews may be conducted at several stages, with specific aspects of the designs evaluated at each one.

Auditors should check to see that there are minutes (or an equivalent record) of design reviews, that they identify actions to be taken to correct any problems or uncertainties, and that the actions have been attended to.

Design and development verification

As described earlier, verification is basic testing/checking of the final design. It should be planned as part of the overall project plan. Typical verification might be:

O   comparing the design with previous ones
O   testing
O   practical demonstrations and walk-throughs
O   analysis via calculation or other methods
O   design review.

For example, a technical product would be verified by using test equipment, a training course might be verified via a design review and walk-through, and a bus service could be verified by simulation.

Auditors should check that enough verification of the appropriate type has been performed, and that any resultant problems or uncertainties are acted upon. Ideally, auditors should be sufficiently competent in the techniques of the design process to make sensible judgements about whether the verification is suitable and adequate (or at least to see whether similar sensible questions have been addressed at design review). It may be difficult for some auditors, though, especially certification assessors, to challenge the design team who are, naturally, the experts.

Design and development validation

This represents field trial or its equivalent. New pharmaceuticals will undergo limited trials on test volunteers, new software will be given to selected individuals and organizations as a beta release, a new traffic control policy will be trialled in a single town before rolling out nationwide and a new theatre production may be given a short run at a provincial house before being put on in the capital.

Sometimes it may not really be possible to provide true validation. This occurs in one-off design projects such as in the construction industry or for those setting up a professional conference. In these cases at least a partial validation should be performed, including such things as:

○   comparing it with a similar previous design;
○   performing as much extension of the verification process as possible;
○   validating individual components;
○   using calculations, simulations or other analyses;
○   design review.

Auditors are looking for similar things here to those sought for verification, with the same thoughts about necessary auditor competence.

Control of changes

When designs are changed there must be a controlled change process which requires proposals to be recorded, reviewed and approved before they are put in place. Consideration will need to be given to any impact on:

○   compatibility (will related items still work with the new design and will there be any interface implications);
○   usability (will there be any human interface implications; will the technical changes made require changes to user instructions);
○   maintainability (how will it affect spares and service);
○   regulatory requirements (will we continue to comply with regulations, or will we need to seek re-approval);
○   service timing (will the change to the service affect its availability or speed of delivery);
○   stocks and work-in-progress (does the change need to happen immediately, or can we use up existing stocks).

Auditors should look to see that the design change process takes all relevant factors into account. Second and third party auditors will probably only be able to see generally that the process is operating, but internal auditors may understand the nature of the products or services sufficiently to look at past design changes and identify whether these considerations are truly adequate, perhaps even directly comparing them to known prior problems.

Purchasing – general

Purchasing must be controlled such that we buy the right products and services to help us fulfil customer needs. With great insight, the writers of the standard have added a statement that the level of purchasing controls should be appropriate to the effect that the purchasing has on the final product or service. This avoids the previous commonly encountered problem of organizations applying strict supplier selection and procurement disciplines to purchases of paper clips and boardroom glassware.

This section also describes the selection of suppliers and sub-contractors based upon their ability. This is the requirement which usually causes organizations to create an 'approved supplier list', which is the simplest but not the only way of proving that the requirement has been met. If appropriate, the organization may also need to create a grading system for suppliers with different levels of supervision and checking applied to each grade.

Auditors should check to see that all purchases are made in accordance with the organization's rules on selection of suppliers. They should look to see that there is some evidence of how the supplier became added to the approved list (i.e. on what basis: prior history, assessment, trial, recommendation, sole source, etc.) and that a single evaluation of the supplier at the beginning of the ISO 9001 system is not the only consideration ever given to its performance. (I have seen many systems where the supplier is on the list because it supplied some sample product which we bought ten years ago, and we have not even asked ourselves the question since whether it is continuing to provide us with adequate products or services.)

A special point to watch out for is the use of supplier questionnaires. They are usually used because a consultant has told the organization that they have to but they really tell us nothing. As an independent consultant (i.e. a one-man business) I was faxed a questionnaire a few years ago to have me 'approved' before I could deliver a training course to a petrochemical company. I answered 'no' to most questions since I did not have a quality manual, a quality manager, a goods inwards area, an inspection procedure, calibrated test equipment or any other of the things that were demanded. Despite this I was awarded 'approved supplier' status only two days later. Plus, when organizations are first putting in a system it must be very insulting to established, high-quality suppliers to be sent a questionnaire stating that, despite their years of good service, they will not be added to the approved supplier list unless they tick the right boxes on this sheet of paper. Auditors should check to see that a meaningful supplier assessment process is used, not one which just 'goes through the motions'.

Purchasing information

When a purchase order is placed, the related documentation must sufficiently describe the product or service to ensure that we receive the right thing, which will include referencing any qualification or approval and management system requirements. (For example, when placing an order for delivery of a training course for our clients we might well state the name of the trainer that we have agreed as suitable, ask for the course syllabus to agreed by us in advance and state that the delivery must include our standard training centre introduction procedures.)

Purchase documents should be reviewed for suitability before release to the supplier. Auditors should thus look for complete information to be recorded and for there to be some evidence of review, for example the signature of the final approval authority. Note that this does not necessarily mean that all orders need to be placed as a written original in the post. Fax orders are acceptable where this is the preferred method. Even telephone orders can be appropriate (in fact, in some businesses suppliers almost insist on telephone orders and discourage written confirmation owing to the risk of duplication) but they should still be recorded. Auditors should determine whether telephone orders are adequately recorded to enable future problems to be resolved and for goods inwards checking to be managed, as well as looking at whether the nature and complexity of the order would make it inappropriate for verbal placement.

Verification of purchased product and/or services

Anything purchased by the organization must be verified to a level appropriate to the risks involved. There are two dimensions to determining risk:

○   How critical the product or service is to satisfaction of customer needs.
○   How much demonstrable confidence the organization has in its supplier.

Auditors should look to see not only that verification is being performed but that the level of verification is appropriate.

Where the risks (including related costs) are very high, some verification may be needed at the supplier premises. For example, if we are buying a large piece of capital equipment from an overseas supplier, the last thing that we need is the huge expense and delay involved if we have it delivered only to find that there is a problem which requires returning it to source for rectification. If we want verification at the supplier premises, it should be written into the original contract or purchase order (otherwise the supplier may not agree to it). There may even be occasions when our customer wishes to make the verification at the supplier (for example if we are buying this equipment as part of a larger, turn-key contract). This should be acceptable (if, of course, the customer has specified it in its original order or contract) but we will have to make sure that we formally tell the supplier of the requirement when we place the business with it. If there is nothing verified at supplier premises then there is, of course, nothing for auditors to investigate. If there is, then auditors should see that the verification has been suitably planned, controlled and recorded. And if customers have done the on-site verification, we should check that the organization has taken its own steps to ensure quality and not left it to the customer (since we are probably still responsible for overall successful completion).

PRODUCTION AND SERVICE OPERATIONS – GENERAL

The main operations of the organization which go towards satisfying customer needs will have been identified in an organization following the standard, as we discussed earlier. For each of these, there need to be controls in place to ensure that the following requirements are fulfilled:

○   Appropriate work standards and instructions are available, with a specific requirement that they be clearly understandable, which opens a door for auditors to look carefully at the nature and format of such instructions. Note that instructions should not be needed where they do not contribute to quality; do not write an instruction to a trained fitter on how to use a spanner, for example (in fact unnecessary instructions get in the way since they make it more difficult to find the important information).

○   Suitable equipment is selected, used and maintained – it is unlikely that auditors will be able to make any judgement about the suitability of equipment within the confines of an audit (although questions could be asked about any selection and commissioning processes) but it is possible to see that there is an appropriate maintenance programme. Note that planned, preventive maintenance is not required, although it may be a good approach in some cases.

○   There is the right working environment, as we have already discussed. For auditors there may be some environments which are specified (for example in medical devices production areas) so that auditing can represent compliance against the rules, but there are other areas where there are few documented requirements but an inadequate environment may lead to poor quality of service (for example an excessively dirty paint factory is likely to result in contaminated product) where auditors may need to make more subjective judgements.

○   The right test and inspection equipment, of suitable accuracy, is used. We will discuss part of this requirement later but it should prompt auditors to identify whether enough test equipment (which includes on-line measurement equipment) is available, at the right place and of the right type.

○   Production and service processes are adequately monitored and verified by use of in-process or end-of-process inspection, testing or checking. Auditors should particularly look to see that in-process monitoring is sufficient and tends to follow the 'prevention rather than detection' philosophy, which will require some judgement rather than strict compliance evaluation.

○   At every stage of processing we know what testing, checking and measurement has been carried out and what its results are (i.e. to prevent misuse of products or mistaken belief that the service has already been proven) – auditing is for compliance here, seeing that everything examined has records or other identification which enables us to tell which testing etc. has been conducted and what its results were.

○   We know when the process has 'ended' and the product or service is released to the customer. Auditors can look for compliance with release procedures via records of prior releases.

Identification and traceability

Items and events need to be identified where applicable, with traceability back along the process if required by the customer or other stakeholders. Service identification will be largely by records of each service occurrence. The 'where applicable' requirement means that there is room for disagreement here as to what identification will be needed, involving a degree of judgement required by both auditors and auditees. This is one area where auditors should use observation as one of their primary tools, looking at items and records to see that they are identified.

Customer property

There must be controls and disciplines in place to take care of all customer property while it is in the care of the organization. Such property might include free issue material, products sent for service or repair, loan samples for development or testing. There are even extreme examples of how this may be interpreted, such as in education and training establishments where the students themselves are considered customer property and so there must be procedures in place to look after their personal safety, security and well-being.

Another common category of customer-owned property is documentation. Not only is the organization expected to look after it and prevent damage or deterioration but there may be a need to preserve confidentiality of designs or other information.

Note that, where items are supplied by the customer for incorporation in the product or service, it should not be assumed that they are satisfactory just because the customer supplied them; the organization will need to undertake an appropriate level of verification.

Auditing this aspect is very much aimed at compliance and so the emphasis varies little between audit types. Auditors should first identify what customer property exists or may exist and look for how items currently on site are controlled. Observation is a key tool here, and auditors should particularly look for controls to identify each item properly and make sure that it cannot be mistakenly used for another project or given back to the wrong customer. They should also watch out for the very tempting practice of 'robbing' things from one customer without their permission, with the intention of replacing them later – this is not permitted unless the customer has given its say-so.

Handling, packaging, storage, preservation and delivery

Everything that affects the product or service including parts, components, materials, tools, etc. must be treated in such a way that it will not be damaged or otherwise deteriorate. This means storing it in such a way that it is protected, as well as observing basic precautions for handling and packaging to prevent damage in transit. It is normally expected that there will be documented procedures for all key aspects, including how we will package things and using what materials. This will also cover special protection requirements including environ-mental storage for perishable items, care of shelf life, electrostatic precautions and any industry-specific special storage requirements.

Auditors should again use observation here, in conjunction with knowledge of proper protection measures for the items concerned to confirm adequate preservation.

Validation of processes

This is the traditional 'special processes' requirement. The idea is that there are often some processes whose output cannot be adequately (or economically) verified by checking, testing, etc. including things which may only come to light after the product has been in use for some time or the service has been delivered. This might include painting, for example, where we cannot test whether the paint we have applied will peel off until it actually does, so we need to have detailed instructions for surface preparation and paint application, as well as testing a sample preparation first. I was once a quality manager in a cable factory where we had to test sample joints for strength since it was impossible to know the strength of the actual joints in real cable lengths. Thus we 'qualified' both jointing staff and jointing machines by regularly testing samples. This 'qualification' principle and the idea of applying extra care to control of the process applies to all special processes.

Auditors should look to see which processes have been identified as needing such treatment, but also check to see which *ought* to have. They should examine the controls to see that they are suitable and adequate, which will require both technical competence and the exercise of judgement.

Control of measuring and monitoring devices

Again this is a well known and little changed requirement; a favourite amongst some auditors who have found easy pickings amongst the technical and logistical complexities of instrument calibration programmes. The requirement is that every instrument whose job is to verify or control quality (including those used to make the process measurements described earlier) should be chosen to be suitable for the job, of the right accuracy and looked after so that its accuracy and use remain suitable. This includes regularly calibrating the device against one or more standards, which themselves are calibrated and traceable back to a national or international standard.

The usual test equipment audit involves looking at a few instruments to see whether they have a label stating that they are currently in calibration, that there is a schedule for calibration and a means of recalling from use for regular checks, that traceable calibration records are maintained and that calibration processes are carefully controlled (many organizations use external calibration centres, but if it is done in-house then control of the standards and techniques used can be quite involved). A favourite question of certification assessors in the past has been to seek defined disciplines for what will happen if an instrument is found to have been inaccurate – does this mean that all product verified with it is now suspect, and what implications does this have?

This is very much a technical issue so there is little here to excite wider management. There are, though, more sophisticated areas that an auditor can explore rather than just looking at labelling and calibration dates. Accuracy and appropriateness can also be investigated. A real example I saw was an assessor at a polymer plant who noticed that the weighbridge had been calibrated at a range of 0–10 tonnes, but in fact most of the lorry loads leaving the premises weighed much more than this. Subsequent investigation showed that the bridge was, in fact, quite inaccurate at the top of its range which had resulted in significant undercharging (nice for the customers, but highly damaging to the polymer producer).

It is interesting to note that there is a specific statement here that any test software should follow the design and development rules contained earlier in the standard. I would go further and say that any software developed or modified internally and used to control or verify any aspect of the quality management system (including things like purchase systems, or stock control programs) should follow those rules. Auditors should always be on the look-out for use of software in any area and identify what controls have been applied.

MEASUREMENT, ANALYSIS AND IMPROVEMENT

General

This is a new emphasis in the year 2000 version of the standard, perhaps the largest change in the whole philosophy. It requires not only measurements of the outputs and partial outputs of main operational processes (equating to process test and inspection) but measurements of all processes, including those often thought of as management or administrative. It also has a requirement to analyse measurements (previously only referred to in the unsuccessful 'statistical techniques' paragraph) and to take improvement actions based on those analyses. These analyses should be one of the sets of inputs to management review where some of the improvement actions may be identified.

This approach follows the commonly quoted management philosophy that we can only manage what we measure and is widely seen as a good development for the use of ISO 9001. There is nothing specific to be audited under this general requirement, although it does lead the audit team in the direction of looking for improvements. Internal auditors should not find it difficult to adapt to this approach since there has always been an emphasis in internal audit on identifying more improvement opportunities than simple non-conformances. Even second party auditors should be able to take a directly relevant approach, with some care. It remains to be seen how this will work with third party certification where it will be hard for assessors to prove that an organization has *not* improved. Or even where they have not improved, it will be hard to prove that they have not tried, especially if they can quote external factors acting against them.

Measurement and monitoring of system performance

There must be defined and systematic ways of measuring management system performance. This includes a requirement to measure customer satisfaction and use internal audits to make sure that the system is working effectively internally.

In addition to looking at each individual set of measurements and analyses as described below, auditors should look to see that an overall system of measurement is in place to provide a good general picture of the organization's quality performance.

Measurement of customer satisfaction

This requires a number of steps:

- ○   continually measure customer satisfaction in a systematic way;
- ○   regularly review and analyse the measurements;
- ○   identify required improvements as a result of the analyses;
- ○   investigate the nature of the actions needed to make the improvements;
- ○   plan and carry out the improvements;
- ○   use future measurement and analyses to confirm the effectiveness of improvements.

It is likely that the use of customer complaints to measure satisfaction will be seen as inadequate for all but the simplest organizations; there will need to be some more positive measure, active rather than reactive. It is entirely possible that many organizations will decide to do this via customer surveys. This will probably be acceptable for certification purposes but we should try to think of other, more imaginative methods and decide whether they might be more appropriate. Otherwise there is going to be a surge of customer surveys to the extent that very few of them will be returned, binned to the sound of customer business managers complaining yet again about the ridiculous quantity of paperwork generated by ISO 9001 systems (similar to the boom in supplier questionnaires in the early 1990s, but worse since they will be regular instead of one-off).

Auditors should look for an appropriate means of measuring customer satisfaction which works, see whether it has been analysed in a sensible manner (there are ways of massaging numbers to either reveal nothing or reveal erroneous conclusions), and see how improvements are identified as a result.

Internal audit

I do not propose to discuss this requirement in detail here since I have explored it at length in the rest of the book. It is worth pointing out, though, that the organization's internal audit programme should itself be subject to internal audit to see whether an adequate schedule has been implemented and whether the programme is achieving the objectives of confirming compliance and assisting the evaluation of effectiveness and efficiency.

Measurement and monitoring of processes

ISO 9001:2000 suggests for the first time that not only do we have to ensure that our products and services have been checked and measured to ensure that they conform to customer requirements, but we also have to measure the processes which create those products and services.

The measurement of processes could include:

O   monitoring technical process conditions during manufacture (furnace temperature, flow rate, etc.);
O   noting turn-around times and other delays;
O   looking at consumption and wastage rates;
O   costs.

There is a wide range of process measures, depending upon the nature of the business or organization. Measurements will be carried out for two purposes:

1.   To enable adjustments to be made to the process to ensure that the final output is satisfactory.
2.   To analyse the process to identify appropriate changes and improvements.

Auditors will need to see that the organization has thought about what measurements need to be applied to what processes (a logical place to do this is when identifying the processes together with their inputs and outputs, as described earlier) and that those measurements are being routinely taken. What is done with those measurements is the next question, with a look to see that system procedures adequately describe how the measurements should be analysed and the criteria for action. Auditors able to exercise more judgement will also be studying the measurements and determining whether they are adequate and sensible (for example the number of customer orders processed in a day is a useful sales metric but may say little from a quality point of view; the time taken to fulfil a customer order from receipt to despatch may be more applicable).

Measurement of product and/or service

This is a renaming of the traditional inspection and testing requirement. The new title for the activity may help to clarify for some service providers who do not inspect anything that this covers the traditional checking and evaluation methods that they have always employed.

Most of the audit requirements here are heavily compliance-based, in that examination should cover whether items have been tested or checked, what the results were, whether they are recorded, and what the actions were if the test 'failed'. Also auditors should check that the responsibilities for deciding that all necessary checks have been completed are clearly defined and that nothing is 'released' to the customer until everything has been thoroughly verified (unless there are suitable controls for resolving the situation if a problem is subsequently discovered). Improvement auditing could look at whether the type and level of verification is adequate, although this is often a tricky area (if the customers are happy with our final service, the argument goes, then why do we need to do extra checking?) and auditors should usually stick to looking for things which could make internal improvements or could directly impact upon known problems encountered by customers.

An interesting point is that auditors should not let organizations get away with saying that the customer inspects it so that is all that is necessary. I have encountered this argument, for example, in training companies (the end-of-course critique sheet is produced as an inspection record) and maintenance organizations (we do not check our work since the customer always signs off to say that they are happy). Customer verification or feedback may be an important element of the work but should not be the only check; the organization itself must have some means for determining whether the work is satisfactory.

Control of nonconformity – general

There must be documented disciplines in place to prevent anything which is not up to scratch being accidentally used. This should include methods for identifying what the things are and what is working with them. This can also apply to services (e.g. taking steps to ensure that hotel guests do not use the swimming pool until the pumping problem has been corrected).

Auditors must pick on specific examples of problems and see how the controls work – if there is anything current that can be examined to see how the controls physically work, so much the better.

Nonconformity review and disposition

'Disposition' here is a usage of the word apparently unique to the ISO 9000 series. It means 'what we do with it'.

Whenever we have anything that is not as it should be, we need to decide our immediate action to put it right. This is where the immediate fix of a problem takes place, not under the requirement of 'corrective action' as so many people appear to believe (see pp. 86–87 for more on this).

The organization needs to have a decision-making discipline which allows it to make the correct decision on what to do about the problem. The permitted decisions include the whole range from scrapping the item and starting again to deciding that it does not matter and accepting it as it is (with the customer's permission, of course, if a customer requirement has been broken).

There must be some record of what was decided and what action was taken, including authorization and what repeat verification (inspection, testing, etc.) was performed if the item was repaired or reworked.

Audit investigation in this area looks at simple compliance to see that a recorded decision was made on each non-conformance and what was done afterwards.

ANALYSIS OF DATA FOR IMPROVEMENT

In the 1994 version of the standard this requirement existed hidden amongst corrective and preventive action but was often ignored, owing to the frequent misunderstanding about the difference between correction and prevention, as already discussed. It has now been pulled out under its own heading which should help to clarify things. The requirement is now to collect data from a number of sources including audits, customer complaints and satisfaction measurements, identified non-compliances and the results of any actions taken. This data should then be analysed to help identify whether or not we are meeting customer requirements and generally keeping them happy and also to see whether the system as a whole is working, has any good or bad trends and whether any improvements are needed (and, of course, action taken where necessary). It is expected that the analysis should be as quantitative as possible. If needed, statistical techniques should be used to help analyse the information. Now, though, the organization will not escape by saying that there are no statistical techniques appropriate; there are enough requirements sprinkled throughout the standard to ensure that some measurement and analysis will have to be performed, even if the analysis is not strictly 'statistical'.

Looking for regular and defined methods of analysis should be one of the key tasks of the auditor, and identification of what is done as a result of that analysis. Internal and customer auditors can also look to see whether the analysis examines the right things and is done in a meaningful manner. All auditors can check that analysis is conducted on all identified measurements and that its flavour is closely tied to objectives (e.g. if one of the corporate objectives is to provide timely response to service requests, then we would expect a process measurement to be applied to response times and that this measurement should be part of the general analysis).

Improvement – general requirements

There is a bold statement that the organization must continually improve. There must be procedures which make use of data from a variety of sources to identify improvements. The way in which we will identify, plan, record and verify appropriate quality improvements must be defined and documented. It is likely that these procedures will be inextricably linked with those for objective setting, measurement, analysis, corrective and preventive action, management review and, of course, internal audit.

Improvement – corrective action

Whenever there is a problem identified, which includes product or service not meeting expectations, audit findings, customer complaints or anything identified by other means which indicates that the quality system or product/service is not performing satisfactorily, there must be documented procedures which cover:

○   identification and recording of what problems occur and what they are;
○   investigation of and recording of why it went wrong;
○   deciding what is to be done to stop it happening again;
○   taking and recording the necessary action;
○   following up to see that the action did actually cure the problem.

This on its own is a significant driver for improvement, since it should gradually eliminate the root causes of problems, so that eventually there is no more opportunity for anything to go wrong! This is a long-standing requirement of ISO 9001 and many people believe that the new continuous improvement requirements are only an extension of what the standard was intended to tell us all along. The public image, though, is that it has previously been all about consistency, not change, so it will be interesting to see how the perceptions alter as ISO 9001:2000 becomes bedded in. All auditors should look closely at this very important requirement; it is disappointing that many audits have skirted around this clause and spent more time on mundane aspects such as document control and calibration.

The first thing to look for is how non-conformance is identified and recorded, and how this leads to the initiation of corrective action. A corrective action form for every instance of a problem may not be the answer: in a factory making thousands of widgets per day there are likely to be a number of in-process and output non-conformances and setting up an action team to investigate each one is not practical or useful. In this sort of case we would look for analysis (yes, this reconnects the previous requirement to this one and there is a logical link between the two) to see where the worst or most expensive problems are occurring and take action on those, using some form of prioritization (Pareto's name comes to mind here). A good place to search for information is also on the second half of the PDCA loop; monitoring for effectiveness and adjustment to make the action really work is often a part of corrective action that is forgotten. All auditors should be able to look at this element in a fairly equal fashion since it is a firm requirement of the standard which itself aims at making the organization's processes better, so the distinction between compliance and improvement auditing here becomes less relevant.

Improvement – preventive action

This requirement has been separated from that for corrective action but otherwise is unchanged from versions of ISO 9001. One problem, though, is that now that the requirement for analysis has been clearly taken out to stand on its own, there is still likely to be some confusion as to what is meant by preventive action. To clarify, it is not about removing the cause of any faults which have been identified. The use of words is part of the confusion here since *preventing* recurrence of a problem is defined as *corrective* action. Thus talking about taking preventive action as a result of any particular problem of non-comformance is meaningless.

Essentially, preventive action consists of looking at the analysis of performance (finding another connection with the requirements for measurement and analysis) and deciding where this indicates that problems could occur in other areas where we have not yet seen them (or perhaps not yet seen them to any great extent). This could mean, for example, that we have had a valid customer complaint relating to the performance of one division which could easily occur in another division, thereby prompting action to ensure that it does not happen in the second division, even though it has never yet occurred. Or we could have an audit finding that a forklift truck driver has no certificate on record which makes us realize that we do not have records of the driving licences or certificates for any of our vehicle drivers or heavy equipment operators. PDCA rules apply just as well to preventive actions as to corrective actions.

This ends the headings in the standard. All that is left is a matrix showing cross-references to ISO 14001. This has two purposes: mostly to assist those who are establishing systems for compliance with both standards, but it also shows that the general management approach to management of any business aspect is very similar. Auditors should concentrate here on looking at the improvement decisions and actions, rather than on results which may only give them part of the picture. Remember ISO 9001 is not intended to be a results-oriented standard and it is in enablers that the emphasis lies (although second party auditors, in particular, may hear loud alarm bells if no positive improvement results are ever seen).

ISO 9001 STATUS

The explanation of the contents of ISO 9001 given here is based on the contents of ISO/CD2 9001:2000, March 1999. It is the second discussion draft of ISO 9001:2000 which has a final publication date of November 2000. Although the eventual year 2000 version is not likely to differ strongly from this draft, there may be detail changes in the final document. Details of the differences between what is described here and the current version can be found at my internet web site at www.conc.co.uk/twothou.

PROCESS ANALYSIS

The year 2000 version of the ISO 9001 standard (and the other members of its family, come to that) leans very heavily towards processes and thinking of each activity in a process fashion. The arguments will undoubtedly fly as to whether this is appropriate for every business, but it seems to be welcomed by most as a good move.

Basing the standard on processes will mean that every organization will have to show that it has thought about how its own operations fit into the process model. For those newly adopting ISO 9001, carrying out an analysis to see exactly which processes are key and which directly contribute to the customer satisfaction loop will be a useful way of setting the scene for the quality management system. Even those organizations that merely update their systems from previous ones based on the 1994 version of ISO 9001 or ISO 9002 will still, though, have to think about their business in terms of its major processes.

This means that everyone will be expected to show that they have decided what their major business processes are, what the main inputs and outputs are for each of them, and which ones lie directly in the path which satisfies customer requirements/orders/contracts. This will apply to every organization, and certification auditors in particular will wish to see that it has been done and is appropriate to the organization (i.e. not just a consultant's standard model with one or two words changed). Both third party and other auditors can request the process analysis data in advance of an audit and use it as part of preparation, helping to understand what goes on and what the main interfaces are.

A typical way of recording the process analysis may be on a table such as that in Figure 4.3.

Process name:			
Inputs	Process steps	Outputs	Customers

FIGURE 4.3   Simple process analysis table

ISO 9000

ISO 9000 has also been revised to create a new version, published simultaneously with ISO 9001. This standard has now changed its purpose to be a document which describes the concepts behind quality management systems, and defines the related vocabulary. As I have already mentioned, the number of documents in the family has been drastically reduced and ISO 8402 is no longer applicable.

The concepts part of the ISO 9000 standard addresses many of the things that I have talked about earlier in this book, including a simple process model and what a quality management system is trying to achieve. There is nothing here that needs to be discussed in detail since the concepts are adequately explored earlier in the book. There is also little value in specifically quoting definitions from the vocabulary section since they can be rather formal and are not always helpful. There is one interesting point worth mentioning though, that the standard no longer tries to give a formal definition of the word 'quality'. Instead it addresses this in an introductory heading *'What is "quality"'* right at the start of the explanation of the concepts. It states that quality is used in the context of achieving sustained customer satisfaction through meeting customer needs and expectations within an organizational environment committed to continual improvement of efficiency and effectiveness. It also states that quality is critical to business success and that customers can be both internal and external. This definition may not help us in our understanding here of how to audit, but I have been told that quality managers may find it useful when asked to give a definition to their colleagues. My own view is that it may be a contribution to the debate, but works to resolve it no better than most other short definitions.

ISO 9004

ISO 9004 retains its general purpose as a guide to how to run good quality systems in an organization. The problem that it does not bear any direct relation to ISO 9001 has now been overcome and we see a document reminiscent of the old BS 5750 Part 4 (which was the guidance standard for BS 5750) where the headings of the contents reflect the headings in ISO 9001.

This standard is intended to give guidance to those who are looking for excellence in their approach to quality, but is not a 'how to implement ISO 9001' document. In many ways it goes beyond the requirements of the certification standard and is intended to provoke thought as to other action that can be taken, whilst maintaining consistency with the ISO 9001 approach. It must be emphasized that this is not a certification standard and third party assessors will not be able to insist upon adherence to any of its principles, although they can perhaps point organizations towards it where improvement to a particular element of the business is required.

It is beyond the scope of this book to explore the contents of ISO 9004 in detail, but it is worth mentioning that auditors whose primary motivation is identification of improvements could use ISO 9004 as a way of seeking those improvements, or at least asking questions about how far the personnel being interviewed are addressing ISO 9004 topics.

ISO 10011

ISO 10011 is the standard which describes how to carry out quality audits. It is divided into three parts, covering the various stages and requirements of running both individual audits and an overall audit programme. It has survived the rewrite programme aimed at producing the year 2000 versions of the family as it has been decided to create a new standard which addresses the requirements of auditing both quality and environmental management systems (environmental auditing is covered at the moment by ISO 14010). The new, combined standard will then be published some time in the future, possibly emerging some time in 2001. It is hoped that the revision will also address the needs of different audits, since it is heavily slanted towards the needs of third party audits in its current edition.

There is absolutely no point in describing the contents of this standard here since the whole book deals with the various aspects. For this reason it should not be necessary for auditors to study ISO 10011, unless they have a special reason to do so, for example to train other auditors.

SUMMARY

○   The ISO 9000 family developed out of international military standards.
○   BS 5750, the UK standard of 1987, is often thought of as the first major commercial quality management standard.
○   The family has recently been reduced in size and now has only four principal members: ISO 9000, ISO 9001, ISO 9004 and ISO 10011.
○   ISO 9000 defines the concepts and vocabulary.
○   ISO 9001 is the certification standard, describing the basic requirements of a quality management system.
○   ISO 9004 gives quality management guidance and will be of use to those seeking to go beyond the basic ISO 9001 system.
○   ISO 10011 describes the conduct and management of quality audits. It has not been updated at the same time as the other standards because it is hoped to create a single standard for both quality and environmental auditing.
○   There are various reasons why organizations might adopt ISO 9001 as a model.

○   The contents of ISO 9001:2000 have much in common with previous versions but there are also some new requirements.

5

QUALITY MANAGEMENT SYSTEM CERTIFICATION

❖

INDEPENDENT CERTIFICATION – PURPOSE AND USE

The ISO 9000 certification standards (now embodied in just one standard, ISO 9001) have always been written not only to describe a logical set of controls that should be applied in order to address quality, but in such a way that they can be independently verified. This allows somebody to check whether you have actually done all of the things mentioned in the standard. This has led, over time, to the formal independent certification system which we all know.

Having the organization's formal approach to quality independently verified has a number of possible purposes:

○ To give a target to aim for, so that we can celebrate a true success at some point in our quality journey.

○ To provide some rigour, so that we do not decide to leave out one or two elements because we do not like them or because they require some thought and effort.

○ To provide an incentive not to let things slide (as can happen with many management initiatives after the initial 'burst') via regular surveillance assessments.

○ To show customers and potential customers that we have demonstrated that we take quality seriously.

○ To reduce the number and extent of customer audits, because somebody trusted has already done it.

An organization may decide to pursue ISO 9001 certification for any one or more of the above reasons. The most usual deciding factor is that one or more significant customers want it.

Once the ISO 9001 certificate is awarded, it is used mostly for its ability to allow access to contracts and for publicity purposes. There are certainly a number of publicity and promotional opportunities. The most basic is that (assuming the certificate was granted by an accredited certifier) the organization will appear in the appropriate national register of 'firms of assessed capability'. Some customers, such as the British Ministry of Defence, use appearance in this register as a prerequisite to tender for any work, and others may look up entries in the register when enquiring for new products or services. Other publicity opportunities mostly relate to the provision of the certificate, which can be proudly displayed in the reception area and copied to customers, and the use of the certification logo.

Registered companies are given permission to use the logo of the certification body, and sometimes also that of the accreditation body, as discussed later in this chapter. The logo can then be placed on headed paper, brochures, compliment slips and even on buildings and vehicles to show that the organization has met the standard. There are various restrictions on the use of the logo, but the main one is that it can only be used in a way which indicates that the management systems have been approved, not the products or services themselves. Therefore the certification mark should not appear on product labels, product packaging, completion or test certificates, etc. since its purpose may be misconstrued (especially since some of the ISO 9001 certification bodies also act as product approvers and the granted logos may be similar).

In theory there may be a benefit of continued certification in that the regular surveillance visits can point out useful areas for corrective action. In practice, though, it is rarely seen as being of real internal benefit since the organization is keen to minimize assessment negative findings to avoid even the slightest risk of the certificate being lost, and third party auditors are narrowly restricted in terms of what useful actions they are either permitted to or capable of finding within the confines of the surveillance visit.

PITFALLS AND PROBLEMS

There are few pitfalls associated with the certification process itself, although some can be encountered on the road towards it. A few of them are discussed below.

○   *Choosing an un-accredited certification body* (see 'Accreditation', p. 100). There are some certification bodies that operate without following the usual rules and obtaining a listing with one of the government-sponsored international accreditation agencies. Managers of most of these bodies will profess that they are giving just as good a service as the accredited bodies, but without the extra bureaucracy and overhead associated with having to gain accreditation. The problem with this is twofold: first, there is no watchdog making sure that the certification company is following the rules and applying equal degrees of strictness to everybody (it is always tempting to bend the rules occasionally if there is nobody watching) and, second, without certification from an accredited body, your company will not appear in the official lists of certified companies so cannot, for example, work for the British Ministry of Defence.

○ *Not allowing enough time to make the system ready for certification.* Many organizations believe that they are almost there and only need a little work to become certifiable. Although this is often true, that little extra work can still take time to complete and to familiarize everyone with it. Also, the assessors will want to see that the system has been fully operational for at least three months before they audit – this is to check not only that the system has been designed well but also that the organization can demonstrate that it works. Six months from the start of work to the day of the audit is a fast programme; most take a year or more.

○ *Not giving the certification company enough notice of the certification date.* These companies rely on selling the time of their assessors. They are only economically viable if the assessors are kept busy. Thus the first available appointment is usually eight weeks or more away, sometimes longer. To be on the safe side, select and instruct the chosen certifier at least three months before your target audit date.

○ *Over-documenting the system.* This represents an enormous temptation before first assessment. The mistake is usually based upon the anxiety that naturally exists about whether the certificate will be awarded or not. Companies tend to overdo things rather than risk major non-compliances. Over-documented systems are not a good idea since, apart from wasting paper, the system is more time-consuming and cumbersome to maintain. It can then be more difficult for users quickly and easily to find the information that they want.

○ *Over-complacency about ways that the standard may be interpreted.* This is one of the most common pitfalls from the third party auditor's point of view. In seminars and conferences everyone will nod their heads wisely when speakers talk about 'going back to the words of the standard' when interpreting a particular activity. This is highly commendable but many assessors forget to do it in the heat of an audit. It is an easy reaction, when confronted with an unconventional (or for unconventional read 'new') approach to a particular requirement. Auditors must remember that organizations can, and should, adopt whatever approach best fits their need and be willing to accept novel approaches on each occasion.

THE CERTIFICATION PROCESS

1. SELECT THE CERTIFIER

The first step in the certification process is for an organization to choose an appropriate assessment body. The availability of certification bodies is discussed later in this chapter, but effectively the choice is similar to that for any other service contractor, based upon reputation, the service offered and, of course, price.

The body needs to be selected at least ten weeks or so before the assessment, perhaps longer. This is because they quickly become booked up and are unlikely to be able to fit an organization in at short notice unless there is a cancellation (and these do not happen very often because most certification bodies levy a charge for short notice cancellations). The majority of certifiers have an information pack that they will send out, typically containing a form which, when completed, will enable them to prepare a quotation and proposal. Some insist on sending a representative to discuss particular needs and circumstances before quoting (some companies like this as it indicates personal attention to the customer, others feel that it just wastes time – which approach you prefer is down to personal preference). The price and length of the certification will depend upon how the particular body structures its fees and the size, nature and scope of the company and its activities. The factors which most increase the fees charged are number of people employed and the number of separate sites involved.

2. THE DOCUMENT REVIEW AND INITIAL VISIT

This stage used to be two steps in the certification process, and is often reported as such, although in practice the two are usually done together in all but the largest organizations.

One or more assessors (usually only one, the intended team leader of the eventual audit team) visit the organization to read through the documentation that has been prepared and see that it is both complete and comprehensive and that the systems appear basically to have been implemented. The review of the documentation often used to be conducted off site, based upon the quality manual. Nowadays, though, it is recognized that:

○　　the top level quality manual on its own is not enough to fully describe the system and assess its adequacy; and

○　　sending a complete set of all relevant quality system documentation to those off site is probably impractical since there is too much of it, and often it is only clear that some of it is needed for reference when reading begins.

So the review normally takes place on the assessed company's premises.

The other part of this step typically involves a tour of the operational areas and brief interviews with a sample of personnel to see that the systems do appear basically to have been implemented (i.e. that the organization has not just written a set of documents in isolation but that they are really working). Nothing will actually be audited at this point, but comments will be made about anything which may represent a risk during a subsequent audit.

If, during any part of this, the auditor decides that the company is not yet ready for certification, which would have been programmed for about four weeks after this visit, he or she can say so. It is the company's final decision as to whether the assessment should go ahead or not, but it is in nobody's interest for the audit to be a disaster so the assessor's views should be taken seriously.

This part of the process has another purpose, to act as part of the audit team preparation for the audit itself. In this the person carrying out the review gains an understanding of what goes on and how it works. At a practical level it also gives the auditor an opportunity to create a timetable for the audit, taking into account the amount of work to be audited in a certain area, any travel time needed and so on. Owing to the rules usually governing the certification, though, the auditor is not allowed to decide that greater time is needed to conduct the audit than was allowed for in the initial quotation, unless the auditor finds something which changes or contradicts the information presented in the early contact stages. The auditor must juggle what has to be audited within the available time.

The output of the document review is a written report of recommendations of things that need to be corrected (but not, of course, how they should be corrected) before the audit itself. Although these are not formal audit findings, it is important to attend to them; one of the worst certification audit performances I ever saw was where a company had taken no action on the initial visit report.

3.   THE CERTIFICATION AUDIT

Organizations seeking ISO 9001 registration often call this the 'final' audit, since they see it as the culmination of their hard work aimed at achieving certification. Assessment bodies, on the other hand, see this as the start of a continuing monitoring of the quality system, so refer to it as the 'initial' audit.

The audit is conducted as described in the various chapters of this book. The emphasis is on seeing that the defined systems meet the requirements of ISO 9001 and that there is evidence that those systems have been implemented effectively (thus this audit can normally only take place after all documented processes have been conducted at least once; although the assessors may allow partial evidence for very lengthy processes taking months or years, or very rare processes, if agreed in advance).

As the audit progresses the auditors will raise major or minor non-compliances if they find them. Some certification bodies have other names for the two categories of non-compliance, but they mean the same thing. Major non-compliances represent a significant risk that customer requirements will not be met, whereas minor non-compliances are small infringements of the defined system which will not have a direct immediate effect on customer satisfaction.

At the end of the audit, there will be a formal closing meeting where the non-compliances and general observations are restated.

If there are any majors, one or more of the audit team will need to return to re-audit and check that they have been adequately addressed. This is usually expected to occur within thirteen weeks of the initial audit; if longer is needed then it is judged that the organization was not truly ready for assessment and the whole process will have to be conducted again, a new application, document review and so on will be needed as and when the system has been made ready. Note that the re-audit within thirteen weeks only looks at the areas considered deficient at the initial audit; it is not a full re-assessment. Assuming that those deficiencies have been corrected, a recommendation for certification is made.

If there are only minor non-compliances, this means that nothing has been found which indicates that customer requirements will not be met. It follows that there is no reason why the certificate should not be recommended straight away. The assessment team will, of course, expect that attention is given to correction of the minor deficiencies found, but this should not be a hurdle in the way of the certificate being granted. The exact way that each certification body deals with this varies from one to another; some will assess the corrective actions at the next audit and some will ask to see a corrective action programme or proposal. In the past, some certification bodies used to insist upon a report sent to the lead auditor providing evidence that the non-compliances had been corrected before the certificate was granted, but today's definitions of the non-compliance classifications mean that this practice should no longer be found.

The recommendation is made by the team leader to the head office of the team's employing certification body. It is reviewed there by technical staff who ensure that the records show that the process has been correctly carried out. Unless there are any irregularities, a certificate is then granted. In practice I have never seen a recommendation from an assessor of an accredited certification body refused, although obviously the rules are there to maintain the integrity of the certification process.

The certificate is sent once the technical review is complete and it can be printed and signed. Some certification bodies will also offer the opportunity for a formal presentation to be made for publicity purposes. With the certificate will also come certification logo artwork with some rules for how and where it may and may not be used. The rules are detailed but boil down to making sure that it is clear that it is the system, not the products or services, that is certified and that any writing and images retain their identity and legibility.

SCOPE

When the certificate is granted, it will come with an associated scope statement. This may appear on the certificate itself, or sometimes as an attachment. The definition of scope is principally there to make it clear to everyone the area of activity that the company is involved in. This prevents organizations who have had their systems assessed promising customers that they have a tested ability to do anything they feel like. Just because a company has been assessed to competently make door hinges, for example, does not mean that it can be considered competent to run a catering service.

Another use of the scope is to specify to which parts of the organization the certificate applies, where only some of the activities have been fully assessed. Examples of this include organizations which have a primary activity which is controlled to ISO 9001, with a secondary activity which is operated at such a low level that it would be complicated and expensive to fully control and certify, or those which have subsidiary offices whose assessment would be disproportionately expensive. Where this happens the organization is expected to take steps to ensure that it does not misrepresent itself. Thus letters relating to uncertified activities, or coming from uncertified locations, should not carry the certification logo or otherwise indicate that they fall within the certification scope.

This does not allow organizations to exclude elements of the business which fall within the ISO 9001 requirements. It is not permitted, therefore, to omit functions such as design, or servicing, or sales quotations from the documented system.

CERTIFICATION COMPANIES

There are dozens of accredited certification companies around the world. The UK alone has almost a hundred. They vary from national standards bodies (British Standards Institution in the UK, SIRIM in Malaysia, SASO in Saudi Arabia and so on) through established inspection and classification companies (such as Lloyds, Det Norske Veritas, SGS, American Bureau of Shipping) to private, profit-making companies set up independently purely to provide an ISO 9001 certification service. These latter are likely to be smaller than those with more established backgrounds, perhaps only employing three or four assessors. Some will also make use of freelance assessors to cope with workload troughs or specialist audits for which the skills do not exist in-house.

Organizations seeking certification can select from any one that is capable and seems to be offering an acceptable level of service. Capability will be dependent upon the accredited scope; just as ISO 9001 organizations have a scope to their certificate, so the certification bodies themselves have a scope within which they are allowed to grant certificates. The larger organizations are likely to have the widest scopes, whereas the smaller ones will probably be more specialized or limited.

The choice of certification body simply depends upon whether the body appears to offer a simple and customer-friendly administration process (the audit processes themselves will only vary negligibly), the price and whether any particular certification body's certificate will carry extra weight in the circumstances. So shipping companies may seek certificates from bodies such as Lloyds or Det Norske Veritas, marketing companies could look to Marketing Quality Assurance and vehicle repair garages might choose the RAC (Royal Automobile Club).

In theory, though, the choice of certification body based on reputation should be irrelevant; as long as the body is properly accredited all should carry equal weight. In the end the choice often boils down to personal preference such as familiarity from experience in previous organizations or recommendations from consultants.

ACCREDITATION

The word 'accredited' is one that organizations who possess an ISO 9001 certificate often apply to themselves. Officially, though, this applies to certification bodies who possess an official 'licence' to operate. The accreditation is provided by an accreditation body which is usually a government agency of some sort. Accreditation is provided in a similar manner to the granting of ISO 9001 certificates: a company seeking authority to assess against ISO 9001 establishes management systems and controls which comply with accreditation body guidelines (which themselves are based on international standards) and subjects itself to an audit. Accreditation is maintained by continuing surveillance, which will include following the occasional assessor during the conduct of an ISO 9001 audit to see that the rules are being followed.

When an ISO 9001 certificate is granted, the associated logo is usually the logo of the certification body attached to the logo of the accreditation body, indicating its authenticity. This is why it should not really matter from whom the certificate is granted; as long as the accreditation logo is present then we know that common, accepted standards have been applied.

There is international agreement to accept the authenticity of certificates granted under different accreditation bodies. Not every country or region, though, has established an accreditation regime. There are only about twenty or so recognized accreditation bodies throughout the world, even though ISO 9001 certification is popular much more widely than this. For those countries where there is no accreditation body, certification companies usually take their authority from one of the more active international schemes. In the Arabian Gulf, for example, where none of the countries has an accreditation body, most certificates are granted under UK or Netherlands accreditation schemes, with the German scheme gaining strength in some areas.

Just as any authentic ISO 9001 certificate should carry equal weight, so it should not really matter under which accreditation scheme a certificate is granted, since they all follow very similar rules.

It should be pointed out that there are some certification bodies in existence which operate without any accreditation, whether or not a valid accreditation regime exists in their country. There is no international regulation which makes this illegal, and usually no national legislation is being breached, but where official recognition is required, such as an entry in an official register of quality certified companies, un-accredited certification does not work. The certification companies who offer such a service range from the purely fraudulent, offering a certificate for little more than the payment of a fee, to those who claim to provide a professional and competent service, but without the burden of having to satisfy an independent regulator. Unfortunately even the best of these often prey upon poorly informed companies by simply not apprising them of the difference between accredited and un-accredited certification; many of their customers simply do not realize that their certificates have no official recognition. For those in the know it is easy to tell – simply look for the accreditation logo on the certificates and other documentation. In the past the only reason to choose such a body was cost, but now that there are so many companies offering an accredited service and some working very hard to undercut the competition, extremely low accredited certification prices can be obtained. Since certification assessors are also prepared to travel internationally and travel costs are continually falling, there should be no real need for anyone anywhere to seek un-accredited certification. As the choice of sources of accredited certification increases and the cost decreases, I hope that the phenomenon of un-accredited assessment will disappear since I believe that it devalues the whole process.

MAINTENANCE AND SURVEILLANCE

The certificate is maintained by continuing to demonstrate to the certification body that the quality system continues to operate and incorporates appropriate improvements. This means that continual effort has to be applied to keeping everything together, completing records, tracking changes and continuing the internal audit programme. It is not enough to forget about the disciplines that should be in place and then try to tidy up just before the external assessor comes.

This has particular importance for internal audit programmes. They can be an excellent way of identifying whether the systems are working and checking that there has been no 'backsliding'. The type of audit schedule which has a 'blitz' every six months may not do the job properly if there has been general organizational laxity in between. It also means that conducting a full audit cycle just before the external assessor's visit also may not be sensible; elsewhere in the book I note that this devalues the internal audit and removes some of its potential, but there is the additional problem that if things have significantly broken down then it may not be possible to put them right before the imminent external assessor's visit.

For the certification company, maintenance of the certificate means carrying out a regular surveillance audit. This requires regular visits, normally six monthly although they may be annual in some cases, most commonly with organizations employing less than about 30 people on a single site. These visits are never wider or more lengthy than the initial audit, but could be of equal length in small organizations (assessors, like management consultants and trainers, hate to sell their time in portions of less than an entire day so organizations with one-day initial audits will probably also have one-day surveillance audits). Where the organization is relatively large, the surveillance audit may not cover everything, but be arranged so that the entire quality system is covered over a period of time. This is particularly true for multi-site organizations where the various sites will be 'sampled' according to a plan.

The auditing process is similar at surveillance visits to the initial audit. The main difference is the conclusions or outcome. Major non-compliances will still result in a requirement to re-audit (usually within six weeks rather than the thirteen allowed initially, because the organization already possesses a certificate and should not be allowed extended periods of operating contrary to its requirements) and minors are still accepted provided that some form of commitment to correct them is obtained. After a surveillance visit, though, the certificate is already in place and remains so (unless the system has broken down so disastrously that the assessor has no choice but to recommend its withdrawal). Even if a major non-compliance is identified, the organization retains the certificate; it just has to take suitable corrective action. It is only if corrective action to address a major non-compliance is not taken effectively that the certificate is in real danger of being taken away. This is not to say that certificates are never revoked. It would be a meaningless exercise if this were so and, of course, some organizations fail to maintain their systems. It is not common, though, and the assessor wants the certificate to remain and will be very reluctant to recommend withdrawal. It is usually only organizations that stop trying who lose their ISO 9001 certificates.

THE IMPLEMENTATION PROJECT

A typical project to prepare an organization for ISO 9001 registration would follow these steps:

1.   Obtain commitment from senior managers to back the project.
2.   Understand the requirements of ISO 9001.
3.   Understand the nature and activities of the business.

4.   Perform a 'gap analysis', identifying where the organization does not currently meet ISO 9001 requirements, and to what extent.
5.   Create an action plan to fill the gaps, including the creation of a quality manual and other system documentation.
6.   Manage the action programme to ensure that it all happens.
7.   Communicate what is going on to all employees as the project progresses.
8.   Continually review the situation against ISO 9001 requirements and adjust as necessary.
9.   Train some internal quality auditors (or find a suitably qualified internal audit resource).
10.   Set a 'live' date at which the organization believes that it has complied with the standard.
11.   Select a certification company.
12.   After the live date, conduct a full series of quality audits (internal, plus possibly a consultancy audit or a certification company pre-assessment) to confirm that the system is working adequately, and act to correct any deficiencies.
13.   Hold a management review meeting to discuss the project so far, to evaluate quality performance and to set the way forward, including any improvements needed.
14.   Submit to a document review and initial visit.
15.   Take action on any resultant comments.
16.   Submit to initial assessment.

The above steps typically take a year to eighteen months in most organizations, although they could take longer in large companies and I have seen the process take as little as five months in small organizations (three months of which was letting the system settle in after the live date).

SYSTEM DOCUMENTATION

Creating the system documentation can often be one of the largest tasks in the ISO 9001 implementation programme. Most of the operational requirements represent common sense and should be practised anyway, but it is likely that the organization will not have a full set of compliant documentation before seeking registration. This is a shame, since the standard is not supposed to be principally about paperwork, but it is a fact of life.

Structure

ISO 9001 quality system documentation is usually structured in a similar fashion to the pyramid shown in Figure 3.1 (p. 41). This is similar to the triangle often displayed and which used to appear in the 1994 version of ISO 10013 (which was a guidance document for the preparation of quality manuals) but probably shows better how it actually works.

At the top of the pyramid are the policy level documents. Other models may show the top document as being just the quality manual, but it may also include other documents such as policy statements, company quality objectives, departmental, project or team quality objectives and so on. The next level down should stem from these and represents the documents that control the main management activities of the organization. These are usually referred to as system procedures or a similar term. There may also be other elements to this layer, such as plans to achieve quality objectives or even business plans. The next level down is the detail level. In fact this can be huge or microscopic, depending upon the size of the organization. In a manufacturing company the detail level will incorporate manufacturing instructions, assembly diagrams, technical drawings, test procedures, user guides, machine manuals, maintenance procedures, prompt cards, specifications and so on. In a simple resale operation the detail layer may be almost empty. The final layer is forms. Forms are still an official part of the documentation system (and so are expected to have the usual document control rules applied) but are different to most other documents in that they are intended to be written upon and become consumed, whereas the rest are reference material.

Documentation advice

Perhaps the most important thing to remember is that not all documentation is on paper; these days it appears as often as electronic copy on the computer screen as in a ring binder.

For those writing the documents, there are a few points to bear in mind:

1.   The documents should be there for the people doing the work, not for the assessor – therefore they should be simple and clear, whilst containing enough detail for the employees to be able to refer to them when necessary.

2.   The quality manual is a standard document containing a description of the organization, outline responsibilities, policy statements of how major activities and controls will be implemented, and a cross-reference to the rest of the system documentation. As such, a model taken from a consultant or another company should suffice and there does not need to be too much time spent on it (although one shipping agency has its quality manual printed in colour and distributes it as a brochure; which at least makes some use of it).

3.   Although we do need to establish some structure to the documentation system (it is very difficult to navigate without it, as I learnt from experience in the early days), it is not there as a strait-jacket. If it is not clear into which category or layer to place a document, or if a procedure document has a paragraph or two of very detailed description then simply make a

practical decision as to what to do about it. There is no need, for example, to create a separate work instruction containing two lines just because the company's guidelines say that procedure documents should not be too detailed.

Similarly there are issues for auditors to consider:

1. Point 3 above for document authors also applies: do not criticize a document for having the wrong title unless it is clearly misleading. As long as the document exists, is suitable and is being used then it has served its purpose and it does not really matter what it is called.

2. Just because a document is not immediately understandable does not mean that there is anything wrong with it. It might be perfectly clear to the people who do, and are likely to, work in the area.

3. Although it is reasonable to allow for some contingencies, do not expect documents to cover every remote possibility (e.g. what happens if it is the night shift, and the weekend, and during a public holiday, and the usual supervisor is off sick, and there is a power cut, and there is a storm raging outside, and the roof has a bad leak...).

4. Unless there is some agreed company standard that should be followed, the exact style of document is a matter for preference and should not be criticized by the auditor. It can include diagrams, text, bullet points, icons, full text or whatever format is preferred. I have seen auditors recommend that flow charts be used for particular processes, when many people do not like flow charts and find them unhelpful. Similarly the way that text is written (instructive, descriptive, present tense, future tense, bullet points, etc.) should be what works internally and not what the auditor prefers.

5. It is the second level down of the pyramid which is usually (although not always, bearing in mind point 3 above) of most interest to auditors. Quality manuals are traditionally of interest to third party auditors at the initial assessment but perform a peripheral role thereafter. Internal auditors should ignore quality manuals, except perhaps in small organizations where the quality manual is used to provide real information to minimize the overall documentation size. Objectives from the top level are, though, of interest since auditors should be looking to see that something is done about achieving those objectives. On the other hand, the level below, the detail layer, is of little interest to auditors in most cases. This is because the contents are too specific, technical or un-auditable. Besides, if an auditor chooses to watch someone performing a detailed task to the requirements of a work instruction, the auditor has the dual problem that the person knows he or she is watching and does not behave normally, and that the auditor may not really be able to follow precisely what it is the person is doing.

SECTOR SCHEMES

There are a number of specialist registrations around, often referred to as 'sector schemes'. These are designed to recognize the fact that certain industries have particular requirements which need to be examined before it can be vouched that they are truly managing quality satisfactorily. The best known of the sector schemes is TickIT, launched by the UK Trade and Industry Department as a specialist certification scheme for software, based on ISO 9000-3. This scheme was UK only and the British eventually lost the fight for universal, international recognition. It has since been made voluntary (until mid-1998, any UK company seeking certification with even a hint of software in its product or service had to go via the TickIT route; one of my clients only reproduced software for sale from a master developed and made by someone else, but was still pushed into having a TickIT certificate). There are also other schemes such as pharmaceutical and aeronautical. An initiative of several years ago was the Stockist scheme, which applied to those whose main job was to act as sellers, dealers or distributors of other people's products; it was withdrawn some time ago since it was perceived to add no value.

Characteristics of these sector schemes are that there are one or more documents which become assessment requirements in addition to ISO 9001, and that the third party auditors who carry out the assessments are required to be specially trained and registered.

As I have already pointed out, sector schemes tend to come and go. Personally, I do not favour them; I believe they tend to create a certain elitism. They can also lead to assessments leaning disproportionately toward the sector scheme elements (such as a TickIT assessment in which I participated in a company where about 3 per cent of the people were involved in software activities yet the TickIT auditor insisted that he would spend three days investigating the software-related activities. I had to spend three days looking at everything else). Since auditors are required to have some knowledge of the areas they audit, and have to take account of other documents such as regulations, specifications, contracts and so on during the assessment, the certification body's own procedures should take care of qualifications, making sector schemes an unnecessary bureaucratic complication.

This is a debate which will go on at a high level, though. From a practical viewpoint, a company needs to be aware that sector schemes exist. If a certification body tells a company that its activities fall under such a scheme, the company's first move should be to find out whether the scheme is voluntary. If so, the company should ask for more details (and obtain more than one opinion) and decide whether it serves its interest to be registered under the scheme, and what the disadvantages are (such as extra cost). If the scheme is obligatory, then the debate is academic and the company will have no choice but to follow it.

QS 9000

QS 9000 is, perhaps, the ultimate sector scheme, since it has evolved to be a separate standard. It is the certification standard used within a large section (although by no means all) of the motor industry. It is a project initiated by Ford, Chrysler and General Motors, aimed at certifying their suppliers to a standard specifically aimed at the requirements of the motor industry. Other motor manufacturers are as keen on good quality but have their own schemes, such as the German VAD 6 specification.

In fact, the whole QS 9000 certification approach is very similar to that for ISO 9001, in that the same certification bodies carry out the assessments as an independent third party. The standard itself is also remarkably similar, with essentially the same management system requirements as ISO 9001, with some extra requirements on forward planning and formalized relationships between the supplier and motor vehicle manufacturer. It is beyond the scope of this book to explore the differences with ISO 9001 in detail, although it should be said that they are at a detail, not fundamental level. The Institute of Quality Assurance has a service which will point those wishing to know more towards suitable reference materials on the subject.

For auditors, the approach is the same. Certification assessors will, of course, have to be familiar with QS 9000 requirements in order to be able to fulfil their function. Second party and internal auditors, though, since they are not usually looking principally at standards compliance, will find it hard to see any difference between auditing ISO 9001 systems and those meeting QS 9000.

PRODUCT CERTIFICATION

We have geared our discussions heavily towards ISO 9001 in this book, and auditing *management* systems. We would be missing out an important section of the assessment industry, though, if we did not mention product certification.

Product certification has been around a long time (UK readers will recognize the famous British Standards kite mark from their childhoods), certainly before management systems certification became fashionable. Product certification requires an organization to prove that the product it makes conforms to accepted specifications, and uses technical testing of regular production samples as a means of verifying compliance. In some areas the use of the appropriate product mark is a prerequisite to being able to offer goods in the market. Examples of this are FCC approval of telecommunications products in the USA or CE marking of electrical and medical goods and children's toys in the European Union.

A development of product certification schemes has been that they have begun to insist upon certain management system controls being present to ensure that every product is satisfactory, not just the ones that are tested. Many manufacturers choose to use ISO 9001 certification as evidence that they have sufficient controls in place. Indeed some product certification regimes go so far as to insist that ISO 9001 is in place before a product can be approved.

Auditors carrying out their investigations where product certification exists should see little difference in the way that they have to examine the processes. For compliance purposes they may need to see that products are being regularly tested internally to show that certification requirements are being adhered to and that records are sufficient to show the results of that testing. Most certification companies who grant ISO 9001 certificates and are also 'competent bodies' for the award of product approvals will carry out the management system certification of both at the same time, usually taking no longer than they would do if only examining for ISO 9001 compliance.

MAKING BEST USE OF THE CERTIFICATE

As I have already mentioned, the best benefits from ISO 9001 do not arise directly from the certification process, but from the improvements resulting from reviewing company operations and putting in the appropriate controls. There are, however, some ways to derive benefits from actually having the certificate:

○   Make sure that all employees know that the company has gained certification, that they can be proud of it and that everyone's combined efforts made success possible.

○   Let every customer know that the company has it and tell them about how good it has been for the company (even if, in the early days, it was a lot of work and the company has not yet seen any direct benefits).

○   Issue a big press release about it – although certificate awards are no longer a big deal nationally, local papers, chambers of commerce or trade magazines are often still prepared to make a story out of them.

○   Advertise by using the certification logo in as many places as possible (although rules about minimum size usually make them look a bit daft on business cards).

○   Display the certificate in the reception area so that every visitor sees it.

Brochures and other publicity material should also regularly make reference to the fact that the company has a registered quality management system and that this illustrates the organization's commitment to quality and customer service.

KEEPING THE ASSESSOR IN CHECK

A final thing to bear in mind when seeking certification is to remember that, despite everything, the company is the assessor's customer. This means that it has at least a say in what goes on. Do not accept everything that the assessors say without asking whether it is sensible.

The first place to apply this advice is when discussing how the certification process will work. It may be that a company wishes to limit the scope of the assessment (remember, of course, that there are some permissible ways to limit the scope and others which are not allowed). Zealous assessors will often try to convince a company to cover everything; listen to their arguments but in the end the company must make its own decision. If a company does not wish assessors to fly to Auckland to assess its outpost sales office there then it has the right to say so.

A recent example I had of this was where a certification company wished to carry out an assessment over three sites using three assessors, each based locally to the respective site. This was organized to keep the cost down, since cost is a prime factor in the choice of many organizations. Cost was not, however, the only consideration for my client and we felt that we would prefer to have the continuity of a single assessor, at least at the initial assessment. The certifiers did not want to agree since it made their planning less tidy but we insisted (and, of course, had the option of the ultimate sanction of taking our business elsewhere) and the certification company acquiesced.

The second place is during the audit itself. Some assessors will be carried away with their own views on what makes for good practice and may try to enforce them by raising non-compliances where they find anything not matching their preconceptions. This must be resisted because it may lead the assessor to think that they can impose other restrictions in the future, and they may be requiring the company to do something that is not in its best interests. A common example of this is assessors who insist that internal auditors keep formal notes of exactly what they have examined during the audit (instrument identifications, purchase order numbers, etc.). Many quality managers find that this is a distraction for their auditors who never use the information afterwards, but they have to enforce the instruction because the assessor says so. Since ISO 9001 does not require this to happen, and ISO 10011 does not really require it either and anyway is only a guidance document, then it does not have to be done.

For any situations like this, the assessor should always be politely asked where that point is specified in the standard. If it cannot be found, or appears to be only a tenuous interpretation of the words, then it does not have to be done. I know it can be difficult to challenge the assessor, especially when a certificate is at stake (and sometimes what is being demanded is so trivial as not to be worth arguing about) but they should not be allowed to get away with making life difficult.

SUMMARY

○   ISO 9001 certification is intended to give external evidence that a company has an adequate quality management system in place.

○ It has some pitfalls which should be watched out for, such as picking an un-accredited certification body.

○ The certification process goes through a number of simple steps, culminating in the initial audit and correction of any problems found.

○ Registration certificates have an associated scope that is covered and it may be possible, subject to some clearly defined restrictions, to have some activities excluded from the scope.

○ Certification bodies should be 'accredited' by a suitable government agency, otherwise their certificates are effectively worthless.

○ A certificate is maintained through regular surveillance visits by an assessor from the certification body.

○ There is a wide range of activities in any project designed to achieve certification, typically taking a year or more to complete.

○ A tiered documentation system is appropriate, although it should not be seen as a restriction.

○ There are a number of specialist sector schemes for certain industries such as TickIT and QS 9000, although auditing these follows the same principles as auditing 'ordinary' ISO 9001 systems.

○ Product certification today usually requires an attendant quality management system and thus has similar audit needs.

○ Gaining the certificate involves a lot of work, so every effort should be made to publicize successful assessment, both inside and outside the organization.

○ The certification assessor is fallible and can be challenged if he or she becomes carried away with insisting upon things which are unreasonable or unjustified.

6
SELECTION, TRAINING AND COMPETENCE OF AUDITORS

❖

AUDITOR QUALITIES

In order for an audit to be done well, we need a good audit team. This requires us to select and train auditors who are able to do the job. The bane of many trainers' lives is the tendency of many organizations to pick internal audit candidates who are willing to participate, or who can be spared, rather than people who are capable of doing the task justice. This is one of the most common causes of mediocre internal audit performance.

When choosing those who are going to be auditors, of any type, there are a number of factors to consider:

○ They should have enough work experience to understand how organizations work and the practicalities of running an operation.
○ They should understand the nature of our work; what it is for and what its main drivers are.
○ They should be confident in their own abilities and knowledge.
○ They should already possess a fair degree of interpersonal and analytical skills.

These are important. With second and third party audits, there is a lot at stake for the audited organization and the organization is unlikely to take it well if the auditor does not appear to understand the basics or have the confidence to pursue a line of questioning. In most cases this problem does not arise. Third party auditors are required to be formally qualified and second party auditors are usually respected experts or someone with an appropriate level of seniority within the auditing organization. It is with internal audits, though, that there is often a greater temptation to select inappropriate people. A youth trainee in administration, for example, may well be quite bright and make a good auditor in a few years' time, but trying to make the transition from school to work, understanding how to deal as an adult with all these experienced people and overcoming adolescent bashfulness are probably enough to cope with without trying to get to grips with quality auditing. Such people are also unlikely to have the confidence to stick to their guns when challenged to justify recommendations which may be unpopular (even good recommendations can be unpopular as managers see them as yet another thing that they have to deal with).

So, choosing the right person is more important than choosing someone who can be spared, or who is willing to do it.

AUDITOR CHARACTERISTICS

It is a favourite technique of most quality audit trainers to discuss, at some point during the training course, what qualities an auditor should display. It breaks up the heavier elements of the course and allows some interaction with the participants. The list produced may look something like that in Figure 6.1.

This list is compiled from qualities typically offered by participants in lead auditor and internal auditor training courses. There is often some debate about a few of the words shown here before they are written onto the flip chart. I usually have to explain the difference between 'disinterested' and 'uninterested' (disinterested means impartial, whereas uninterested means finding it boring) which then leads to a debate as to whether an auditor is, or should be, truly disinterested, especially internal auditors. Some participants also question 'friendly'; they say that in order to perform a good examination they need to stay a little remote, rather like some driving examiners tend to do. I usually disagree with this – auditing is only a part of work and it can be conducted with a degree of cordiality without compromising integrity.

The most frequent comment given is on the list of qualities as a whole. I am often told that this list represents a super-person and can never be attained. People might also comment that the list is very similar to that of desirable and undesirable qualities for any professional business person, and certainly does not describe anybody that they have ever met. I agree with both of these sentiments to some extent, especially the one about the list applying to anybody; after all auditing is just another facet of our working lives. Whilst I do accept that nobody is quite as perfect as this, however, I do feel that we tend to think of auditing as a special activity and thus mentally prepare ourselves for it better than we might for other tasks. This means that auditors can come closer to the ideal than others might, even though they all should be exhibiting similar sets of behaviours.

SELECTION OF INTERNAL AUDITORS

As I have already mentioned, choice of internal auditors is often badly done. I was

GOOD	BAD
Polite	Distracted
Patient	Arrogant
Trained	Appeasing
Empathetic	Directive
Disinterested	Uninterested
Prepared	Intimidating
Tenacious	Intimidated
Inquisitive	Argumentative
Factual	Careless
Learner	Vague
Punctual	Nit-picking
Friendly	Patronizing
Thorough	Trivial
Open-minded	Opinionated
Fair	Self-absorbed
Enthusiastic	Uncommunicative

FIGURE 6.1   Attributes of an auditor

pleased once to be able to present a 'Continuous Improvement Review' course for a pharmaceutical sales company that had deliberately chosen all candidates as middle and senior managers. This was to enable them to understand the issues that they were exploring in detail and make their recommendations with sufficient credibility for them to be taken seriously. The company had even changed the name from the old internal audit label to show that it was taking a new and more serious approach to the subject. For that company, selection of the right people was critical to the success of the project.

Criteria for selection could be:

O   at least three years' work experience after full-time education;
O   a level of expertise or seniority in the organization that means that the
     auditor's reports will be respected;
O   ability to devote enough time to prepare for, carry out and report internal
     audits commensurate with the demands of the organization's own pro-
     gramme without regular cancellation, postponement or skimping;
O   a belief in what the audit programme is trying to achieve.

As well as these, audit candidates will need to have a general understanding of
what the business is about and its key success factors (although not necessarily
specific technical understanding of every aspect, as we will discuss below), will
have to undergo suitable training and carry out some real audits, perhaps super-
vised or in a learning capacity, before they are considered to be fully competent.

SELECTION OF EXTERNAL AUDITORS

THIRD PARTY CERTIFICATION ASSESSORS

The main criterion here is easy: assessors have to be registered with one of the
appropriate registration schemes. There are a number of international schemes,
some of which are described later in this chapter, and some national regimes have
their own qualification rules (particularly where the state standards body is the
only nationally accredited certification body).

There are other requirements though. It is normally accepted that certification
auditors should have had a reasonable level of 'real' work experience before
becoming auditors. Without this they are unlikely to understand the practicalities
and real world requirements of what they are examining and may not make good
judgements. This is almost universally practised and we rarely see young investigators with a freshly acquired MBA but no practical experience acting in these
roles, as might often be the case with traditional management consultancies. In
order to obtain best value from their employees, certification bodies also rather
like to appoint auditors who have, or are quickly able to acquire, an understanding of the operations in a wide range of industries and organizations, so that they
can service a broad client base.

It should be noted that some of the certification bodies also make use of sub-
contractors. These are freelance, qualified, third party auditors who carry out
examinations on behalf of the certification body on an as-required basis, usually
working on a daily fee. The certifiers make use of this option to avoid the overheads of full-time employees, to cope with exceptional workload peaks, or to
bring in specialist knowledge which is needed only rarely and does not exist
amongst the permanent staff. Some certification bodies make copious use of such
resources while others would only call upon them in extreme need. As auditors,

they act exactly the same as full-time employees and there should be no real difference in the quality of the audit carried out. They can have the advantage of possessing a broader perspective than auditors who carry out the same type of audit every day for the same employer (since, for example, auditing may be only one of the many ways they earn their living) but they are less likely to be familiar with the administrative processes and the rules about certification under unusual circumstances.

SUPPLIER AUDITORS

The rules for selection of those making up a team to audit supplier and subcontractors are much simpler. Organizations will normally choose employees who are trusted to show good technical judgement in the areas that the audit is intended to cover. Ideally they will also have received some instruction in audit techniques. If the audit is to cover a wide set of objectives, for example looking both at their technical ability as well as at their administrative techniques for dealing with customer requests, then more than one expert will be sent, one to cover each specialization. Most supplier audit teams comprise a commercial expert (someone from the procurement or finance departments) and a technical expert (from engineering, operations or production, for example).

TRAINING

It is always expected that every auditor has been trained in audit techniques. The details of how that training could be conducted varies, though, between the audit types.

Third party auditors will need to have attended and passed a suitable training course in order to be able to gain their qualification. The training is not lengthy, typically a single five-day course, which explores the concepts from background through to the actual conduct of the audit. The course for most registration schemes incorporates an examination, which must be passed if candidates wish to become qualified to conduct third party audits.

Internal auditors are also always trained, since this is a specific requirement of ISO 9001. The way in which they are trained varies. They can attend the five-day course for third party auditors (although much of the emphasis on such courses is inappropriate for internal audits), a formal registered two- or three-day internal auditor course or a non-approved but still formal training course, or they can be trained in a less formal manner, including self-study and on-the-job training or personal instruction. Some true form of recognized training is expected, though. It is not enough simply to follow an experienced auditor around on an audit and then be left to do it on your own. There must always have been some training in the theory behind audits and explanation of how it should and should not work.

The best way of achieving this is in an approved two-day course (sometimes extended to three days) or an equivalent. In most cases I would judge that anything less than a day of training is insufficient for most internal auditors, with perhaps very few exceptions (I once instructed an internal auditor who intended to conduct examinations in an organization which employed only three people, and managed in this case to pare it down to just under three hours).

Second party auditors are the ones least likely to receive any actual training in how to go about auditing. It is quite usual for procurement executives, accompanied perhaps by a technical expert, to be simply told one day that they will have to visit a supplier to decide whether they can be used, or to monitor their general performance, without any instruction in how to do so. This occurs partly because there is no actual dictate from anywhere that the auditors should have been trained (unlike for third party and internal auditors) and, for many, it is an infrequent activity. The latter should, of course, be no excuse; internal auditors often only spend a few days per year in carrying out audits yet still become trained.

The five-day course aimed at training third party auditors does claim to be suitable for supplier auditing, and many case studies used in the courses are based on supplier audits, since they allow a little more flexibility than certification assessments. In practice, though, much of what is taught in these events is irrelevant to most second party audit teams whose main objective is not to confirm compliance with ISO 9001, especially if the company already possesses a third party certificate. Unfortunately there is no standard product in the quality audit training market to teach the necessary skills. I once gave an in-house course on the subject, specially tailored for the needs of a number of supplier auditors in a large organization, and employing a suitable trainer to do this is always an option if appropriate. If you have only one or two people who need such training, then perhaps a reasonable approach would be to use the basic investigation and management techniques described in this book as a starting point, then conduct a workshop with the people who will do the audits, maybe also involving one or two interested parties such as the quality manager or the procurement manager, and discuss exactly what needs to be examined, keeping notes so that it can be revisited later if the exercise needs to be repeated.

LIVE AUDIT TRAINING

This may be an interesting place to mention a key difference between some of the audit training courses on offer. All of them, as is good training policy, include some exercises in audit practice to reinforce the instruction material. Most of them, especially those run as open, public events, use an imaginary case study, possibly with some role play, to provide the basis for the practice audit. Others, with in-house courses often using it as a tool, have the participants carry out a practice audit on actual operations, with the trainer in attendance and providing feedback on what went well and what did not. I am not a huge fan of the live audit as an integral part of training, mostly because the participants are going to carry out practice audits after the training anyway so why do it in the course itself? From a training point of view there is also the problem of not knowing what they will find, if anything. Then there are the logistical difficulties of setting it up and the absolute certainty that they will not be able to cover the range of circumstances, problems and pitfalls that can be contrived in a case-study based exercise. However, the fact that the two forms exist is one of the main differentiators between the various audit training courses and can be used as an aid to training selection.

INDEPENDENCE

It is an accepted rule of all quality auditing that auditors must be independent of the activity that they are auditing. We have already explored in an earlier part of the book how this applies to assessors, supplier auditors and internal auditors.

In terms of the auditors' own integrity it is important for them to reveal if there is any reason why they should not carry out the audit. Whilst preparing the manuscript for this book I was approached by a certification company to conduct a surveillance audit of a computer training company (as both a trainer and auditor, training company systems have become a mini-specialization of mine). I was not especially busy at the time and therefore reluctant to turn any work away, but felt honour-bound to say that the company was actually owned and run by my brother-in-law so that I would not be truly independent in my role as assessor.

RELEVANT EXPERIENCE

This is a topic which often gives rise to debate in training courses, and one which is particularly difficult to answer. Some authorities on the subject will often be heard saying that direct experience of the activities in the area being audited is not important; once a person understands the techniques of auditing then it is simply a case of following the investigation trail to its resolution. This argument might, at first sight, seem valid for strict compliance auditing (I can see whether or not you have signed this form; I do not need to know what the signature implies or how you decided whether or not to sign it) but even there is a little weak. There are many occasions when something a little unusual happens and, as we have said before, the auditor needs to decide whether the action taken was *reasonable*. It is not possible to make that judgement if you do not understand what is going on. Remembering, also, that ISO 9001 permits the absence of documented procedures where it does not adversely affect quality, then how can we decide whether it adversely affects quality or not if we have no understanding of what the activities are all about? This becomes even more important when we begin to look at whether suitable plans are in place to achieve objectives and examine the adequacy of improvement projects.

On the other hand, people who are too familiar with a particular discipline, and have themselves been in the auditee's position, will sometimes accept one of the standard excuses:

○   This level of failure is typical for our industry and is unavoidable.
○   Everyone knows that these rules never work.
○   That's the way everybody does it.
○   That's a basic assumption.
○   You can only pick this up through experience.
○   We don't pay them enough to insist that they follow procedures.
○   We all know that the work has certain limitations.

Whereas somebody with a completely fresh mind may be naïve enough to question basic assumptions and identify real areas for improvement.

On balance, experience shows that if we can only choose one auditor, then it is better to have somebody who understands the details of what they are examining. Certainly this is the approach taken by third party certification bodies who keep lists of which organizational types each assessor is permitted to audit. If we are fielding a team, however, we have greater flexibility. We can choose a team leader who has direct experience of the work being carried out and a team member who is more of an outsider. This way we can obtain the advantages of close understanding coupled with a completely fresh approach. It should be pointed out, though, that even the second auditor must have some basic understanding of what goes on; it is impossible to audit effectively if you do not understand a word of what is being said! This often arises in engineering environments, for example. I have met several people, in private life, who explain that as soon as I start speaking about engineering or technology they can feel their mental shutters coming down and we are no longer really communicating. If this happens to you then you should avoid auditing those areas. A similar approach needs to be taken to auditing jargon-heavy professions such as software, accountancy and the law; stay away from them if you find conversations about the subject intimidating.

As I have said, third party auditors tend to have rules about auditor competence for a particular industry. Second party auditors typically cope with the issue by sending a team containing a procurement executive for commercial aspects and a technical expert chosen for his or her understanding of what the supplier does. The question of familiarity can be most problematic for internal auditors. Resources are always limited, so although the organization will train and develop a number of internal auditors, it is not practical to have very large numbers (anyway, they would probably then not conduct enough audits to 'keep their hand in'). This, combined with the fact that they are not permitted to audit their own area of responsibility, means that auditors may well find themselves asked to examine an area of the organization with which they are not terribly familiar. Internal auditors do have an advantage, of course, in that they must understand the basics of what goes on since they do, at least, work in the same organization. Beyond this, a rule of thumb which I always apply is to ask the potential auditor whether or not he or she feels comfortable investigating this area. If you feel that you will be able to ask reasonable questions and make judgements as to whether the answers are sensible, then you can perform the audit. If not, then you cannot. Again, if it is possible to use a team of two or more, then overcoming the lack of relevant knowledge of a single internal auditor becomes less of a problem.

TENURE OF SERVICE

Quality auditing is never, at least as far as I have observed, a lifelong career. As I have already mentioned, it is not something that we move into straight after leaving full-time education and is, again as far as I am aware, never something that school, college or university careers advisers include on their list. It is something that most people fall into.

One of the reasons that it is not a major career path is that most of us do not do it full time. Internal quality auditors are usually selected from a wide range of other jobs within the organization and asked to perform a few audits per year. Even where they are quality professionals auditing only occupies a small portion of their working time. Supplier auditors follow a similar pattern. Even third party auditors are rarely employed as full-time certification assessors. The largest third party auditor registration organization, the International Register of Certificated Auditors (yes, I too wonder at the word 'certificated') has approaching 10 000 registrations. Yet there is not room in the market, even internationally, for that many assessors to be carrying out 150 or so audit days per year each. In fact only a small proportion are employed as full-time assessors; the others are consultants, trainers, quality managers, second party auditors or freelance people with 'portfolio' careers. Some of these may conduct no more than one or two audits per year. Even I, who consider myself an *aficionado*, spend no more than about a third of my time in audit-related activities, and approximately half of that is spent in training others how to audit, rather than actually carrying them out myself.

As a result, we never meet anyone who avows to having spent their entire career as an auditor. There may be career-long quality assurance professionals (although many of these also drift into it from other disciplines) but they have much wider roles than simply auditing.

Third party certification assessors can, though, remain a considerable time in their jobs. Although they may not move into it until they have acquired some commercial/general experience in an operational role, they can still enter the job in their thirties, giving them up to 30 years as a professional auditor. In fact once they become assessors it becomes more difficult for them to find and move into other jobs. Where a consultant might be poached by a client and take up a position as a full-time manager, the nature of the relationship and the often rather distant approach precludes this for assessors. Even at a simple logistical level it is difficult to attend job interviews when one's diary is booked ten weeks or more ahead. On the other hand, I would be concerned about an assessor who had done nothing but audit ISO 9000 systems for 30 years. It is very easy to become stale in such a role and end up going through the motions, as hundreds of audits are carried out one after the other with many of them seeming the same and little looked at in depth or for any sustained period. This is a serious problem, since there is much at stake for the organizations being audited and their customers.

Fortunately this does not really seem to happen. Most assessors who stay in the field tend either to broaden or change their roles to audit against other standards (many quality assessors have expanded their remit in the last few years to become environmental auditors, or have taken interest in other areas such as data security or even social accountability). Alternatively they may move into management positions within the certification body, only performing the occasional audit to maintain their registration. It remains to be seen how this will develop in the next few years, however, since in recent times the certification industry has expanded enormously, taking on a new breed of younger assessors who will not be prepared to leave the profession for retirement in a few years' time. Certification body management will have to consider how to deal with a long-standing workforce whilst maintaining the standard of certification service.

For second party auditors, this is rarely a problem. When they carry out a supplier audit, it is usually an integral part of their main role or a wider business project, so has a direct relevance to them and can be seen in broader context. This, combined with the fact that this type of audit is usually only carried out sporadically, means that the danger of familiarity and staleness does not really exist. There is little problem with professionals such as procurement executives conducting supplier audits on and off throughout their working lives.

This is quite an interesting issue for internal auditors. In most cases they do not conduct audits as a full-time activity so do not quickly encounter the same problems as certification assessors, yet they do not have the advantage of a wider context for the audits since they are self-contained tasks outside the remit of their normal jobs. In fact, the lack of regular and constant interest in the subject can be a problem in itself and result in boredom and sameness setting in earlier than might be the case with those whose livelihood directly depends upon conducting audits. For these reasons, it is as important for internal auditors to pursue continuing professional development (CPD), as discussed below, as for full-time assessors. Even where CPD is an integral part of company support for internal auditors, there may be a time when individual auditors simply feel that they have done enough. This could be because they have become bored with it, feel that they are no longer identifying valuable improvements in the way that they used to, or just that their career has moved on and it is no longer appropriate or convenient to be a member of the team of auditors. I usually tell my trainees that there is nothing to be ashamed of in asking to be rotated out and let somebody fresh take their place, as long as they have done enough audits reasonably to repay the investment that the company made in training them. I find that some companies routinely schedule an audit training course every two or three years to replenish the stock of auditors since they know that there will be a continual level of drop-out.

CONTINUING PROFESSIONAL DEVELOPMENT (CPD)

All auditors need to pursue a continuing programme of keeping up to date with developments, polishing and enhancing their skills and increasing their knowledge. This is aimed at keeping the audits effective. It is not possible to audit effectively if, for example, you do not understand the requirements of the latest version of ISO 9001 or current thinking on best practice application of its requirements. For those regularly auditing the same organization for improvement, early examinations may easily reveal potential gains. Later audits, however, will require greater understanding of the work and objectives of the area being audited in more detail.

These days, most professional qualification schemes require a formal programme of continuing professional development. Third party auditor registration also has a CPD requirement. Those organizations in possession of the Investors in People award (popular principally in the UK at the time of writing but gradually spreading to other parts of the international community) will also have their own, most likely more informal, CPD schemes for all employees. Even where such schemes are not already in existence, some procedures for continuing development of skills and knowledge for auditors should be created and employed.

All auditors will need to:

O   understand the requirements and implications of ISO 9001 and any other standards relevant to the organization that they are auditing;
O   constantly seek to study different approaches to quality management systems;
O   share information and opinions with other auditors;
O   find ways of enhancing their audit skills; and
O   keep up to date with changes in recommended audit practice.

The various types of auditors will also have specific objectives for their own CPD programmes. For example, assessors will need to understand certification rules and how they develop, as well as continually trying to expand their scope of competence in order to be useful to their employer. Internal auditors should take a keen interest in the markets, pressures, objectives and plans of their organization in order to be able to fully understand what is happening and why (employees should probably do this anyway, but being an auditor, as explained earlier, sometimes gives us that extra incentive to be dedicated and professional).

One of the problems with encouraging CPD is that most everybody's first reaction is that it costs money, and that training budgets are limited. In fact continuing development is never intended to include only classroom training courses; these alone cannot provide the range and depth of knowledge and skills intended. Even if we were able to find enough courses of the right type that could be tailored to our specific needs, it would be a very costly and time-consuming way of going about it. CPD may well involve some traditional, instructor-led training but will also include reading books and articles, attending exhibitions and lectures, audits carried out in new organizations, research, internal workshops, distance learning and evening classes, self-study (paper or computer-based), watching training and information videos and so on. In fact when you start to look at it, it is likely that most of you already do some of this to a greater or lesser extent. When we think about it more rigorously, however, we can identify where we are supporting our skills and knowledge and where there are gaps, so that we can take action to fill them. To aid in this process, and as part of good general practice, it is a good idea to maintain some form of CPD log.

REGISTRATION AND QUALIFICATION

Every auditor needs to become qualified. This is with a small 'q', meaning that they should gain sufficient training, skills and experience to attain a level of competence which is acceptable to their employers and/or clients. In most cases, though, there is no actual requirement for them to possess a formal qualification, even if sometimes it is preferred as an employment criterion. This equates to most other jobs in industry such as engineers, accountants and personnel specialists who may be accepted members of their professional institutions but do not need to be in order to perform their roles.

The exception to this is third party certification assessors. Under accredited certification schemes the auditors are required to be registered under a formal system, the requirements of the largest of which are described below. Some consultants and advisers also become registered assessors in order to show that they have equivalent skills to those who will be conducting the investigations leading to award of a certificate. There are optional schemes for other types of auditors. I also know of only one professional general qualification scheme for quality auditors, aimed not at allowing auditors to perform a specific job but more like a professional qualification found in other professions. Again, this is described below. If a more general qualification is sought, auditors should speak to the appropriate national or international quality management institution (such as the Institute of Quality Assurance in the UK or the American Society for Quality) who operate professional qualification schemes for quality practitioners, based upon levels of membership in the same manner as for professional institutions in other areas.

IRCA

The largest of the auditor registration organizations is the International Register of Certificated Auditors (IRCA). This is based in the UK and was originally formed as a division of the Institute of Quality Assurance (with a different name in those days) but now operates independently, relying only on the IQA for 'pay and provisions'. It was created to register third party certification auditors but has extended its remit to also register internal auditors, and runs schemes to approve external and internal auditor training courses as part of formalizing the requirements for auditor registration. In fact the approval of training courses is a significant proportion of its activities since this is time-consuming and complex, even though it is seen as being secondary to the main purpose of auditor registration.

The details of auditor registration schemes are given below. At the time of writing, the IRCA has approaching 10 000 registered external auditors and a few hundred registered internal auditors.

Course approval involves setting a syllabus, checking that submitted course designs match the syllabus requirements, confirming that the training organization has the right management and administrative processes to enable the courses to be run effectively (via an audit), checking the qualifications of trainers (the instructors have to be registered auditors and demonstrate some competence as trainers) and monitoring one of the first delivered training courses to see that everything is being done as planned. Thereafter regular surveillance audits are carried out of the management processes and real courses are sampled to see that everything continues to meet the IRCA requirements. There are very large numbers of registered lead auditor courses (aimed at training external auditors) and slightly fewer, although still quite numerous, internal auditor courses. This proliferation of approved training providers has resulted in fierce competition, especially in some parts of the world, so that a five-day lead auditor course can, choosing the UK as an example, be bought for as little as £300.

The IRCA can be contacted via the IQA web site at www.iqa.org

IRCA LEAD AUDITOR

The lead auditor qualification used to be called 'lead assessor' and that is the name still used by many. The title was changed to 'auditor' to provide greater international conformity and to emphasize that what they do is perform audits. It is a registration scheme intended originally for those who carry out assessments for ISO 9001 certification bodies, although it is also used by second party auditors who feel that they require some formal recognition of their competence and by consultants who wish to be seen as having comparable skills to certification assessors.

There are three grades of registration within the scheme. These are provisional auditor, auditor and lead auditor. The first of these is for those who meet the basic academic and training requirements but have not yet gained sufficient experience; it is taken up only by people who wish to place their foot on the ladder with a view to upgrading at a later date. The other grades are fully qualified positions, the main difference being that lead auditors have demonstrated the ability to direct a team containing more than one auditor. Certification assessors are not usually allowed to audit on their own or manage teams until they have attained lead status, so the grade of auditor is also seen as a temporary stepping stone to the fully qualified lead auditor. The exception to this is consultants or some supplier auditors who wish to show that they have a qualification but do not have the opportunity to lead teams since they always work alone and thus stay at the grade of auditor.

In order to become an IRCA registered auditor a candidate must fulfil the following requirements:

○   Attend, and pass the examination and assessment of, a registered lead auditor training course or its equivalent (if the course is not an IRCA registered lead auditor course then you should check with the IRCA before proceeding) no longer than three years before applying.

○   Demonstrate academic achievement through a suitable programme of study. This is deliberately vague to allow for variations in international education schemes, but must be after the age of 18 years, have involved at least 600 hours of study and required some form of test or examination. A university degree meets these criteria as do some other further education programmes and some vocational qualifications, such as ship's master or airline pilot may also be acceptable. This requirement may be waived if a suitable case is made although such candidates will have to pass an interview and carry out many more audits before being accepted.

○   Have had at least four years' work experience. There is a rider about relevance of the experience but most work qualifies, although some schemes which involve little business interaction may be excluded (such as freelance proof-readers working from home etc.) At least two years of this must be quality related. Again, it is often possible to argue that most work, especially that of a managerial or supervisory nature, is quality related.

○   Have completed at least five audits. The audits must be attested by somebody as having been conducted in a competent manner. They also must be conducted on another organization than the one employing the applicant, where there is a complete and operational quality management system in place in which the auditor has had no prior involvement – this excludes many audits which are carried out by consultants for their clients.

For lead auditor, applicants need to fulfil the same requirements, plus they must have conducted an additional five audits as leader of a team of more than one.

Registration is renewed annually through payment of the appropriate fee. Every three years auditors and lead auditors must submit log sheets to show that they have continued to audit regularly and have been pursuing a continuing professional development programme.

IRCA INTERNAL AUDITOR

The internal auditor scheme arose entirely because there was an external registration scheme yet nothing equivalent for internal auditors, even though every ISO 9001 registered organization had a complement of trained internal quality auditors. The scheme is entirely voluntary and there is no requirement for internal auditors to be registered. The benefits of registration are simply that it at least represents some recognition of competence and looks good on the c.v. or résumé. Since it costs money and the benefits are thin and tenuous, the take-up has been low.

To qualify for internal auditor registration, a candidate must:

○   have successfully completed an approved internal auditor course. There is no requirement for an examination on this course but participants are monitored to make sure they fully attend and participate and that they appear to have grasped what is being taught; some training organizations do use an examination simply to provide consistency with the lead auditor course;

○   meet a number of simple education, knowledge and experience requirements which should represent no hurdle at all for anyone who is not freshly out of education and understands the basics of their employer's quality system;

○   have conducted at least ten audits of a minimum of three hours each (including preparation time).

Registration involves submission of a log sheet identical to that used by registered external auditors, plus the appropriate application and registration fees. Continuing registration requires no CPD, but simply a three-yearly verification that a very small number (much smaller than I would recommend as a sensible minimum but which is probably set at a practical level for a registration scheme) of audits have been carried out since registration. Booklets and supporting data on the scheme, and for IATCA registration can be obtained from the IRCA offices.

IATCA

IATCA is the International Auditor and Training Certification Association. It was set up by a number of independent auditor registration bodies, notably those of the UK, the USA, Australia and New Zealand, to provide a single, common registration qualification. This was done in answer to some concerns from international organizations that they were not seeing a consistent approach, and from some auditors that they were having to make multiple registrations in order to operate internationally.

When the scheme was first envisioned, it was thought that ultimately all certification assessors would register with IATCA, leaving the national schemes such as IRCA for first and second party auditors and consultants. At the time of writing, though, the national schemes are still going strong and IATCA has still to find its niche. It is early days, however, and it will be interesting to see how it develops.

Application is normally made via the national registration body. The criteria are very similar to those for IRCA auditor and lead auditor (IATCA has auditor and senior auditor). The differences are as follows:

O   Corporate membership of a recognized professional institution is recognized as a suitable academic qualification.

O   Attendance at one of the traditional national registration body courses will suffice for an interim period but after this the course will have to be recognized as meeting IATCA criteria.

O   The requirements for what the audits must cover are very specific in that applicants must demonstrate that they have audited a whole business (not just departments or individual processes), been involved in the whole audit process from planning to action completion and have covered every requirement of ISO 9001.

O   The requirements for auditor grade are that at least 30 days have been spent in auditing, at least 20 of which must have been on-site (i.e. not off-site document reviews or planning). This time must include at least two audits where a decision on the acceptability of a system had to be made (i.e. excluding routine surveillance audits).

O   All audits must have been witnessed by, and under the guidance of, a verifying auditor (normally someone who has been a registered IATCA senior auditor for over a year). This requirement is the one which represents the main departure from national schemes such as the IRCA and with which anyone other than those working for a certification body will find it hard to comply (and even the smaller certification bodies may have difficulty in coping with this). At least two different verifying auditors must have witnessed the various audits.

O   For senior auditor, applicants must have conducted five witnessed audits as trainee leader of a team of more than one, at least three of which must have been of two days duration or more.

It can be seen that IATCA registration is more difficult to achieve. In some ways it makes sense that someone competent should specifically watch to see that the audits are done in a satisfactory manner but this may introduce excessive practical difficulties and burdens for hopeful registrants.

There is, again, a three-yearly re-assessment process which requires a programme of CPD to be undertaken plus a small number of audits. It should be noted, though, that 50 per cent of audits carried out by registered senior auditors are expected to be as leader of a team of more than one. In practice, I am sure that this will result in auditors not submitting records of all audits for re-registration; they will simply show enough to qualify for re-registration and balance them so that 50 per cent are as a team leader. Otherwise even the most active assessors working for large bodies are unlikely to requalify at the end of three years.

IATCA also has a web site, at www.iatca.org

ASQ

The American Society for Quality (ASQ) offers the only auditor qualification scheme of which I am aware that is a true qualification rather than the basic registration scheme offered by bodies whose focus is primarily on ISO 9001 assessment. The Certified Quality Auditor (CQA) qualification which they administer is primarily for USA residents but has been adopted in many other areas of the world where there is a strong American influence. It is a qualification intended to indicate suitable status for quality professionals involved in audits of any type.

To qualify as a CQA, applicants must fulfil the following requirements:

○   Have eight years work experience directly related to one or more areas of the body of knowledge defined by the ASQ. At least three years of this must be in a 'decision-making' role. Higher academic qualifications such as university degrees may reduce the experience requirement.

○   Be a suitably qualified person such as a full member of the ASQ or equivalent professional institution, or a Professional Engineer (equivalent to Chartered Engineer in the UK) or have two recognized professionals attest to the candidate's ability and professionalism.

○   Pass a written examination of multiple choice questions based on the body of knowledge.

A more detailed description of the CQA qualification and entry requirements can be found on ASQ's web site at www.asq.org/standcert/certification/cqa.html

SECTOR SCHEMES

The various sector schemes that exist are usually subsidiary programmes of the national external auditor registration systems. They are too numerous to mention here but are typically the same as for 'standard' auditor registration, except that the training course attended should have been recognized as being tailored directly to the sector and the candidate will need to demonstrate specific experience and knowledge of the industry, usually by interview.

Most auditors registered under specific schemes are usually thought of as quite capable of auditing areas outside their sector scheme qualification, although they have to demonstrate their basic competence in the area in the same way as any other auditor.

Sector schemes are universally applied to external auditors. Since the registration or basic competence requirements for internal auditors usually include some knowledge of their organization's own quality system then it is expected that they will understand what is going on in the area that they audit.

FUTURE OF REGISTRATION

It is hard to make a detailed prediction of what will happen to auditor registration in the future. Apart from independent qualification schemes such as ASQ's Certified Quality Auditor, it is intimately tied up with the future of ISO 9001 certification. If this continues to flourish it is certain that auditor registration requirements will continue to develop and be applied internationally.

Certainly it is highly unlikely that we will continue to see requirements for professional, accredited ISO 9001 certification without seeing a parallel requirement for qualification of auditors. In fact the rules appear to be growing stricter, as we have seen with the IATCA requirements. This is inevitable. Since I became involved in the field I have seen tightening of rules in all areas such as certification body appointment, assessor registration, interpretation of standards, certificate scoping and internal auditor training. As each level of capability is reached then the target is moved, in line with the modern striving for continuous change and increased effectiveness and efficiency. If we assume that this will continue, then we could see even stricter requirements for certification assessors and even a need for supplier and internal auditors to possess some formal qualification (such as formal registration to one scheme or another) in order for their organization to pass ISO 9001 assessment.

SUMMARY

O   All auditors need to possess a good degree of technical understanding, experience and confidence, and suitable interpersonal skills.

O   Auditors need to display personal characteristics that can occasionally appear unattainable, but need to be strived for.

O   We have to select auditors who possess those skills and those qualities, as well as having some interest in the auditing process.

○   All auditors must have some training; those requiring formal qualifications will need to attend prescribed approved courses.

○   Independence is usually important for the audit to work well, although it is recognized that internal auditors and supplier auditors cannot be totally impartial, nor would it necessarily be a good thing if they did not express their opinions.

○   Team members must have some understanding of what they are looking at, otherwise the audit will be meaningless or very slow, but they do not necessarily need to be technical experts.

○   Very few people take up auditing directly from education; in particular certification assessors need a good understanding of how 'the real world' works before adopting auditing as a full-time job. Internal auditors may perform the function for a while and subsequently let someone else have a turn.

○   Every auditor needs to keep their knowledge and skills up to date. Those in a registration scheme will need to show formal records that they have pursued a programme of continuing professional development.

○   There are a number of auditor qualification and registration schemes which have many similarities, but each serving a slightly different purpose.

○   It is likely that formal qualifications of some sort will be a continuing requirement for auditors and the registration criteria will inevitably become stricter.

PART TWO

RUNNING THE AUDIT

❖

7

PLANNING

❖

AUDIT PLANNING

Whilst the actual preparation for an individual audit can often be dealt with in some detail by training courses and reference materials, the subject of planning is sometimes glossed over. Indeed preparation and planning are often spoken of as one and the same thing, with the only real reference to planning being a reminder that some form of schedule needs to be prepared.

In fact there is a great deal of coordination and planning needed to make any audit programme work. Although much of this is not carried out by the audit team themselves but as part of audit programme management, since it is a necessary part of the process it is important that we address it here. And, of course, some of its elements, such as the audit scope and the investigation procedures, directly affect what the audit team will do.

Just as with any other form of planning, it is not an activity which is conducted once and then forgotten about until the next cycle. Planning and execution are integral functions, requiring plans to be updated as work progresses and changes are required or new information comes to light. Monitoring of progress against a plan is also a key management function and may itself result in plan modifications and updates.

DEFINING INDIVIDUAL AUDITS

A key part of planning is to identify exactly what has to be done. The work breakdown structure tool used in project management, for example, is there simply to decide what work has to be covered within the planning remit. The equivalent in audit planning is to identify what audits have to be done in order to satisfy your objectives, and how big they are (i.e. to know roughly how much work will be associated with each one).

Planning horizons are typically six months to a year. One certain feature of plans looking this far ahead, especially twelve months forward, is that it will be impossible to create a list of all audits and their sizes that will be exactly right for the whole duration of the plan. Certification bodies, in particular, will not know which new clients they will win in that time, who could book new assessments at only six weeks notice. Part of the identification of forward workload, then, will be based upon market forecasts of the number, size and type of new contracts gained and of existing clients lost (although there is always the hope that the latter will be zero). There will, of course, be existing clients whose audits are due at particular times, but they will represent only part of the picture. Supplier audit programmers will have an easier time, although there will inevitably be new suppliers taken on during the year whose scope, size and timing cannot be predicted. Internal audit coordinators have the easiest task, simply having to divide the organization into sensibly manageable chunks. Even they will find that organizational or staff changes, availability difficulties, the need to schedule extra audits or re-audits and so on will entail review of the schedule at some point in the planning timeframe.

Setting exactly what a single audit will include always causes some intellectual effort. For a certification audit there is the discussion with the client as to exactly what the client wishes to include and what not to include and balancing this with what it is sensible or permissible to include. Once this has been agreed, the duration of the audit is probably fixed by accreditation rules and all that is left for the planner to decide is how many to set for the audit team (e.g. should it be one auditor for two days or two auditors for one day?) and whether to allow for travelling time. There is always the question of whether or not an initial visit's findings will delay the initial audit, but at this stage allowing a month between the two is the best bet.

For surveillance audits, it is normal for the audit team leader to recommend at the initial audit how the activities will subsequently be sampled, so that all the planner needs to do is study the recommendation to see what has to be covered. Certification auditors and planners should watch that this is done well. As a sub-contract auditor I have often been left to decide for myself what to look at in a large or complex organization, without much knowledge of whether or not I was doing the right thing. It is good practice for a strong procedure to be in place to handle this planning, thus avoiding humming and ha-ing at the time of audit preparation and reducing the risk of something important being missed.

DEFINING THE INTERNAL AUDIT

For internal audits, the way that any individual audit is defined varies enormously from one organization to another. As we have already discussed, those which follow a direct audit trail and cross several functional boundaries (pursuing the horizontal loop, in ISO 9001:2000 terms) should only be used by very confident and experienced auditors, or in project-based organizations where this approach is natural.

Most auditors will take the converse approach, looking at all activities within a single functional area or place. A common way of addressing this is to select the scope of a single audit procedure document as the boundary of the individual audit. In most organizations this does not really work well. Single documents usually describe too narrow a set of activities to make the audit meaningful. There are not enough interfaces between activities and too few opportunities to look at 'the whole picture'. It can also result in important aspects being ignored simply because they do not fall within the selected procedure. It is better to define the audit by function or physical area and then be prepared to examine anything that is going on within it.

CREATING A SCHEDULE

Once you know all the things that have to be audited, you can create a schedule aimed at covering them all within a given time period.

For third party certification this is relatively easy since there are rules about frequency and timing so we simply need to put them on our plan, then do a little bit of juggling to make best use of resources.

Other audit programmes need to give more consideration to how often the audits should be carried out. It is normal to define a minimum frequency for investigating each area, then think about where extras may be needed. Reasons why an organization or area may need to be looked at more often than the minimum could be:

O   it is crucial to the success of the business;
O   it represents high risk;
O   it is new and therefore an unknown quantity;
O   it contains many problems or improvement actions whose progress need to be monitored;
O   it is large, meaning that the sample size in an audit only examines a tiny proportion of the work.

The schedule is then created by trying to spread the set of needed audits throughout the year, or the length of the planning cycle. This is done in the same way that any other schedule is created, by looking at what has to be covered and who is available, trying to spread the work reasonably evenly. Some flexibility should be allowed so that, for example, audits of an area examined twice per year do not have to occur exactly six months apart. On the other hand, you need to be 'reasonable' about it so that you do not plan two audits only four weeks apart with the next then scheduled for eleven months later.

When planning several months, or even a year, ahead it is usually not practical to set the date of the audit too rigidly. If the schedule defines the exact date for something that could be happening up to twelve months away the chances are we will not make it and will have to re-arrange. For all types of audit programme, setting the month is often good enough. This enables us to perform rough resource planning and gives the auditees an idea of when they can expect the next visit but does not tie anybody down too rigidly. Then, whenever the normal planning horizon for the organization involved approaches we can set the actual date(s). I am often asked what this planning horizon should be but there is no hard and fast rule; it differs from culture to culture and organization to organization. A French company that I have regularly audited has never provided a date earlier than eight weeks from the time of my telephone call yet in the Arabian Gulf organizations seem reluctant to commit to any appointments further than a week away but will be happy to accommodate a visit tomorrow. Those responsible for setting the specific audit dates need to become familiar with the preferred planning cycles of the auditors and auditees and balance this against their own needs. Note that trying to set the date too far in advance is not a good idea: I was recently with a quality manager who was in a quandary because his certifier had asked for a date seven months hence and he had no idea who would be available then or even whether the business would still be occupying the same premises!

Although the audit programme coordinator establishes the overall schedule, he or she need not necessarily set the precise time and date. If the coordinator has full control over the auditor's diary, as with full-time certification assessors for example, then it may well be considered best for the coordinator to set the date. Otherwise it is usually best for the audit team leader to deal directly with the auditee representative to avoid long message delays and potential for confusion. This is especially important for internal auditors or consultants who have many calls on their time outside the influence of the audit programme coordinator.

TAKING ACCOUNT OF CIRCUMSTANCES

In setting the dates for the schedule you need to take account of various, fairly obvious points:

○   If the auditors only consider it a part-time occupation, then they are unlikely to want to do all their audits together and thus take too much time away from their main job at one go.

○   Even if the auditors are full-timers, they will still need time clear in their diaries for continuing professional development, reading correspondence and formal instructions, reviewing corrective actions (see Chapter 11) and to allow for unplanned emergencies (sickness, transport delays, last minute client cancellations, etc.).

A number of other factors which may affect scheduling also need to be taken into account:

○   Long national holidays or other celebrations (Christmas, Ramadan, etc.) can make audits impossible not just for the duration of the holiday but also for a week or two either side.

○   Some organizations have shut-downs or popular holiday periods which have extended effects.

○   It can be too much for an organization or area to cope with if there is more than one team of auditors in at the same time, so take account of financial or other audits plans.

○   Travelling time is wasteful, tiring and has to be paid for in some form or another, so try to arrange distant visits to occur together; an audit today in Edinburgh, tomorrow in Dover and the day after in Newcastle is not good planning.

○   Auditors have basic human needs such as eating and sleeping. Schedules need to allow for this and not include too many late nights, early starts or meals on the fly.

○   Fatigue from travelling, especially flying between time zones, has to be accounted for.

Except in the most basic of audit programmes, then, creating the schedule is not a simple task and is likely to involve an element of data gathering and several iterations. Then, when the detailed dates have to be arranged as part of the short-term scheduling, the same issues will have to be revisited, with the recognition that at this stage there is less room to shuffle dates around once they have been agreed.

REVISING THE PLAN

Once the schedule has been agreed it becomes a controlled document and will need re-authorization and communication if and when it is changed. Since changing it can be complex and may affect many people, it is best to minimize the number of changes to the long-term plan. One way of achieving this is to keep the short-term planning activity of setting specific dates and times separate from the overall longer range planning. In this way everyone sees a copy of the long-term plan which, if prepared well, should change rarely, and the short-term details are communicated only to the auditors and auditees involved by use of confirmation letters or forms etc.

If the full schedule does have to be revised, then of course you must consider all of the factors mentioned above as important for its initial creation. Where you are re-scheduling the efforts of a full-time auditor it will be obvious that you cannot just move one assignment, another will also have to move to accommodate it. Indeed you may need to juggle several proposed audits to enable the schedule to fit your needs once more. Even where this is not the case and the auditor is a consultant or employee with other responsibilities whose other work does not require fixed appointments, it may still be a good idea not to move one audit in isolation. The entire programme has a tendency to shift inexorably backwards if, when encountering an inevitable delay, you do not bring another audit forward to compensate.

IDENTIFICATION OF RESOURCES

We will discuss recruitment of resources in more detail later as part of programme coordination. It is, however, impossible to divorce this from the planning function. Setting the schedule, for example, is difficult to do until we know what resources are available and deciding what resources we need is hard until we know what the schedule is. They are mutually dependent processes.

For the planner, it is most important to ensure that the audit is carried out when intended. This is vital if you are subject to review by an external regulator or assessor who will complain if you are not doing what you said you would. On a more practical level, failing to meet the date could mean that you have missed the 'window' within which the auditees are able to provide their fullest cooperation; at other times they may be busy with other audits, on holiday, launching a project, completing a project and so on. There also could be a good reason why you wished to audit at that time, such as witnessing an installation which only happens rarely or examining a project at a critical stage. All of this means that you must have the right resources available at the right time.

Resources means auditors in this context. Since there is nothing required for most audits other than the audit team and the cooperation of the auditees, it is the availability of people with which the planner is concerned. This is why many planners assign the auditor or audit team to an individual audit at the very beginning when the schedule is set. If auditor availability is not a problem, or the programme is such that the schedule is typically highly fluid (such as in some service organizations with very short planning horizons - my own commitments are usually completely unknown beyond six weeks from today, for example) then the auditors can be allocated nearer the date. If dates are critical, though, it is better to assign them in advance.

Another factor is auditor competence. If one or more auditors need special skills or experience for a particular area then we must make sure that the right skills are available at the right time. This may involve planning to recruit the right person in sufficient time, or arranging a training and development progamme to provide existing personnel with the necessary capabilities and qualifications. This is especially important if some formal qualification is needed as it always takes longer than anticipated to apply to awarding bodies for a qualification, even after the necessary training or education has been received and the requisite examinations passed.

Every planner should have some idea how to obtain external resources to assist with the programme if necessary. Modern business has recognized the benefits of employing interim managers and contract or temporary staff at all levels. Auditing should be no different. Some organizations like to make extensive use of such personnel to give maximum flexibility. Thus certification bodies use many sub-contract assessors; in fact some have no full-time auditors at all thus enabling them to have a range of skills available without incurring excessive overheads. Purchasing managers often will use consultants to examine their suppliers for them and some quality managers even use outside experts to assist with their internal audits. Others may prefer to make more use of full-time staff, only employing contractors and other outsiders if specialist or rare skills are needed for particular jobs. Even where the organization and its planners believe that they can fulfil the audit schedule entirely with full-time staff or have a policy against using consultants and contractors, a prudent planner will have details of external personnel to hand in case of unforeseen circumstances to ensure that every option is available when considering how to resolve the situation.

Of course, many of the issues raised above become academic if the audit regime is resource-limited. Many planners find, particularly in small organizations, that the question of finding enough resources to fit the schedule is academic; the powers that be impose a limit on resources and planners must work within these constraints. This limit is usually imposed for budgetary reasons and may define the maximum number of full-time auditors that can be employed, or even something as small as how many internal auditors they can afford to have trained. Other constraints can arise where the audit resource diminishes through natural wastage or withdrawal from a voluntary scheme (such as with many internal audit programmes). In such cases the planner may have to start from the resource availability as a given, fitting the schedule within the resultant boundaries. This may require withdrawal of some 'nice to have' elements and could result in reduced audit frequency, smaller audit teams, complete elimination of peripheral audits or reduced audit duration.

SELECTING THE AUDIT TEAMS

The first issue that a planner needs to consider is the size of the audit team. This task can be removed if the audit team size is a matter of policy. A large number of internal audit regimes, for example, assume a team size of one. Others always send pairs of auditors and I have seen one where four is the standard size – in an environment highly geared towards improvement where a large team is employed to enable one or more auditors to spend time analysing and measuring key aspects in detail whilst the rest of the team continue with the overall investigation. In other cases, the size of team may be flexible, either to make the best resource use for fixed working days or to decide how deep the examination should be for fixed duration. In this case the planner simply needs to decide what is best on a case-by-case basis. Remember that two auditors for one day tends to be less efficient than one auditor for two days owing to the doubling of person hours spent in meetings and the need for team coordination. This inefficiency is made worse if there is international travel involved since you double the travel time and have twice the flight costs (which inevitably far exceeds the extra accommodation costs incurred by having fewer auditors stay for longer). Another factor which could affect the size of audit teams is whether a mix of specializations is required that cannot be embodied in a small team; this may often be found in second party audit teams that are assessing the supplier for a variety of competences.

Once we know how large the team is to be the next step is to decide who is to be in it. This will be a decision based upon availability, individual workload and skills or specialization. There are also a number of other factors to be taken into account:

O   For internal audits, teams should be selected so that they do not audit their own area of responsibility.

O   For external audits, team members should not have any personal interest in whom they are auditing – this will exclude them from organizations run by their family members, companies that they buy things from at home, businesses against whose activities they have taken a moral stance, etc. (although this cannot be taken too far otherwise telecommunications carriers and utility companies would never be audited).

O   Where a team of more than one auditor is used the mix of the team should be considered: do they work well together, or do they have complementary styles which will ensure a wider coverage?

O   How far will they have to travel from their home base or their previous day's work?

O   How often has this auditor audited the same organization before? – to some extent continuity avoids having to learn about the processes afresh every time but taken too far it can lead to stagnation.

SCOPING THE AUDIT

The auditors need to understand what it is that they have to examine. The way to achieve this is carefully to define the scope before the start. Although it is a good idea to look at anything that goes on in an area, this may not be acceptable in some external audits and not practical for all internal audits.

The third party assessment should define the scope as part of contractual arrangements and so it should be relatively easy to define for the audit team. It is common practice for the precise wording of the scope statement to be confirmed by the lead assessor at the initial audit, but there is rarely any room for real movement here; the auditor is only looking at minor points of interpretation. This can be very important to get right. Many companies operate a variety of business activities and will sometimes consider some of them to be trivial or not requiring certification and so will not want to pay the assessor to look at them. This must be clearly understood in advance so that no time is wasted in debate or in examining the wrong things.

Supplier audits are examinations of one commercial organization by another. This is not the same as being assessed by an independent third party and there are often system elements which suppliers may not wish their customers to see. These could include large amounts of financial data and anything which relates to the business of other customers. Whilst the scope of a supplier audit is rarely formally defined for supplier audits, other than a broad statement that they are being investigated for their capability and competence, audit teams must understand that they are only permitted to examine system elements which apply to their contracts and which do not represent commercial secrets (many businesses jealously guard the details of their processes to prevent imitation; Coca Cola is probably the most famous example of this).

When auditing internally many of the restrictions of external examinations do not apply. In fact the usual approach is to allow the audit team to look at anything which they consider could affect quality or the service that is provided to customers. This is fine in most cases but can be overwhelming if visiting areas with large, diverse or complex operations. If there is too much to look at the audit team are in danger of investigating everything superficially, ignoring key issues, picking exactly the same sub-set as at the last audit or simply running out of time. In such cases the planner will need to divide the area or process into smaller parts and explain to the team what is to be covered, ensuring that those aspects not looked at are covered by another item on the audit schedule.

COORDINATION OF THE AUDIT

There is a wide range of small details that need to be sorted out before the investigation visit itself. These are the administrative details essential to the smooth running of the audit. As discussed under management of the audit programme, there are practical reasons why much of this should be handled by the audit programme coordinator, but there could also be occasions when some details are dealt with by the team leader.

Examples of the sorts of things that need to be arranged are as follows:

○   Travel arrangements, especially if an audit team is travelling separately when coordination will be needed to ensure that they arrive together and perhaps have a few minutes to discuss the audit before meeting the auditees. Travel arrangements could also include arrangements for conveying the audit team between airports, railway stations, etc. and the place of audit.

○   Start times and required departure times, especially if timed transport is involved (for example the closing meeting will have to finish by a certain time if the team have an aeroplane to catch).

○   Ensuring that the auditee management has provided any necessary support such as guides (see below), office space, word processing or copying facilities, safety equipment and protective clothing, security clearance, meeting rooms for introduction and feedback sessions, and local transport, as appropriate to the needs of the individual audit.

PROVISION OF AUDIT COLLATERAL

Auditors will require access to a variety of information in order to be able to carry out their investigation successfully. A large proportion of this information will have to be created by the audit programme coordination as part of defining and establishing the overall audit system, but there is also a planning element in making sure that it is made available to the audit team before their investigation commences. The documentation needed for preparation, which may also have to be collected by the audit programme coordinator, is discussed in the next chapter. Additional documents that the team must possess for use during the investigation and reporting stages include:

○   blank forms for creating the standard report such as corrective action requests, observation sheets and summary report forms;

○   ancillary forms for recording extra information such as certification or approval recommendations, change of details, trainee auditor evaluation, forward planning sheets and auditee feedback forms;

○   assistance documents such as business sector guides, interpretation documents, key regulations and standard checklists;

○   any other supporting information or guidelines not made available at the preparation stage.

GUIDES

One of the key details that needs to be planned for on many occasions is the provision of guides. A guide is a member of the auditee organization who knows his or her way around, is familiar with the systems, plans and objectives of the processes being audited and knows the people involved.

One of the guide's most important roles, usually in external audits where findings need to be formally acknowledged and witnessed, is to act as the signatory for the points raised by the auditor that the guide has accompanied. The guide is often used to perform this function rather than the interviewee or the quality representative or a senior manager. The interviewee may not be somebody closely involved with audit planning and arrangements and may be uncertain what is being signed for, and therefore often reluctant to sign. Indeed, some interviewees may feel very nervous about signing as they may believe that they could be 'told off' as a result. The manager of the area, or any other manager spoken to later, may have difficulty in signing to confirm that the facts are correct since he or she was not there at the appropriate time. The guide is always present and should be selected to be confident enough to confirm findings and so be the ideal person to act as witness. Specific responsibilities of guides include:

O   showing the auditor around;
O   introducing the auditor to interviewees;
O   helping to clarify any planning issues (e.g. helping the auditor to understand which area is responsible for what);
O   obtaining any information, documents or other materials requested by the auditor other than that which can be provided by the interviewee (photocopies, stationery, business plans, brochures, etc.);
O   helping with administration and support such as meals, refreshments, travel arrangements, security, accommodation, office facilities and rescheduling;
O   assisting with clarification of key system elements but not to answer for the interviewee. This is important. The guide may often be an experienced person such as the quality coordinator who feels able to explain things to the auditor's satisfaction but the auditor wishes to hear the answer from the person doing the work. If you are auditing and are lumbered with a talkative guide you may need to politely but firmly ask the guide to keep quiet and simply observe. The guide should be permitted, though, to explain that the auditor is asking the wrong person, mention who else could provide the required information, explain company policy and anything else that the interviewee would not reasonably be expected to answer. This can be especially useful in avoiding a waste of time if nervous interviewees are asked questions completely outside their area of responsibility yet feel that they need to try to answer the auditor anyway;
O   help with time management by reminding the auditor (who may not have looked at a watch for some time in the heat of the interview) about progress and deadlines;

O   to stay with the auditor throughout the investigation and not leave him or her alone, risking times when the auditor wishes to move but does not know how to get there or who to ask for. The exception to this is when the auditor specifically asks to be alone, such as when writing up reports or findings.

Guides may also be interviewees at some point, at which time they will temporarily fill both roles. If the audit team comprises more than one person, one guide should accompany each auditor.

Note that guides are not needed in every case. If internal audit interviewees are confident, known to the auditor and the team is familiar with the workplace layout then there is little for an audit guide to do especially if the system does not require finding sheets to be countersigned. They are a good idea for most external audits, however, and certification assessors will certainly expect them.

MONITORING PROGRESS

There is no point in having a plan and schedule unless we monitor to see that the plan is being met. It is a key responsibility of programme coordinators to look at the plan regularly and see how well the audits are progressing.

If each audit is arranged when scheduled, and postponements are compensated where possible by audits brought forward, then there should be little problem with the plan being effective. Small problems and delays can be cumulative, however, so a careful watch on progress needs to be made.

A particular eye needs to be kept on audits and events which are believed to be in the pipeline but for which no firm arrangements have yet been made. These could include:

O   new certification clients who have not yet set dates;

O   possible new certification clients who have indicated acceptance but have not yet formally signed up;

O   potential new suppliers;

O   existing departments to be added to the remit of the audit programme;

O   known forthcoming extensions to the audit programme of any type where the dates have not yet been set (e.g. extensions to certification scope, new business departments being established, new supplier facilities);

O   planned training of more auditors (they will need to be given audits to do soon after their training to build up their experience before they forget their training);

O   specific events which need auditing (installations, plant shut-downs, etc.) but whose date of occurrence is not yet known.

All of these will have implications for scheduling and resource usage. The planner will need to play with the allocation of tentative dates and audit teams in an attempt to predict how best to manage them. It will be important to chase for exact dates and details as far as possible in advance to avoid dangers of plans not being adhered to or commitments not being met.

SUMMARY

O A great deal of planning and coordination of audit programmes is needed to make them run smoothly and effectively.

O Defining what comprises the individual audit forms one of the first planning tasks, deciding what will be looked at during each audit and ensuring the whole of the system is covered.

O The frequency of audits for each area then has to be decided.

O A schedule can then be prepared.

O Preparing the schedule and deciding what resources are needed are mutually dependent activities.

O Scheduling and planning needs to take account of emergencies and changing circumstances.

O The size of the audit team can be fixed or variable and can represent a useful planning tool.

O Audit teams should be selected not only on availability and relevant experience but also taking account of auditor development needs and team dynamics.

O The scope of an audit has to be set to enable the team to concentrate on relevant subjects.

O Somebody must take responsibility for organizing the support elements of an audit such as travel and accommodation.

O The team will have to be provided with reference materials and standard formats to enable them to carry out the audit adequately.

O Guides need to be provided for external audits, although not usually for internal programmes.

O Guides provide general local support but also act as witness to non-compliances.

O The schedule and its progress needs to be tracked to make sure that it does not fall behind and that future events are confirmed as early as possible.

8

PREPARATION

❖

WHY PREPARE?

It is generally said that if we are adequately prepared for something then we are less likely to encounter problems and are more likely to make our activities successful. This is why actors rehearse, musicians practise and ships' masters plot their courses in advance. This is also well understood in business where careful preparations are made for presentations, negotiations, important meetings, customer visits, office moves and so on.

Audits are no different. They are lengthy, complex activities which could easily fail to meet their objectives if not managed well. Since preparation is a key factor in good management, it follows that audits, too, have to be adequately prepared for.

Audit preparation needs to equip the auditor for conducting the investigation. The auditor will have to understand what goes on in the area or organization, how it works, how big it is, who is involved, what the interfaces are, what processes operate and how they are controlled. This knowledge has to be a mixture of the global and the specific. Thus auditors need to have a good overview of what is done and what it is intended to achieve, as well as appreciating some of the detail control and disciplines which are used.

It can certainly be embarrassing not to be well prepared. External auditors who arrive at an organization's premises and ask 'What do you do here then?' do not advance their credibility or create confidence.

At the detail level, too, there are good reasons for being well prepared. Many of you, I am sure, will have seen the exercise used in some training courses where participants are given an instruction sheet which they are told to follow (usually with a comment that we are running behind schedule, so please do it as quickly as possible) which asks them to perform progressively more ridiculous tasks until, right at the end, the sheet tells them that they should not have done any of it. This

147

can happen to ill-prepared auditors. If you are trying to follow documentation that you have not previously looked at you may be tempted to go through it line by line, checking that each step is followed. The document, though, may well have been written by someone who was simply asked to put their thoughts down on paper (i.e. not a professional technical author) and may decide to put a small comment at the end to remind readers that all of the above only applies to the night shift, or when the emergency plan has been invoked, or when the managing director is away on holiday.

Finally, I am often approached by people who suggest that when they become good at auditing, they will no longer need to prepare. Good auditors, they say, do it 'off the cuff'. This view comes from observation of certification assessors who appear to have no checklists or other notes of what to cover, and to be unfamiliar with the related documentation. This is only partially true. For the initial assessment, auditors working for ISO 9001 certification bodies do conduct a fairly detailed preparation in the form of an initial visit which is intended to familiarize them with what happens in some detail. Through commercial and time constraints, however, they are unable to do this for subsequent, surveillance, audits. Such auditors will, though, usually admit that surveillance audits are often fairly shallow and do little more than give a general impression that things are still being controlled well and perhaps pick on only one or two items with any degree of thoroughness. And they *do* have checklists. The difference here is that they are looking specifically to see whether or not the organization is meeting ISO 9001 requirements, so their checklist is against ISO 9001. Most of them are so familiar with the requirements of the standard that the checklist used is largely in their head rather than on paper, but it will always be there, informally or formally. Some certifiers also have more detailed checklists written for specific industry sectors, which are used by auditors when such organizations are visited. Thus certification auditors do believe that preparation is important, it is just that the way the system operates sometimes means that full preparation for every audit is impractical.

WHEN TO PREPARE

This may sound slightly obvious. After all, everybody knows that you have to prepare for something before you do it. This is true, but it is probably worth taking a few lines to discuss exactly when.

My own view is that preparation should be done just before the audit is conducted, immediately prior to the start. To go straight from a time of preparation to conducting the examination is ideal or, if the audit is to start first thing in the morning or will be lengthy (thus involving lengthy preparation), then the day before should be set aside. Certainly preparation several weeks before the audit is not sensible, since by the time that you come to do it you are likely to have forgotten much of what you had learnt. Sometimes this can be difficult. Certification assessors, for example, who are full-time employees of certification bodies, are allowed very little preparation time for anything other than the very first, initial audit designed to award the certificate. Thus they have to snatch whatever preparation time they can, which in practice is often in front of the television the previous evening.

The other problem with leaving preparation to the last minute is that there is more danger of failing to do it. If you are off to start an audit which will take you away from your desk for three days, then there is a great temptation to spend the afternoon before making sure that everything likely to come up has been dealt with and put to bed, instead of doing the preparation work that you had intended. Similarly, if somebody gives you an urgent task which must be done now, there is no opportunity to put the preparation off until later. If an improvement audit is planned, involving the collection of a wide variety of data from a number of sources, it may not be instantly available in a single binder or network directory, and some time will be needed to collect it. Auditors will have to learn for themselves what represents the best time for their organization and the type of audits that they conduct.

The final thing to remember when considering when to begin preparation is that good preparation can be time-consuming. If you are considering a routine surveillance or regular internal audit in an area with which you are very familiar and there has been little change, then a short reminder of how it all works and an update on performance measurement will suffice. Where you are looking at something completely new, however, simply collecting the relevant data may take some time. In this case you may still leave the actual study of information and the preparation of points to investigate until the afternoon before, but you should gather the papers and documents that you will need in advance, so that you are ready to study them when you begin your preparation. This may be especially important for customer auditors who wish to audit in some detail but will have to specifically request every piece of information that they wish to see, so will need to clear it and obtain access to it well in advance of wanting to read it.

DATA GATHERING

Before you can refer to information on the area that you are to audit, you will need to gain access to it. The first phase of audit preparation, therefore, is data gathering. The way in which this is done varies depending upon the type of audit being conducted, particularly on whom the auditors are working for.

THIRD PARTY AUDITS

Certification assessors have little need for directly associated data since they are principally auditing against ISO 9001. They do, however, require a basic understanding of what the organization does and how it works. Before the initial audit, then, they should attempt to obtain brochures and organization charts, together with product and/or service descriptions and specifications where possible.

Ideally these should be sought before the initial visit which is used by certification companies as part of the preparation and planning cycle. This simple set of data should be enough to understand what they do and how the people are organized, and avoid any embarrassment during the visit created by a failure to understand what the organization itself is all about.

Sometimes this is not possible (e.g. some types of organization do not produce brochures and have no published organization charts). In this case the equivalent information, perhaps obtained through questioning rather than reading, will simply have to be obtained at the initial visit – at least it is then available for the initial audit itself.

Certification auditors used to collect information about detailed operations by asking organizations to send quality system manuals and then conducted the documentation review off-site. These days this is rarely done. It was found impractical to ask organizations to send copies of the complex series of documents that make up a quality management system, and the old practice of sending only the top level quality manual gave little information since most quality manuals look so similar. The document review is now, most often, carried out together with the initial visit, so that a specific understanding can be obtained at this time. The main objective of the document review, however, is to confirm that the documents adequately address the requirements of the standard.

Preliminary data gathering, then, for third party auditors is principally to gain basic information on what the company is and what it does. This would also apply to assessors conducting routine surveillance audits who have been newly appointed to audit this particular organization.

In common with all other auditors, the other piece of data that an assessor should collect before the start of an audit is the report of previous assessments.

SECOND PARTY AUDITS

Customer auditors have less need to find out generally what goes on at their suppliers since, presumably, they already know. Or at least they know about those things in which they are interested, which amounts to the same thing.

In terms of data gathering, customer auditors will find some parts of the job easier and some more difficult than will third party assessors. Certification assessors are usually trusted to be independent. Most companies are, therefore, willing to let them investigate and have access to anything they wish. When the audit team comes from a customer, though, there may be things that the company does not wish them to see, such as pricing data or information relating to other clients. On the other hand, audit teams from the customer will have a direct understanding of, and interest in, the contractual relationship and thus will be able to appreciate its requirements and niceties just by looking at it from their own point of view. Since much of quality management, and modern business thinking in general, is about understanding the customer's viewpoint then second party auditors should start from a strong position.

Before the start of the audit, the audit team should certainly gather information about what is expected from the supplier by their own organization. Thoughts on what is not liked or appreciated in terms of past performance should also be garnered, where appropriate, and comparative performance against other similar suppliers, if available. It would also be a good idea to have some contact with the supplier itself to gain an understanding of what it is looking for in the relationship. For example it could be that the low volumes or infrequency of orders, whilst important to you when they happen, may be a distraction to the supplier who draws significantly greater profit from other contracts, or it may find your administrative requirements difficult to cope with and so on.

INTERNAL AUDITS

A lot depends here upon the objectives of the audit. If the purpose is compliance verification, as might happen with an organization newly adopting a formal quality management system and not using it for business improvement, the information needed in advance will simply be the description of operational requirements (such as system procedure documents) that apply. If, however, the objective is to help the business move forward, then there is a wider, or perhaps completely different, set of information that is needed.

One of the key features of ISO 9001:2000 is the requirement to create a cascading set of policies and objectives, then to establish quantifiable targets and measure performance against those targets. Collecting information on this should, then, be one of the primary data gathering tasks for an internal auditor. It should also be remembered that true objectives do not only come from quality documents created to satisfy an ISO 9001 assessor; they will also be defined in business plans, change programme project definitions, cost reduction initiatives and so on.

Since the standard also relies heavily on the concept of process management, with a requirement to identify key processes together with their inputs and outputs, it should also be possible to identify who the customers of the audit area are and to gather data from them (or from appropriate documented information) in terms of their requirements, performance targets, complaints and irritations, and general expectations.

The set of data that might be collected by internal auditors includes:

O   general business and quality objectives
O   area-specific business and quality objectives
O   reports of general and specific performance measurements
O   definitions of customer requirements and expectations

O   customer complaints and satisfaction measurement results
O   improvement action plans
O   improvement project progress reports
O   service-level agreements (if used)
O   previous audit reports, including resultant actions
O   quality cost data
O   key process definitions
O   process maps
O   system procedures.

Some of this information may not be available directly and will need to be sought out. Some of it will be only indirectly available at all; this might require general information to be collected to enable further analysis later, or at least to find the right questions to ask. An example of this could be quality costs: unless the area prepares formal quality cost reports, analysis of prevention and failure costs may only be possible through a collection of financial reports, production figures, inspection reports and so on. In such cases it may not be practical to collect everything necessary for the audit team to calculate the costs themselves, although the simple absence of the right data could lead to some useful areas to investigate.

If some of the information related to external customers is not directly available, the audit team should not ring them up and start asking questions. Even where the most candid relationships with customers exist, that relationship still needs to be handled carefully to ensure its continuity. After all, an audit has definitely not achieved its purpose if you lose a customer through a badly chosen remark, or simply irritation at the number of times they are being telephoned by internal auditors. If the information is not there in published form, the audit team can consult with the quality manager, marketing manager or whoever is responsible for managing the customer relationship and ask how the information can be acquired. Sometimes it will be necessary to conduct the audit with little of such data if it is not already available; this in itself will give rise to concern since it should have been collected and analysed by the management of the area itself.

As I have mentioned earlier, this type of comprehensive data gathering can be very time-consuming, particularly since it can rarely be achieved by simply wandering into the area and asking to borrow the appropriate file. Apart from beginning the collection activity early enough for everything to be available before the audit, it may be a good idea to find someone who will carry out the initial data collection on behalf of the audit team. This could be the quality coordinator or somebody else directly involved with the administration of the audit system whose role does not normally include such activities, leaving the auditors only needing to free themselves from their 'real' jobs in order to conduct the audit itself.

MAKING USE OF THE BACKGROUND DATA

Once the background data has been collected, it is time to use it to prepare. This is the preparation that I described earlier as being best done very shortly before the start of the investigation itself. The data gathering may be done some time in advance but the actual preparation needs to be conducted just before the audit to avoid everything being forgotten.

In principle, the preparation involves simply reading all of the data that has been collected and absorbing it. This enables the audit team to understand what should be and/or has been happening in the area or organization that they are going to study. This will in turn let them ask sensible questions, understand the answers that they are given and not waste their time in basic understanding or pursuing irrelevant topics.

The theory of this is quite sound but it does have some practical difficulties. I remember being asked to read a bulging lever arch file full of documentation in preparation for an in-house environmental audit course that I was about to present. The idea was that I would teach in line with company policy and would be able to answer any questions in the context of their own procedures, polices and objectives. The problem was that there was a huge amount of information there, much of which was unlikely to be relevant to the scope of the course and I found myself losing interest after a few minutes each time that I tried to read through it. I also forgot most of it by the time that I came to the course itself.

Higher education students are familiar with some of these problems. The accepted way to overcome the difficulty of concentrating upon the printed word and absorbing the key points is to make notes as you read. Team members preparing for an audit should do the same. It is not enough simply to read large quantities of data and hope to remember it; you need to reinforce your study by writing down principal elements as you go. I like to think of this as 'active' preparation, in that you do not just sit there and let the words and numbers flow through you but do something constructive as you read.

When you prepare, though, do not write everything down that you read; this would be a pointless exercise and would result in notes that are simply a lengthy précis of the original data itself. The best approach is to look through the documents and seek things that either seem to require verification (a typical compliance issue might be the need for senior personnel to approve purchase orders above a certain value) or where you need to ask further questions (some highly bureaucratic purchase order approval systems might require up to six signatures – you could decide to ask why, and ask how long it takes to have an order authorized).

The points that you wish to check for should be chosen carefully. Usually you will only have a limited amount of time and therefore will not be able to look for every little detail. Thus pick those things which you feel represent the highest risk of failure, or are likely to represent inefficiency or deviation from company plans.

The fact that each auditor will have a slightly different view of what is important and what is not does not represent a problem. In fact it helps the audit programme stay fresh and lively, as the same auditor is not always sent to the same area time after time.

What you decide to omit from your notes is as important. First, do not decide to ask about things which you know will be well understood. I spent a few meetings with a major electronics manufacturer with a view to performing some manufacturing training; the training never happened but I learned a lot from the early discussions. One of the key values in the organization was the respect for the individual. This topic was so strongly emphasized that it was continually talked about and used as one of the benchmarks for proposed actions. As an auditor, it would have been pointless to investigate whether employees knew that this was a stated value and what it meant, because it clearly was a fundamental driver of the business.

Similarly there is no point in attempting to check what is obvious or unverifiable. For example, there might be a local instruction which calls for the first person to enter the office area to turn the lights on. Unless you are sitting there in the dark it is obvious that somebody must have switched on the lights so the question would be a bit academic. And anyway it cannot really be verified. If you were to find out who first came into the office and ask them if they turned the lights on as soon as they came in, they would undoubtedly answer in the affirmative since they know they are being audited. You would not really know whether they did or not and could not verify it from any documentary evidence. Verifying the occurrence of telephone calls represents a similar situation (I suppose you could look at PBX records and see whether a call was made from one number to another at a certain time, but it still does not tell you what was said). If it is obvious, automatic or not possible to confirm directly, then it is best to leave it and make notes about something more worthy of investigation.

AN AUDIT SCRIPT

What you are not trying to create with your notes is an audit script. It is not sensible to use them to read the first question from the page, listen to the answer, then read the second question. Auditing does not work like that (or if it does it is being done badly). For a start you never know exactly how people will answer questions, so the second point in your notes may not arise logically from the answer to the first. Also you are excluding yourselves from following up on interesting things that interviewees say if you try to stick to a script.

The actual questions that you ask will arise from your innate investigation skills and not from a piece of paper. Your notes are reminders of the topics that you wish to cover, rather than actual questions. Many of the questions are likely to be based upon those topics but will not be read directly from the page.

USING THE NOTES

The way that auditors actually use notes is as reminders – they are often spoken of as an *aide-mémoire*. First, you ask questions designed to gain information and follow these up with further questions, intended to clarify or expand upon what you have already heard. Then when you reach the end of a particular questioning cycle and have asked all of the questions that occur to you, you can then examine your notes. It will usually then be apparent that you have actually covered a few of your intended points, but that there are some that have not been addressed, or there is a completely new topic to be discussed. You can then ask for a detailed explanation of the missed item or begin with searching questions on the new topic.

By ticking off the items in your notes as you go (perhaps marking off several together when you reach a natural pause), you can keep track of everything and ensure that nothing important is forgotten.

TEAM PREPARATION

Preparation time is even more important if a team of auditors are involved. In addition to gaining an understanding of what is to be examined, the team will have to decide how they will work together during the audit.

It is normally expected that a team of auditors will separate during the investigation phase, coming together again only to compare notes and to decide what will be reported. Most organizations consider pairs of auditors walking around virtually holding hands an expensive use of resources and also intimidating for the auditees. It can, though, be a valid technique if one or more of the auditors is new to the practice and lacks confidence, or if the dual viewpoint of subject matter expert and complete outsider is sought. Thus part of preparation will involve deciding exactly who will look at what and whether the audit team will be together or apart for each stage of the investigation.

Where the audit team are given adequate time to fully prepare, then each auditor should make their own notes about what they wish to look for, within the remit and coverage that they agree to or are assigned by the team leader. Where this is not possible, such as in certification assessments, the team leader will at least need to devote some time, perhaps prior to the opening meeting, explaining to the team what they are expected to cover and how those areas contribute to the overall picture.

A key part of this team preparation will be decisions as to when the team will meet again (quotations from the opening scene of *Macbeth* are popular at this stage) to check progress and to inform each other of what is happening. This is important to include in any audit programme; if one auditor finds a real show-stopper then it is not really appropriate for the rest of the team to wait until the end to find out about it. Meal and refreshment breaks can be a good time to get back together, and times for these should be pre-arranged by the team.

Team members will also need to be certain of what exactly they are expected to cover. It is always a danger in team audits that an area or topic will not be fully covered unless the team carefully prepare and ensure that their plans cover investigation of all necessary aspects.

In third party certification audits, team members are rarely given the opportunity to prepare fully. What little preparation is carried out is done by the team leader. In every case where preparation is possible, though, each auditor should prepare their own notes and read the documentation relating directly to what they will audit. If they leave it all to the team leader there is a strong chance that they will not fully understand what is going on or what the prepared investigation topics really mean. They will then be almost as badly off as an auditor who has not prepared at all.

PROBLEM IDENTIFICATION

One phrase often used in the context of study of documentation prior to live investigation is 'system audit'. A system audit is a detailed look at all documentation relating to an audit organization or area (and remember that this may not just be traditional quality system documentation but also business plans, objectives and so on) with the objective of finding out whether or not that documentation is adequate. This is certainly the objective of the document review carried out by certification assessors prior to an initial audit. It is also taught on some registered lead auditor courses as a key part of any external audit.

In this book I have not tried to emphasize the system audit too much, concentrating more on the preparation aspects of any review of documentation. This is mostly because, apart from the essential review by certification assessors to see that an organization seeking registration has addressed all ISO 9001 requirements, document audits of this type are largely academic; the organization knows what it has to document and, if it has reached the stage of submitting itself to an audit of any type, is unlikely these days to have made major omissions in its documentation.

Certainly auditors looking at organizations where no similar audits have been carried out before will need to look at the suitability of documentation and point out any apparent flaws. Otherwise, though, the time is better spent in preparing for interviews rather than time-consuming comparison of documents with defined requirements. This said, there may be some occasions when problems are identified, even though this was not the intention. Although documents are being studied for the purpose of identifying what is to be asked later, things may arise which appear to be direct contraventions of policy, contract requirements or standards. If this happens, auditors should not immediately reach for their pens and write out a corrective action notice. Even if it is fairly certain that there is a problem with documentation, it is better to make a note to ask about it than to pre-judge the issue before even speaking to anybody.

There are a number of reasons for this approach:

O   It avoids giving the impression that the auditors have made up their minds in advance about what they will find.

O   It gives the people concerned the opportunity to explain a legitimate justification for the apparent discrepancy.

O   There could be other documentation, available to the people in the workplace, but for one reason or another not supplied in advance to the audit team, which covers the situation.

O   If it does prove to represent a problem, it allows the auditees to better understand why it needs attention since they were involved in debating its circumstances, rather than just being presented with a 'parking ticket'.

USE OF CHECKLISTS

Some readers, reaching this point, will wonder why I have constantly referred to notes. 'He's talking about checklists', they might say, 'so why doesn't he just say so?'

In fact I did consider avoiding referring to checklists altogether, in the hope that new auditors would not become burdened with the concept. I realized, though, that some readers may already have had some auditing experience and all would probably be involved in some form of training which would mention the topic. The reason that I tried to evade the word was that it is one of those turn-off phrases that seems to antagonize people. I was at a seminar held by a large certification body, for example, where the speaker told us, with a look of disgust, that he hoped that the use of checklists would wane as auditors became more competent. For some reason many auditors hate the idea of checklists, although they may accept, without apparent contradiction, that good preparation is vital.

The difference between preparation of the notes that I have described and audit checklists is often in their formality. Checklists are usually considered to be something created on a standard form which becomes part of official audit records, whereas pre-audit notes are simply informal jottings by the auditor which are thrown away after the final report has been created. Many auditors hate the formal variety but are quite happy with the informal approach.

There is something to be said for using official checklists. Using a standard format, such as that shown in Figure 8.1, can:

O   provide a thorough audit record which might result in a reduced amount of required reporting at the end of the audit;

O   provide a more rigorous framework for preparation;

O   enforce more discipline on auditors who might otherwise be tempted to skimp on preparation.

AUDIT:	DATE:		TEAM LEADER:		AUDITORS:	
AUDIT SCOPE:						
DOC. REF.	QUESTION	SAMPLES SEEN		OK?	COMMENTS/CAR REF	

FIGURE 8.1   Checklist form

This type of standard form can also be used to provide a record of what happened during the audit. The centre column can record what was actually looked at (batch identifications, file sequences, contract names, instrument numbers, etc.) with the fourth column to say whether or not everything was satisfactory and the fifth to record comments or cross-references to corrective action requests. In fact, although I have included the middle record column on the form for the sake of completeness, I do not necessarily recommend its use. When I am auditing I find the need to record everything that I studied an extra chore that I could do without, and I have doubts about what purpose, if any, that information might be put to afterwards. Many people that I speak to, however, like the practice and want to do it; if so, a formal checklist format is the ideal place to do so.

On balance, I rather like the use of checklist forms on which to write down what I wish to examine during an audit, rather than simply using a notepad which is likely to become untidy and difficult to follow. Individual auditors will probably have to follow corporate policy on the subject. Those running audit programmes can choose how they would like to manage it, depending upon the needs and preferences of their organization and its auditors.

STANDARD CHECKLISTS

One reason that checklists could be disliked is the common use of standard versions. These are lists of questions, or topics to cover, which are prepared once and then reused every time that an audit of that type is carried out. They are most often used for internal audits where they can be written around a particular department or process, so that each auditor simply needs to take a checklist and follow it to ensure that all important items are covered.

There is nothing to stop you using standard checklists if you like them. Many audit programme coordinators feel that it ensures that full coverage is obtained and helps the auditors by giving them direction and reducing the amount of preparation time needed. Whilst I do accept these arguments, the benefits are not as strong as the drawbacks and, although the reduction of preparation time is a strong factor in many cases, I do feel that that they have greater disadvantages:

❍   Auditors are tempted not to prepare at all, relying solely on the checklists which results in them having only a thin understanding of what the area is all about and how it works.

❍   They are also tempted to rely on the checklist and not on their investigation skills, resulting in shallow audits which never vary.

❍   Standard checklists can rarely take account of frequently changing aspects such as improvement plans, quality objectives, targets and measurements and current customer requirements.

Second or third party auditors relying on standard checklists find these problems exacerbated. Checklists are unlikely to be directly relevant to the individual organization being audited and are much harder to keep up to date with changes. Audits based on them will be very shallow, taking little account of the specific circumstances of what is being audited. Most second and third party auditors only use standard checklists (often based on ISO 9001 requirements) for initial training and development of auditors. This is just the way it should be and no assessor should ever be auditing against a 'vanilla' checklist.

A PROCESS-BASED APPROACH

An interesting alternative to the creation of a simple textual list of points to cover when auditing is to create a process diagram similar to the model shown in Figure 8.2. Auditors use this single sheet to write a description of the process and its key steps. They then fill in the other boxes, noting major inputs and outputs, and the supporting elements common to all processes. These supporting elements are sometimes known as '5 Ms and an E'. They stand for:

- O   Machinery (equipment and facilities)
- O   Materials
- O   Manpower (personnel)
- O   Methods (standard operating practices, techniques and technologies)
- O   Measurement (process and performance monitoring and feedback)
- O   Environment (the external conditions affecting the process).

The auditor can then select each item written on the map and ask about it, how it is controlled, its results, records, associated responsibilities, risks, problems, examples and so on.

I have only ever seen this approach employed once as a formal part of the audit process, although I have found several individual auditors who have liked it and added it to their toolkit. Interestingly, I saw the organization that used this approach when the 1994 version of ISO 9001 was still relatively new and the auditors had to reinterpret procedure documentation into the process map. Now that ISO 9001:2000 is with us, key processes will have been identified, together with their inputs and outputs. One idea is to define these in such a way that it is easy for auditors to take the standard description and add the 5 Ms and E to it, together with any supplementary information that they garner from plans, objectives, measurements, etc. As long as this does not go so far as to represent the equivalent of the standard checklist, it could be an excellent middle point between the time-consuming preparation on a blank page and the limiting and ossifying list of standard questions.

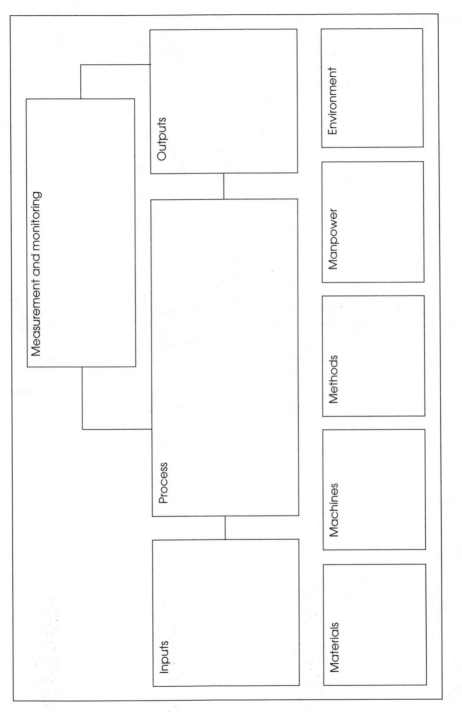

FIGURE 8.2 Process preparation sheet

SUMMARY

○   Preparation for any activity increases the chances of success; auditing is no exception.

○   Everybody needs to prepare as much as possible, even experienced auditors, but the restrictions on some programmes such as third party assessments make the desired amount of preparation difficult.

○   A lot of data will need to be gathered, beyond the simple binder containing the quality system manual and procedures.

○   Data gathering may well need to begin some time in advance of the audit, although studying the data should be done as close to the start of the investigation as possible.

○   Active preparation should be used, taking notes as the data is studied, in order to make best use of the information and to ensure good audit coverage.

○   Audit notes are not a script and should not limit the audit.

○   Teams of more than one auditor need to allocate responsibilities for the various elements, each one to prepare accordingly.

○   The purpose of preparation is not usually to find problems, although some potential problems may be uncovered at this stage, which need to be confirmed by questioning during the investigation stage.

○   Notes of points to cover can be informal or use a standard sheet.

○   Pre-prepared checklists are sometimes used but have disadvantages.

○   The use of a process diagram or similar map can be an interesting alternative mode of preparation to the creation of textual checklists.

9

CONDUCTING THE AUDIT

❖

CONDUCTING THE EXAMINATION

The steps in conducting the examination phase are given below:

1. Auditors arrive.
2. Introduction.
3. Audit team separates.
4. Auditors find individual auditees.
5. Interviewing and investigation.
6. Repeat steps 4 and 5, as necessary.
7. Auditors retreat to consider findings and audit team re-convenes.
8. Auditors agree and document findings.
9. Auditors feed back findings.
10. Audit report completed.
11. Auditors depart.
12. Auditees take appropriate corrective and preventive action.
13. Auditing organization tracks action.
14. Auditing organization confirms acceptability of completed actions.

There are slight variations and expansions on this theme, depending upon the type of audit and its purpose. The basic sequence, though, applies for all. Steps 1 to 11 are discussed in more detail in the remainder of this chapter. Steps 12 to 14 are discussed later in the book.

ARRIVAL

Auditors always go to the place of work; nobody ever comes for an audit at the auditor's own desk. Thus the responsibility for turning up at the audit venue rests with the auditors. It is most important for the team to be ready at the agreed start time. If the auditors arrive late:

O   it ruins their schedule;
O   it gives them less auditing time;
O   it sends the message that good time-keeping is not important;
O   it sets them off on the wrong foot and may even put them at a disadvantage.

If there is a team of more than one, it may be necessary to pull the team together before arrival at the auditee organization. This enables the team leader to ensure that everyone is there and to present a united approach (in the same way that football teams run out onto the pitch together, rather than in dribs and drabs).

When auditing at a remote location (i.e. anywhere other than the auditor's normal place of work) suitable travel arrangements will have to be made. Allow some leeway to cope with delays. If it is a long way to travel, then staying overnight locally can be a good idea; it also helps to ensure that the team arrive 'fresh'. In fact, it is advisable to arrive at the other location at least fifteen minutes before the scheduled start of the opening meeting. This allows for delays with security, reception, necessary toilet visits, and making your way to the meeting room, as well as dealing with the initial hellos and pleasantries.

If the audit is multi-site, with travel between locations during the audit, someone needs to make the travel arrangements. If the client or auditee are helping with those arrangements, then the lead auditor should still double-check that they are in place, complete and adequate.

OPENING MEETING

The nature, style, content and formality of opening meetings vary greatly between the types of audit. There is a similar approach for second and third party audits, with small differences, but they are almost inapplicable for internal audits. We will discuss first the opening meeting structure for a second or third party audit, then look at the differences when auditing internally.

THE PURPOSE OF THE OPENING MEETING

The first thing that needs to be pointed out is that opening meetings are not intended for auditors to see how stuffily they can act. This is a business meeting. As such it should be handled professionally but not rigidly. If the nature and type of issues to discuss at an audit opening meeting are pre-defined in the organization, make sure that they are not read out as a script. Auditors should be able to explain their objectives and procedures, not read them from a book.

The purposes of an opening meeting are:

O   to perform preliminary introductions;
O   to ensure a common understanding of what the audit is about;
O   to explain the methods and procedures to be employed by the auditors;
O   to confirm the timetable for the audit (including the time of feedback/ closing meetings);
O   to resolve any access/security/availability problems;
O   to deal with any questions or concerns from either side;
O   generally to 'set the scene'.

'Setting the scene' should emphasize the positive nature of audits (since the way that audit results are reported concentrates strongly on negatives). They are not intended to find fault (auditors should *not* feel elated when they discover a problem). In particular, it should be emphasized that the audit is not an attempt to blame any individual or group. Faults are always 'against' the system, not 'against' any person. No criticism is implied; reported deficiencies are simply an indication of where enhancements can be made. Some would argue that this lack of blame should be emphasized at the start of every audit (as long as we do not become too rigid about it) but it certainly should be done if the people involved are not familiar with the process of auditing (or with the particular process applicable to this one).

So, a typical agenda for a first opening meeting would be:

O   say hello;
O   introduce the audit team leader;
O   introduce the rest of the audit team;
O   introduce the auditee representatives;
O   remind everyone of the scope of the audit (i.e. what it will cover);
O   explain what the audit will be conducted against (e.g. ISO 9001, regulatory standards, contract requirements, industry codes of practice, etc.);
O   explain what the audit results will mean (e.g. certification, granting of approved supplier status or not);
O   tell them what the reporting process will be, including feedback/closing meetings and written reports;
O   review the timetable and check that it is sensible; make adjustments as necessary (agreeing or confirming the time of the final closing meeting is vital);
O   ask for audit team support – this could include such things as office/desk space, photocopying and printing facilities, food and refreshment;
O   explain the role of the guides;

○   emphasize the blame-free nature of auditing;
○   find out what health and safety and security precautions will have to be taken by the team;
○   discover if there are any confidentiality or secrecy issues to be addressed;
○   identify anything which might be a barrier to the audit, such as absent employees, emergencies, building works, recent organizational changes, employee/trade union disputes, accidents, etc.;
○   explain that anything you see or hear will be entirely confidential;
○   answer any final concerns from either side.

This is a fairly comprehensive list, but there may well be other things that auditors wish to discuss. Do not feel inhibited from discussing them just because they are not mentioned here. On the other hand, do not feel that you must say something about every point on this list. If there are some items which are inappropriate, then just leave them out. This is particularly relevant for audits which are repeats of those conducted several times before. Thus the list of topics could be severely trimmed, for example, at routine certification surveillance audits in a company which has held its certificate for many years. (Of course, if the certification body rules insist upon a full opening meeting every time, then the auditor has to do it, but could also offer a suggestion that the rules could be changed to make them more practical.)

WHO SHOULD ATTEND AN OPENING MEETING?

Attendees at an opening meeting should include the following:

1.   All of the audit team. Do not let the team leader do it alone. Auditors who are not present might miss something important. Also, their absence may send signals to the auditees that they do not care.
2.   The person responsible for the quality system in the organization being audited.
3.   For important audits, the chief executive or chief operating officer (managing director, general manager, etc.). Important audits include the initial ISO 9001 certification audit, or an initial supplier approval by a major potential customer. The chief executive should be aware that, if they do not attend, the auditor will realize that they do not see it as important. For internal audits, the equivalent here is the most senior person responsible for operations in the area audited.
4.   The audit guide(s).
5.   Anyone else that the auditee management would like to be there, as long as it does not become a crowd.

When the audits are routine, not only might the meeting be made shorter and less formal but it may also have a 'thinner' attendance than at other audits. Often at such meetings the quality management representative may be the only person there on behalf of the auditee.

OPENING MEETING RECORDS

There is no need to generate minutes of an audit opening meeting; it is not that type of event. In the typical ISO 9001 spirit of recording everything, it is possible that sometimes there may need to be a simple record that the opening meeting took place. Certification companies may, for example, wish to do this. In this case, the simple ticking of a box on a checklist should suffice. If really considered necessary, perhaps the names of the people attending could also be recorded (although it has to be asked to what purpose this information could possibly be put).

DIFFERENCES BETWEEN SECOND AND THIRD PARTY OPENING MEETINGS

In broad principle, second party audits (customer/supplier audits) and third party audits (usually certification or accreditation) have similar opening meetings. The same sorts of issues need to be discussed. The main difference, probably, is in flexibility. Certification companies need to try to keep a degree of consistency between audits, to avoid any danger of one certified company being treated substantially differently to another. Thus their opening meetings tend to be rather formulaic and fixed. When a customer team is auditing a current or potential supplier/sub-contractor, however, this is not the case. The way in which they view that supplier will depend upon the product or service that they offer, how central that is to their own business, the history of the relationship, their own internal quality control disciplines (e.g. if we do no goods inwards inspection on these items then what the supplier does is critical) and so on. Therefore, second party opening meetings may vary more depending upon the specific aims of the audit leader and the audit team. Third party audit opening meetings will probably follow a more predictable structure which will vary only minutely from one event to another.

INTERNAL AUDIT OPENING MEETINGS

Where teams are carrying out an internal audit, both auditors and auditees are members of the same organization. This means that they probably already know each other. It is also likely that the purpose and style of the audit is familiar to both sides. For these reasons, the opening meeting conducted at other audits is largely inappropriate.

In extremes, the internal audit opening meeting may not exist at all; the auditor(s) will simply arrive and get on with it. Typically, though, some form of quick 'hello' to the head of the area involved will happen. A script for such an opening meeting may look something like this:

Auditor:	[*poking their head around the department manager's office door*] 'Hello. I'm here for the audit.'
Manager:	'Ah, yes, come to give us a hard time again. Come in. Sit down.'
Auditor:	'Actually I won't, if you don't mind. I've probably got no questions for you personally today, unless there's anything I need to clarify near the end. I'll just get straight on and talk to your staff, if that's okay.'
Manager:	'Fine. You'll find that John's off sick and Mandy's not in until after lunch, but otherwise take your pick.'
Auditor:	'Right. Still okay for a feedback session at four o'clock?'
Manager:	'Yep.'
Auditor:	'Good. See you then.'

There are, of course, occasions when a slightly more formal meeting may be desirable to start off an internal audit, for example:

O   In a very large organization where the various participants do not know each other, perhaps when the auditors and auditees are from different sites or divisions.

O   Where auditing is a new experience for the auditees, where the audit team leader will need to explain what it is all about, what will happen and what the findings mean. The team leader should pay special attention to reassuring them that no blame will be attached to any negative findings.

O   If the audit has been arranged for a special purpose, in which case some time will have to be spent discussing the specifics of the audit.

O   If there is any other reason why extra discussion or explanation is needed, for example if the audit methodology has changed, or if there are new standards or requirements to be met.

CONCLUDING THE OPENING MEETING

Once the opening meeting is over, it is vital that the auditors clearly mark the distinction between the end of the meeting and the start of investigation. It is tempting, especially in smaller organizations or areas, simply to start asking questions, straight away, to the people in the room. The problems with this are:

O   it can confuse the auditors;

O   it will waste the time of the people in the room who are not involved in the questions;

O   it may mean reduced access to information; data is far more accessible at the place of work than in a conference room;

O   the auditors will concentrate on managers rather than on coal-face workers (in some small organizations, the manager may be the only one that can be audited, but in most cases it is far better to go out and speak to the people who do the 'real' work – the manager is only then audited at the end, if there are questions that only he or she can answer).

In general, it is much tidier to 'paragraph' the audit by making it clear that you have finished one step, before moving on to another. Even in small, informal situations where the auditor does, in fact, have to interview the same manager with whom the opening meeting was held, it still needs to be pointed out when the audit investigation has begun.

WHO SHOULD DO THE TALKING?

Since the main purpose of an opening meeting is to set the scene, then the only person from the audit team who usually needs to plan to say anything is the team leader. Of course, the auditee representatives will say and ask what they wish.

This does not mean that other audit team members are not allowed to speak. If they think that the team leader has forgotten an important point, or they have a specific question that occurs to them, they certainly may join in. Similarly, if one member of a team is a specialist (such as an external TickIT auditor), he or she may wish to clarify items relating to that specialization. For example, a second party audit team may well comprise a technical specialist, a quality management expert and a commercial auditor. Each of these will have different objectives which they may wish to check for themselves.

Remember that auditing is just another facet of business management. This means that audit meetings are simply business meetings. The rules that apply to other business meetings will also apply here; it is not a role play.

PITFALLS

Opening meetings are simple enough for major difficulties to be encountered only rarely. There are, however, one or two things to watch out for, which it is worth exploring here.

Time-wasting

Do not spend too long on the opening meeting; the investigation needs to be completed in the time allowed and delays are not welcomed. By all means begin the meeting with one or two pleasantries, but do not then spend half an hour on the state of the economy, sharing personal problems, discussing favourite sports teams or listening to the managing director explain company plans for the future. Particularly watch out for the prepared video or slide presentation on the company; auditors may wish to have a very brief introduction (although this really should have been sorted out beforehand) but no more than two or three minutes.

If something grander is offered, suggest that it happens over lunch time, while everybody is enjoying their sandwiches.

Nervousness

If the people at the opening meeting are nervous then it is the audit team's job to put them at their ease. Auditors are not ogres and the process will run a lot more smoothly if everyone is relaxed. There is no need to be stiff and withdrawn, like the cold style of many British driving examiners.

Misconceptions

It is the audit team's responsibility to communicate the message correctly, not the auditee's responsibility to hear it (Harry Alder, *NLP for Managers*, Judy Piatkus, 1996).

OPENING MEETING CHECKLIST

- ○   Arrive on time and start on time.
- ○   Describe the audit purpose, scope and process.
- ○   Revisit audit timetable.
- ○   Explain possible outcomes.
- ○   Allow questions in both directions.
- ○   Resolve any access issues (security, safety, travel, etc.).
- ○   Keep it brief, to the point, and not too stuffy or artificial.

COMMENCING THE INVESTIGATION

When the opening meeting is finished, it is time to begin the investigation. In most audits, the interviews begin immediately. It is not good practice to have a long break (perhaps to go and do some other work) between the two. Normally then the investigation will commence away from the meeting room, out in the work-place. The temptation to sit in the conference room and have files and people brought to you must be avoided. It will only succeed in passing control from you to the auditee. It will also result in only limited investigation. The only place that a real audit can be carried out is at the place of work.

If the audit team consists of more than one person they should split up at this point to audit different parts of the organization separately. There is absolutely no point in having a large audit team simply so that they can walk around mob-handed and watch each other. The team leader should have built the need for the auditors to split up into the plan. This means that where guides are used, each auditor will require their own guide.

The only exceptions to the separation rule are as follows:

○   Where one of the auditors is considered to be under training or acting as an observer.

○   For some elements of the audit where it is desirable for the whole audit team to be present for information and education, for example a brief discussion at the beginning with the chief executive about the approach to quality and customer care, where the organization is headed and how the personnel structure works.

○   Where in-depth examination is sought and it is felt that two investigators might spot something that one would not (e.g. in advanced internal programmes).

BEGINNING THE INVESTIGATION

The auditor, led by the guide if present, arrives at the area where the investigation is to be carried out. The first thing that auditors must do is understand exactly where it is they are and what they can reasonably look at here. It is embarrassing and time-wasting to start asking questions which would be more appropriate in another area and it reduces the auditor's credibility. This should be sorted out with the guide or the area management before arriving.

On arrival, accepted practice is first to introduce yourself to the most senior person in the area (or, perhaps, the person representing the area for the purposes of the audit). This is a courtesy and also lets those responsible for smooth running of the area know what is going on. You must not, though, now go and have another opening meeting with this person. Stay in the workplace and ask to speak to a worker, not a manager or supervisor. If the manager suggests that he or she could answer the whole range of questions better than the workers, thank them politely and say that you will come back to them at the end if you have any questions. For the same reasons that the opening meeting must end and the auditors disperse, the audit must not be conducted from the warmth of a supervisor's office. Similarly, unless it adds real value, the presentation of the department's role or the grand tour should be avoided.

The next step, then, is for the auditor to pick somebody to interview. Notice the way that this is described: the auditor should pick, not the manager. It is typical for managers to say something like 'Oh, speak to Hussein, he'll be the best one for you.' There may be several reasons why Hussein has been chosen. Cynics might say that he will have been trained in the best answers to keep the auditor away from any danger areas. This may be true, but there are more likely to be innocent reasons. These could be that the manager thinks that Hussein will give the best impression and he or she likes the department to have a good image (which is only human); the manager might believe that Hussein is on top of his work and will be able to spend an hour or so with you; it could be that Hussein is quite confident and any other employee in that area would be too nervous; there could be a number of other reasons. The danger with accepting this is that the reasons will not change between one audit and the next, so Hussein may always be the one interviewed, resulting in a poor audit sample. To avoid this, auditors should choose whom they wish to meet.

Selecting somebody can be difficult, especially for external auditors. Internal auditors will not have too hard a job since they probably know the people in the room or area and can pick someone by name. Second and third party auditors cannot usually do this. There are a number of ways to to solve the problem:

○   Pick someone based on information previously acquired, for example 'I'd like to speak to the commercial agent responsible for the QRS contract.'
○   Ask specifically to speak to somebody who was not audited last time.
○   Have a look around and see who stands out, then just ask to speak to 'that person over there'.
○   Ask the supervisor to explain the detailed division of responsibilities, then pick the person who most fully covers the points on your checklist.

Of course, there are often practicalities to be considered. Sometimes, for example, there is nobody other than the manager (in small companies there is often only one person involved in a particular function and they are usually given a managerial title). Or, the only person other than the supervisor may be a secretary who carries out clerical tasks as instructed but has no functional responsibility (the auditor may still wish to interview the secretary briefly to make sure that is really the limit of the role). One must recognize, as well, that it may not be practical to interview the person selected. To take an extreme example, when auditing a bomb disposal operation it would not be sensible to pick the person lying underneath an explosive device armed only with a pair of wire clippers; they will not be able to stop what they are doing to speak to you. In the same way, the supervisor may ask you to leave an employee alone because he or she has an urgent report for a customer to finish today, only joined the organization yesterday and does not even know where the canteen is yet, or is manning the telephones alone, etc. As long as the auditor believes that they are not being misled to divert attention away from a poorly trained or indiscreet employee, then these are valid reasons to choose someone else (making a note, of course, to seek out that person next time).

Auditors usually prefer that the manager or supervisor of the area does not lean over their shoulder during an audit, that interviewees are given the space to answer questions themselves without having their boss as well as the auditor breathing down their necks. In many cases the guide is present anyway and having the supervisor standing there makes the whole exercise a little cumbersome. If managers express a desire to do so, though, and insist that they would find it extremely valuable and would prefer to tag along, then it is very hard to refuse outright. Just make sure that they know to whom each question is being posed, telling them politely but firmly to shut up if they keep trying to answer the questions on somebody else's behalf.

Once the person is selected, the auditor approaches them, permitting introductions by the guide and/or manager as appropriate, or introduces him or herself, and ensures that the interviewee understands the purpose of the interview. The manager should have done this beforehand, but it is always worth checking. In some cases it may be necessary to give a very brief explanation of what is going on, emphasizing the blame-free nature of the exercise.

THE INTERVIEW

At last, the real auditing can begin. The auditor asks the person selected to explain his or her work and conducts a general discussion of what happens, and how it is controlled.

Note that the initial discussion is general. The auditor should never begin the audit by looking at a checklist and asking something directly from the page: 'Right, I want to check that every purchase order contains a *full* set of data as described in procedure number 32, paragraph 6.2.3.'

First, this is likely to feel threatening to a nervous auditee. Second, and probably more importantly, little information will be gained. All that will happen is that a purchase order will be produced which shows the information. No description of working practices, problems and so on will be given. The interview will thus be staccato and of limited use.

A better approach is to begin with a general question asking the person to explain what he or she is doing, or how the job is done. For example:

> I wonder if I might start by asking you to describe to me what your job involves?

or,

> I'd like you to begin, please, by explaining to me how we go about placing a purchase order.

or, for an internal auditor where such questions might seem too naïve, then:

> I know basically what we do for quotations, but since I don't work in this department I don't understand it in detail. I wonder if you'd be good enough to take me through it step by step?

These questions are naïve, and intended to be so. If the interviewee looks at the auditor strangely and wonders what the hidden motive behind the question is, then an experienced auditor often laughs it off with a bit of self-effacing humour:

> Yes, I know it's described in the procedure document but I've read so many of them now that my brain can't cope. Assume you're having to explain it to an inexperienced trainee and that's just about the level I'll be able to cope with.

When lucky, an auditor will receive a moderately full and detailed explanation of the process in hand. If not so lucky, then the answer may be brief and the auditor will have to prompt for more information:

> Yes, I see. So exactly what information is it that you're looking for when you take the enquiry?

From what is said, the auditor can ask more questions to expand and clarify the picture. Further questions are also prompted by 'alarm bells'. Competent auditors develop internal alarm bells which ring when something is said which needs investigation. Examples of when alarm bells ring are:

○   elements of the process are skipped over ('then it goes through various checks and so on, then we release it');

○   conditional phrases are used ('if it is an existing customer, then we do this');

○   indications are given that sometimes there are short cuts ('if we have time...', 'we should really do this...', 'the *official* system is...');

○   there are suggestions that the procedures are not taken seriously ('well, officially, we do, but...');

○   moans and complaints ('it's all very well writing all that stuff in the manual, but the boss should come out here and see what it's really like');

○   negative attitudes ('this quality stuff's a waste of time');

○   hints of failure ('I'll admit to you now that we're not as good at following up as we should be');

○   lack of knowledge ('I've no idea');

○   lack of communication or education ('nobody ever told me I had to do that').

The list can be endless. Each auditor will gradually increase the sensitivity of their own alarm to areas which they have proved can lead to potential problems. It ought to be emphasized, though, that when the alarm rings, auditors have not usually found a problem yet; they have just discovered an area where more questions need to be asked.

As the questioning proceeds, it is likely that the discussions will become more detailed and specific, until the subject finally comes around to where information is recorded. For example, the interviewee might mention that a form is filled in, or a database entry is made. At this point the auditor should always ask to see an example of some actual work. This might seem obvious but many find that, during the heat of an audit itself, it is tempting to become carried away with understanding the process, rather than checking its results.

SELECTING EXAMPLES OF RECORDS

The auditor then chooses the example to look at. For the same reasons as when selecting the interviewee, do not let the department personnel pick the example. In fact it is even more important here. If it is left up to the interviewees, they will select the 'Blue Peter' example ('here's one I prepared earlier') which will be perfect. This is not necessarily devious; people simply prefer to show their best work (just as when I arrive home in the evening and my youngest daughter has some drawings to show, the first one that she proudly displays is the one that she likes the most).

It should not be too difficult to pick the example. Second party auditors will, obviously, choose something directly related to their own contracts. Internal auditors usually have a very good idea of the range of work carried out and can easily come up with something. Even third party auditors will probably have some idea. If not, then it is easy enough to browse through the file or list to pick one that attracts the eye. If it is absolutely essential to let the auditee pick the first example, then this will provide an opportunity for the auditor to narrow down the choice for the second example ('Thanks, that was one from three months ago, do you have one from last week?'). Always look at more than one example (everybody can think of an exception to this rule, for example auditing an organization that manages royal coronations will not permit many current examples, but it applies in the majority of cases). The reason for this is that one example does not give a complete picture.

A way of explaining this is to think of a fruit cake. If I simply take a single slice, looking to see whether the fruit is evenly distributed, one slice will tell me nothing. If, however, I take three or four, and they all have a roughly equal amount of raisins, then I can assume that distribution is fairly even. If one slice is all fruit and no mixture and the other two are all cake and no fruit, we can tell that something has gone awry. This illustrates that auditing is a sampling exercise; it is not necessary to eat the whole cake in order to gain an idea of what is going on. To choose the examples, it is best to select as wide a range as possible. If the first calibrated instrument examined is a multi-meter, then the auditor should ensure that not all examples are multi-meters. We can use the cake allegory again here; we will gain far more information about its composition if we take four slices at 90° apart than if we take four right next to each other.

There is no hard and fast rule about how many samples are taken. It depends upon how much time is available and how complex each individual item is. A good starting number, though, is three or four.

IDENTIFYING PROBLEMS

The most important rule for an auditor, and no apology is made for repeating this, is that when something is seen or heard that does not *seem* to be right, no problem has yet been found. It simply means that some more questions need to be asked. A good auditor will keep asking questions and looking at more data until he or she is absolutely certain that there is, or is not, something to report.

Another vital element is to see the evidence. There are almost no circumstances where a problem should be reported simply based upon someone's verbal statement. This is true even where the person being interviewed seems to state that something is not going to plan. Examples could be:

○   'No, I don't think we've had a meeting for some time.'
○   'I never sign them.'
○   'Elizabeth hasn't been trained.'
○   'It's not identified.'
○   'It's stored dangerously.'

In all of these cases it sounds as if the auditor is being given a 'freebie'. In truth, though, all they are is pointers to where to look. If the interviewee says that documents are never signed, then the next step is to go to the file and see if they have been signed. If they say that Elizabeth has not been trained, then the auditor goes to the training records and checks to see whether this is indeed correct.

There are a number of reasons why you have to confirm everything via evidence. The first, and probably most important, is that the interviewee may be wrong. This could be because:

○   they misunderstand the auditor's questions;
○   they misunderstand the process;
○   they are not responsible for what they are describing;
○   they are nervous and speaking without thinking;
○   they are deliberately trying to cause trouble (although this might seem unlikely, auditors will often find that interviewees complain about their employer, in many cases without real justification).

Another reason is so that you can report exactly what you have seen, enabling those responsible to carry out proper investigation and correction. If the final report, for example, simply states that some documents are not dated, based on hearsay, then it will be very difficult for the manager subsequently to examine those documents and identify what is going wrong.

The final reason is to preserve your own credibility. At the final feedback session, managers who are confident in the excellence of their own department (or at least do not wish it to be found wanting by an outsider) may challenge any negative findings. If the only support to an audit report is somebody saying that they thought there was a problem, then you will have great difficulty in standing your ground.

NOTIFYING PROBLEMS

Once the auditor has found something negative to report, he or she should inform the interviewee immediately. It is extremely unprofessional to take secret notes and wait to 'hit' the auditees with the observations at the closing meeting. Again, there are good practical reasons for doing this. One of these is to make the auditor's job easier. If only non-committal noises are made at the time, then at the closing meeting a barrage of non-compliances is reported, the manager may rightly protest that he or she has spoken, in the interim, to the interviewee, who reports that no problems were discussed. Most significantly, though, it gives the auditee an opportunity to explain that there is obviously some misunderstanding. Remember that being audited is a strange, and sometimes nerve-racking experience. This means that auditor's questions may be misunderstood or misinterpreted. Likewise the auditor may misinterpret genuine answers. So, if auditors state that they are going to report a problem, but the interviewees believe that they have described and demonstrated a water-tight process, it gives them the chance to say 'Hang on a minute...' and explain it more clearly. Again, there is nothing more embarrassing than reporting the wrong thing at a closing meeting.

Imagine the following:

Auditor:	'The next non-compliance relates to supplier control. There is no ongoing analysis of supplier performance. I asked Alan if he did supplier performance reviews and he said that he didn't. I asked to see a supplier review file and he said he didn't have one. I asked if he had any records on supplier review and he said that he didn't.'
Manager:	'Quite right; he doesn't. That's nothing to do with Alan so, of course, he doesn't have any files. I do all of that and have the files right here.'

Now we could argue about communication and awareness issues here, but this seems to be largely the auditor's fault. Many people are taught to answer the auditor's questions directly and not volunteer further information. Thus if you ask 'Do *you* have any files?' the answer may simple come back 'No, *I* do not.'

There may be some occasions when it is not appropriate to tell the interviewee, but to point it out to somebody else. I was once auditing a print company and saw an operator making a very sloppy job of packing up some boxes of brochures. Rather than say to the operator himself that his work was not good enough, a quiet word was had with the guide, who took immediate control via the area supervisor. It was still important, though, to mention it immediately rather than leaving it until the closing meeting when it was both too late and harder to justify.

If something really serious is found, for example a major non-compliance in a third party audit, or something which will preclude approved supplier status in a second party audit, then the auditor must make doubly sure that this is brought to the attention of someone in authority straight away. It would be unreasonable to allow a severe problem to wait several hours until a closing meeting. Even if the auditor is unsure, at the time, whether or not this is a major or minor issue, but has doubts, then the auditor's thoughts must be communicated to somebody in charge.

MOVING ON

Once a problem or suggestion has been identified, and communicated to the interviewee, the auditor should move straight on to the next topic. What should not be done is:

○   waste time by continuing to double-confirm the problem by finding the same thing again;

○   be so pleased that one has actually proven some auditing ability that it is 'thrashed to death';

○   batter the poor auditee by repeating the same finding again and again;

○   lecture the auditee ('This is very important, you know. If we don't fill this in properly we won't know what's happened and it will make life very difficult. You really will need to pay some attention to this in the future to avoid serious problems.').

Once the auditor has determined that there is something here worth reporting, the auditor should simply say, 'That's not as per the policy, so I'll include that in my report. Now I'd like to move on to...' (I prefer not to be too precise here. Whenever possible avoid saying that it is a non-compliance, for example, to allow for some flexibility at the end when actually writing up the report).

USE OF THE CHECKLIST

Some readers may have noticed, by now, that they were told that preparing a checklist is a good idea, but that there has been no mention of how to use it during an audit. Of course, just having gone to the trouble of preparing it in advance will have been of some benefit since the auditor will be familiar with the contents of the related documents. There is, however, a specific use of the checklist during the audit itself. This is as a prompt for the auditor, to jog the memory for those things that ought to be covered or aspects that have not been mentioned during general conversation. Typically, the auditor will not look at the checklist at the start of the interview, but will begin with a broad question. Then, when the series of points arising from initial questions have been exhausted, and the related records have been examined, there will be a pause for breath. At this point, the auditor will glance at the checklist. Several points will have already been covered and can be ticked off. There may, though, be one point which has not been addressed, perhaps because it is highly specific or only happens occasionally. The checklist enables the auditor to remember that it is a key part of procedures and ask a question about it ('Ah, just a point before we move on, the document says that there are special rules for dealing with this during the night shift, I wonder if you could explain that to me please.'). Then when the auditor is sure that all relevant items related to that subject have been covered, the checklist is useful again to identify the next topic of conversation ('Fine. I think we've covered as much about purchase orders as I'd like to look at for now, perhaps we could move on to talk about how you choose and monitor suppliers.'). It is a good idea to make notes on the checklist as the audit proceeds, to help cross-refer to any specific issues raised in the report.

RECORDING WHAT WAS LOOKED AT

Almost every auditor training course teaches the participants that they should take careful notes of everything they have seen. Thus if the auditor examines three project files as the selected sample, then the identifications of those project files should be written somewhere, perhaps on the checklist or a separate auditor note sheet. When asked what the benefits are of such note-taking, some of the following are given as answers:

O   It means that, if asked, auditors can prove that they actually did look at a reasonable sample (this seems to be the favourite reason).
O   It provides for a certain degree of rigour.
O   It helps the auditor to pursue an audit trail when moving from one area to another.

The first of these is a terrible reason; business practices should never be introduced for no reason other than to show something to another auditor. Indeed, one leading certification body told its auditors some time ago that they must keep records of what they saw, but that the company does not want to see them; they should be held by the auditor at home until called for by the accreditation auditor, if required. This is an open admission that the records have no use other than to keep the regulators happy. Sadly, ISO 9001 implementations are full of this sort of thing. Only the third reason shows any sense, but even then might be better handled by informal notes.

I do believe that keeping such notes has some actual disadvantages:

O   It is yet another task to manage – alongside questioning, listening to the answers, referring back to documentation and checklists, thinking of the next question, and making specific notes of things that need to be followed up.
O   It destroys audit flow – in the midst of an interesting line of questioning, the players have to stop while the number and dates of the form just seen are written down, even though there was nothing wrong with it.
O   It is yet another record that takes up space in the filing cabinet but will never be looked at (subsequent auditors are unlikely to read them since they will be wishing to audit more current information so that there is little chance of overlap).

Given these disadvantages, and the rather tenuous reasons in favour, I do not support the practice. I recognize, however, that this is not a majority opinion and readers must choose their own path. If these details are to be recorded, then adding a suitable column to the checklist form is an excellent way to deal with it. More discussion of note-taking is given in Chapter 12.

STICKING TO THE CHECKLIST

Yes, auditors are permitted to ask questions about things not on the checklist (and, it follows, not mentioned in procedures). The audit looks at the way that the process or function is being managed, not just what is written in a manual. Indeed, auditors may find an immediate problem to report simply because an activity is identified which is not adequately covered in documentation. The common argument that 'you can't audit that, it's not in the procedure manual' is invalid. If it is being done and it affects quality, then it is auditable.

ENDING THE INTERVIEW

When general questions have been asked, the answers given and explored, evidence examined and all points on the checklist covered, it is time to end the interview. Do not, simply because the next appointment is not for another half an hour yet, sit around and waste time, or go over the same things again. If the interview has finished early, there is always more preparation that can be done, or possibly some reporting. To end the interview, simply thank the person(s) involved, summarize what findings are going to appear in the report (and state any good points here, as well as reminding the interviewee of any negative findings) and say goodbye. The interviewee, or the guide, can then direct the auditor to the next appointment.

THE SERIES OF INTERVIEWS

The audit will probably comprise several interviews in order to cover every aspect of the system or area being looked at (a notable exception to this was an ISO 9001 certification audit that I carried out on a two-man company in Cornwall, where one of the partners was absent on the day owing to a domestic crisis). Once the line of questioning has been exhausted with one interviewee, it is time to move on to the next subject and pick whoever is responsible for that area.

It is worth noting that auditors may, of course, audit more than one person who nominally do exactly the same thing. This would be in an area of some size where there are large numbers of employees with the same basic responsibility. So, in an insurance office, for example, we could have dozens of agents. It would not be sensible, in this case, to pick just one but the auditor would probably speak to several. Indeed, unless it is a very small function with only one or two people involved, then you should always try to speak to more than one person. The same reasons for this apply as discussed earlier when looking at selecting examples of evidence: if you only speak to one person then it is just like taking only a single slice of cake.

FINDINGS REVIEW AND WRITE-UP

Once all of the interviews are complete, and everything has been covered, it is time for the audit team to decide exactly what they are going to say in the final report. Time will have been allowed in the programme for reflection and writing up the findings.

The first step is for the team leader to understand all of the points that each auditor intends to raise (and has told the interviewees will be raised). The lead auditor can then decide whether, in the light of the larger picture, to adjust the content and style of what is to be reported. Although this might seem strange, since the auditor has been diligent and investigated until the point has been proved one way or the other, and the leader was probably not there so does not know all the details, there are many cases when the team leader may decide to change the nature of the reported findings. Examples could be:

○   if the auditor is less experienced, or knowledgeable about this specific industry, than the team leader who can point out that certain things are accepted industry practice;

○   if the finding is altered by a finding made by another auditor (this is the most common reason, e.g. what the auditor thought were missing controls are actually managed by another department seen by a different member of the team);

○   if the team leader is aware, from prior contact with the organization, of action programmes that are under way to correct this very problem;

○   if the team leader considers that the auditor has misjudged the severity of the problem (e.g. if it is too trivial a point to raise, such as a minor typographical error on an internal document, or perhaps where the auditor has suggested a minor finding which the leader considers should be raised to a major concern owing to duplication of the finding by other audit team members).

At this time the team should also write out their findings. These should include all non-compliances and suggestions/observations. This is to enable them to be presented at the closing meeting. Without doing this, there is a danger of confusion. If non-compliances are written out some time after the final meeting, it is possible that they will say something slightly different to the understanding received by the auditee management when they were discussed. If nothing else, this will lead to delay while the confusion is clarified.

If it is normal practice in the audit regime to ask someone from the audited area to witness findings, now is the time to ask the guide (preferably or, if not, somebody else who is both competent and understands the nature of the findings) to sign the written reports. It is better to do it now than to ask for it at the closing meeting where there is greater potential for argument and the time of large numbers of people could, potentially, be wasted.

The next chapter discusses exactly how to report and write the findings. Some auditors also write out the full report of the audit before the closing meeting. The advantages of this are:

○   that the exact form of words used in the report will be known by both sides;
○   that it can be written while the details are fresh in the auditor's mind;
○   that after the closing meeting the auditor's job is over; there is no report 'hanging over' to be done later (rather like attending a meeting and being asked to take the minutes; for most of us writing them up afterwards is a chore which tends to be put off as long as possible).

Certainly professional auditors, such as certification assessors, usually write the report before the closing meeting. This is purely for practical reasons, since tomorrow they probably begin another audit and do not have time to write a report later for today's audit.

The main disadvantage is that it does not give the opportunity to document any discussions or issues which arise at the closing meeting. In the end, there is no rule about this, it is up to the preference of the individual team leader (or perhaps the policy of the audit team leader's employers or client). A compromise might be to draft certain elements of the report in advance, with some blank space left to add details from the closing meeting if needed.

It should be noted that this time still needs to be allowed for even where the team consists of a single auditor. A reflection of exactly what is to be reported is still required and the non-compliances and other reports will still have to be written.

CLOSING MEETING

Exactly as for opening meetings, the nature of closing meetings varies greatly between the types of audit. Whereas opening meetings are often ignored for internal audits, closing meetings are essential for all types of audit. This is because it is most important to explain to whoever is responsible for the area what has been found. No auditor should ever complete the audit by disappearing and subsequently sending in a report. This will only alienate the personnel involved, and removes any chance to debate the issues while they are still fresh in every-one's minds. After a long period of disruption by the auditor(s) and permitted access to normally confidential information, it is only courteous to spend some time afterwards explaining to whoever had allowed the access what the results are.

THE PURPOSE OF THE CLOSING MEETING

The main reason for holding this meeting is to report any findings which require some action. This reflects the fact that quality audits are, generally, a rather negative exercise. Despite the continual protestations that they are constructive and positive, essentially they are about identifying what areas should be improved or corrected in a department or process. This can be as constructive or as diplomatic as possible, but in reality everybody is interested only in what the auditors think can be made better, not what good elements exist that can be learnt elsewhere. This would be the outcome of a benchmarking exercise which would be approached in a different way.

There are, though, some secondary purposes: to report what was examined, to offer thanks, to permit detailed explanation and to discuss further actions.

What is said about actions required should not be a surprise to the area personnel as a whole since the auditors will have informed them of anything that is to appear in the report as the audit has proceeded. It may be new to the most senior person present – he or she will probably not have been present during most of the audit itself – but it will have been told to somebody.

The closing meeting is certainly not the place to 'hit' the auditee management with a surprise revelation. If there is something big or serious to report then the auditors should have made every effort to tell people before it reaches this stage.

The purposes of a closing meeting are:

○   to tell the auditee management what has been looked at;
○   to recap on some of the opening meeting points such as scope, standards and confidentiality;
○   to thank the organization for its assistance, cooperation and hospitality, as appropriate;
○   to report positive and negative findings;
○   to discuss the nature and implications of, and possible solutions to, findings, as required by the auditee management;
○   to ask for action on any negative findings;
○   to explain the consequences or result of the audit and its findings;
○   generally to report anything that the auditors wish to say, and to hand over written reports.

Part of the recap on opening meeting explanations should be to re-emphasize that any negative findings are not to be seen as criticisms or blame of an individual, but merely areas where the system can be enhanced.

A typical agenda for a closing meeting would be:

○   say that the audit has finished (or state what elements of the audit could not be finished in the time allowed);
○   explain what was looked at;
○   thank the personnel involved for their time and cooperation;

O   report the good things seen (there must be *something* good, otherwise
     the organization would be in trouble);
O   report the non-compliances, in order of importance;
O   report any formal suggestions and opportunities for improvement;
O   mention any suggestions and opportunities for improvement which have
     not been written down;
O   discuss and explain the findings, including reasons why they are being
     reported;
O   if the auditee management require, discuss what actions could be taken
     to correct the problems;
O   remind everybody that the auditors will treat the findings professionally
     and in confidence;
O   remind everybody that no personal criticism should be attached to any
     findings;
O   state the implications of the findings (e.g. certification will be recom-
     mended, they will be added to the approved supplier list, or simply that
     they have a few actions to take);
O   remind the people involved of the requirements of the corrective action
     process;
O   ask for, and answer, questions;
O   discuss arrangements for future audits;
O   close any gaps of understanding from either side.

Just as with opening meetings, the topics list could be lengthened or shortened as
appropriate for the particular audit.
    To expand upon some of the above:

Non-compliances

These should be described one by one, in detail. It is best to mention them in
approximate order of importance. If they are described in the order that they were
found there is a danger that significant time will be spent explaining trivia before
really important topics are arrived at. Neither should they be simply summarized.
Managers should have the opportunity to understand each finding, even if it
appears to take some time to go through them all.

Suggestions and improvement opportunities

These should be discussed in the same way as non-compliances, with a clear
explanation of the meaning of the different categorizations. Auditors should not,
though, trivialize their suggestions. They would not have been made unless it was
believed that real improvements could result; thus they should be presented with
equal gravity to non-compliances.

Verbal observations

The closing meeting also provides an opportunity to mention points which have not been, or will not be, included in the written reports. There are a number of reasons why this might be done. The two most common are if the finding is too trivial to warrant a written report (e.g. a number of typographical errors, which do not lead to confusion, in an internal document) or are too sensitive (e.g. a personal complaint about the abusive behaviour of an individual member of staff).

Corrective actions

The final responsibility for what action is to be taken must lie with the manager. It is not up to the auditor to tell the manager what to do (except for consultancy audits by a technical specialist). In some audits, especially second party assessments, the team may have strong views about what they want the audited organization to do, but these can never have stronger force than recommendations. After all, the management of the business (or department, process, site, etc.) are responsible for the correct and successful running of its functions. They may, of course, wish to discuss possible solutions to the problem with the audit team, but in the end the corrective action always must be owned by the auditee. It is never the general system auditor's responsibility to tell the audited organization what to do.

Corrective process

Especially where they have not been subject to this type of audit many times before, the auditee management will need to be reminded what they need to deal with, who they have to inform, how they should record their actions and what follow-up will be carried out (see Chapter 11 for more details).

Everything which will be mentioned outside or which will be included in a final report must be discussed at the meeting. It is totally unacceptable for auditors later to complain about something that they have not said to the manager at the time. Certainly if I were a company manager and I discovered that auditors had been saying things about me, my staff or my systems which I had not had the chance to debate, then I would be very annoyed. It would also mean that I would have no trust in the auditors and would never permit those people to intrude into my area again.

WHO SHOULD ATTEND A CLOSING MEETING?

Attendees at a closing meeting should include the following:

1.   All of the audit team. A mistake that is often made is to allow the team leader to present all findings. This does not work well. Most managers

will want to ask questions about findings and the team leader will not be able to answer them if she or he was not there when the details were seen.

2. The person responsible for the quality system in the organization or area being audited.
3. The most senior operational person (the chief executive, department head, etc.).
4. The audit guide(s).
5. Anyone else that the auditee management would like to be there, as long as it does not become a crowd.

As with opening meetings, the attendance list may be shorter for routine audits. However, you often find that more people are interested in attending the closing meeting than wanted to be there for the introduction. This is because the closing meeting feeds back the results which may have serious implications (for example do we keep our certificate, or will we be on the tender invitation list for future work?). In the end it is usually up to the auditee management to decide who should be there, within reason.

CLOSING MEETING RECORDS

It should not be necessary to generate formal closing meeting minutes. In most cases, though, it is a good idea to have a mechanism to record key discussions or questions arising. The final summary report is a good place to do this, which is perhaps a good reason for not finishing the report until after the final meeting has been completed. As with opening meetings, it may be required at very formal audits to record who was there. Certification auditors who have strict rules to follow may also need a checklist to tick off, ensuring that they do actually cover all of the necessary points.

DIFFERENCES BETWEEN SECOND AND THIRD PARTY CLOSING MEETINGS

Opening meetings probably vary between the different types of audit more than closing meetings do. All audits need a closing meeting where the findings are individually described and explained. It is only the supporting discussions which are likely to vary. Second party audit closing meetings, as with all elements of such assessments, are likely to be more prescriptive. Companies often have fixed ideas about what their suppliers need to do and their auditors can be rather strict in the expectations of corrective action. Third party auditors are typically more reserved in their judgements and will carefully explain that the organization itself must identify suitable actions. Otherwise the items discussed in the meeting are extremely similar. Both are likely, for example, to emphasize that they will treat anything seen as confidential and will set timescales for the actions to be taken.

Those conducting a supplier audit will set maximum corrective action times in line with the needs of the business or project involved. Certification audits usually have a pre-set maximum time allowed for correction of non-compliances. This is discussed in more detail in Chapter 11 as part of follow-up disciplines.

INTERNAL AUDIT CLOSING MEETINGS

Unlike previous comments about opening meetings for internal audits, closing meetings are just as appropriate here as when the auditors are not from the same organization. This is because the only way properly to conclude the investigation stage of an audit is to tell the people responsible what has been found. Many internal auditors, pressed for time, are tempted to knock off the report quickly and drop it on the manager's desk, arguing that they are always at hand later if the manager has any questions. This is poor practice and should always be avoided. Reasons for this include:

O   simple courtesy;
O   a report can rarely explain things as clearly as a face-to-face discussion;
O   if there are contentious issues then communicating them in writing is likely to lead to dispute and resentment;
O   it looks as if the auditor does not care enough about the results to take the time to explain them;
O   the report will not be taken as seriously if it just another set of papers that hits the manager's desk.

Thus even internal auditors must take the time to meet the head of the area audited and explain the findings. The meeting is unlikely to be as formal as one with external auditors (for a start, there is usually less at stake) but similar matters will be discussed. It is certainly an opportunity to discuss what actions should be taken as a result of the findings. Even on an internal audit, where both parties are from the same company, the auditor must never impose an action on the personnel involved. The person in charge of the area carries the ultimate responsibility for how an area should be run and thus must make the decision as to how it is managed. The audit team can, however, provide some input to the decision process and it is entirely appropriate for an internal auditor to do so.

Even some of the formal reminders used by certification auditors, such as the blame-free nature of the process, or the fact that there may be non-compliances not found owing to the sampling nature of the audit, may also be necessary to mention, especially if the auditors suspect that there is some misunderstanding about these issues.

CONCLUDING THE CLOSING MEETING

This is less of a problem than for opening meetings. Basically, the meeting is over when all of the findings have been discussed and all questions answered. Apart from a responsibility of the auditors to ensure that the management understand the nature of the findings, what they mean and what has to be done next, there is little else to say. Auditors should, though, try to keep control of the meeting and keep it to a reasonable length without too much heated debate.

WHO SHOULD DO THE TALKING?

This is not a forum for the lead auditor to hold court. The team leader should perform the initial introductions and discuss the general issues but each auditor should report their own findings. To allow anyone other than the person who found the observation to report it is risky; if the managers attending should ask for explanation then discussion stops if the person reporting is not familiar with the exact circumstances. Of course, the auditee management will want to discuss the findings; auditors will need to be ready to explain and justify their judgements. The team leader should allow each of his or her colleagues to speak on their own, but be ready to step in if they need some support.

PITFALLS

There are many things that can go wrong at the feedback meeting. Examples are discussed below.

Argument

This is the most common pitfall, that managers argue with the auditors about the validity and/or reasonableness of findings. Sadly, this has become common owing to defensive and protective attitudes by managers and unprofessional approaches by auditors. This means that auditors must be prepared for some debate. If, however, the auditors have proved their non-compliances beyond doubt, and emphasized that their observations represent the opinions of the auditors rather than hard problems, then the debates should be minimal. Direct and factual is the key, avoiding criticism or personal interpretation.

Pressure to withdraw

This is an extension of the 'argument' problem. Sometimes the argument from auditee managers will be persuasive to the extent that auditors will feel under pressure to withdraw one or more findings. This is most likely to occur when auditors raise non-compliances based upon subjective rather than objective information. If the auditors have done their job properly then there should be no need to withdraw anything. If it is an observation then there should be no need to withdraw it since the manager is able to ignore the finding, provided that the manager has adequate justification. There are also occasions when auditors are tempted, to avoid conflict, to 'downgrade' non-compliances to observations. This represents a misconception. An observation is not (or should not be) a weak non-compliance; it is a different thing. It is, therefore, not simply a low-grade non-compliance and downgrade is not an appropriate response to managerial resistance.

Proving of auditor error

Sometimes arguments from managers will eventually prove that the auditor was wrong. This is rare, but can happen. For example, sometimes staff may not be aware that their boss looks after a particular activity and thus believe that it does not happen at all. This misunderstanding may be corrected at the closing meeting. If so, the auditor may decide to withdraw the non-compliance (although may raise another non-compliance or observation relating to awareness and communication). There is nothing wrong in such withdrawal if the auditor is definitely mistaken, but it should not happen simply because the manager wishes to argue.

Unrealistic expectations

Managers may sometimes expect that the auditors have found everything that needs action. That is, there are no problems existing in their processes other than those reported by the audit team. This is clearly untrue since auditing is only a sampling exercise. There may, in fact, be many problems which the auditors simply did not see since they were in areas or examples not selected for examination. The auditors must make this clear. At certification audits it is typical to include a formal statement to this effect at the closing meeting. Other auditors will need to bear it in mind, explaining the situation if there is any doubt or confusion.

Anxiety

Auditing often makes the recipients nervous. Auditee management become especially anxious if there is something at stake, for example the award of an ISO 9001 certificate or a major supply contract. This may make them over-anxious and eager to please, frightened or highly defensive. Auditors should be aware of the underlying anxiety and be both reassuring and firm.

Hidden agendas

It is quite common for managers to have one or two serious pressing problems on the go at any one time. These problems can appear so grave that they swamp everything else. As a result anything that the auditors report will be attributed to the problem at the top of the manager's mind. There are two points to watch out for in this. The first, and simplest, is that auditors should pull the auditee management away from interpreting every finding in exactly the same way; each will need to be looked at individually to determine the root cause and best course of action. Just because, for example, the managers involved believe that they do not have enough staff it does not mean that every problem is a result of insufficient personnel. The second danger is that auditors become drawn into a sensitive political situation. Auditors should not be seen to have directly advised something sensitive such as, for example, the dismissal of an employee. This might sound extreme but it can happen if the organization or area management feel that an individual is to blame for the negative findings or for a wider set of problems. If this happens then the audit team must ensure that they distance themselves from any political or controversial action.

Trivialization

When managers are defensive, or see the auditing process as having nothing to do with 'real work', they may try to make the findings seem unimportant and offer ways of correcting them which over-trivialize the auditors' efforts. Although it is not usually the auditor's job to tell the manager what to do about a problem, the auditor does need to ensure that proposed actions are reasonable. This means that if managers try to trivialize a report ('Oh, I'll just add a line to the procedure document to allow for that') auditors will need to draw their attention to the requirement for audit findings to be adequately investigated and considered, rather than being addressed by 'quick fix' solutions.

Sympathy

We are all only human (well, most of us) and auditors are not there to give people a hard time. Thus they may feel embarrassed or hesitant if auditees take the findings very badly, or when they are reporting something which will be difficult and lengthy to solve. There is a temptation in such circumstances to withdraw a non-compliance or suggest that a 'quick fix' will do. Although auditors should not be frosty and aloof, they should not change what they have found simply because they feel sorry for the people at the closing meeting.

Corruption

This is often warned about at lead auditor training courses but rarely happens in practice. Despite its rarity, though, it still can occur and should be watched out for. It is most important for auditors to show the utmost integrity when reporting audit findings. The most obvious, and rarest, form of bribery is the outright, 'I'll give you £2000 if you make the report more favourable.' This is too obvious and extremely dangerous (the penalties are severe if the parties are caught at it). Less obvious and more likely is, 'What would we have to do to convince you to rethink this report?' This type of statement is unlikely to be innocent but is couched in such terms that attempted bribery can be denied if there is a challenge. Auditors should identify when this is happening and make it absolutely clear that their integrity is not for sale (at least, not at the price that most auditees are willing to pay). Indeed, such comments may be traps with no real bribe at stake but simply to test the auditor's steadiness. An even less direct attempt at buying the way out of a bad report is persuasion of the form, 'Oh, come on, I thought you were on our side when we were enjoying that expensive dinner together last night.' Again, auditors must not be swayed by any generosity, even if it has already been received and accepted. For this reason many audit organizations refuse to accept any form of gift or hospitality. This is probably being too strict, after all if a certification assessor, for example, has to stay overnight locally, then the client is paying for the evening meal anyway, whether or not the client is also present at the dinner. And accepting a company promotional mug or T-shirt is hardly going to make any difference, although a family holiday in Barbados is probably going too far. Auditors have to decide what is 'reasonable'. Bribery as a ploy is almost non-existent for internal audits, so auditors do not need to worry about being too vigilant under these circumstances.

CLOSING MEETING CHECKLIST

O   Lead auditor controls but does not dominate.
O   Each auditor reports their own findings.
O   Auditors must be prepared to discuss and justify findings.
O   Thanks are expected from both sides.
O   The meaning and implication of the findings should be discussed.
O   A commitment to (and, if possible, the specifics of) corrective action should be obtained from the auditee management.
O   Both sides should understand what happens next.
O   Again, keep it informal and businesslike.

MANAGING THE PROGRESS OF THE AUDIT

Dealing with the simplest option first, there is not much to managing the overall internal audit. These are usually restricted to a single functional area, so that an auditor simply has to go through the steps of preparation, introduction, investigation, decision, feedback and reporting. The audit is then over. For second and third party audits, though, a little more thought is required. These are typically a series of horizontal audits conducted over the period of somewhere between half a day and two weeks. If the audit is to be completed within a single day or less, this is not too complicated. There is an opening meeting at the start of the day. The investigation then proceeds with a simple introduction in each department and basic thanks as the auditor departs for the next area. The time to consider findings and write up findings takes place after all interviews have been conducted and all areas visited. There is then one closing meeting to report the findings in all areas, together with a single report summarizing the whole. If the organization being audited requires an interim update, or an audit team needs to come together to prepare notes, this can be done informally at lunch time (note: usual practice is to keep breaks, such as lunch, as short and informal as possible – 'sandwiches on site' is a traditional UK approach, although this takes other forms around the world).

For audits occupying two or more days, it is normal practice for the auditors to sit quietly and gather their thoughts at the end of the day, probably also writing out their findings at this time. An informal feedback to the organization's management of the previous day's findings would then be given at the start of the next day, at which point the auditors may well ask the guides to witness the written reports (see Chapter 10 for more explanation of the writing out and witnessing of non-compliances and other findings). Otherwise the pattern is the same, with a single opening meeting at the start of the first day and a closing meeting at the end of the last day.

As part of managing the progress of the audit, the team will, of course, have to consider things such as lunch and break times and normal working hours. For example, office staff may well be flexible as to when they can be interviewed but shop floor personnel are more likely to have fixed hours. A common practice is for Friday afternoons to be reserved for overtime working; auditors will have to be aware that they should visit production areas in the morning if auditing on a Friday.

CONSULTANCY AUDITS

Although it is not one of the 'official' types of audit, it is still valuable to look at what happens when an external business consultant is brought in. If consultants are there to assist with the internal audit programme then they will be asked simply to conduct themselves as any other auditor (although their improvement recommendations may be given more weight than those from a true internal auditor).

If the consultant is there to determine readiness for ISO 9001 certification, as often happens towards the end of a consultancy project, then in theory the consultant is offering a service directly comparable to the pre-assessment audit offered by certification bodies. In practice the consultant is likely to conduct a full audit in a similar manner to the initial audit by the external assessors, but with a stronger emphasis on identifying enhancements and improvements, including some recommendations on not just what should be corrected, but how. Consultants will typically always break the rule that auditors will not tell managers what to do; they are being employed for their expertise and auditees usually expect them to explain the best way of dealing with a situation.

The biggest difference to standard audit practice described in this chapter is the consultancy improvement audit. This is where consultants are brought in to look in detail at one or more areas of the operation and to employ their professional expertise to recommend enhancements and improvements. These audits are not particularly concerned with compliance with standard procedures and auditors are not expected to employ the impartial judgements seen elsewhere. They are likely to be very prescriptive in their evaluation of the area. Their questions and investigations are also less likely to be general in nature; they will be evaluating performance directly in their particular area of expertise. Reports and feedback will also concentrate far more on what should be done, rather than simply pointing out areas which require attention and leaving it up to auditee management to decide upon corrective action.

The fact that an auditor is an external expert does not, though, absolve the auditor from the duty to be sure of the facts before making a pronouncement. For the audit to be of maximum benefit, the recommendations must offer a real improvement over the existing process ('I prefer it like this' is not a good justification for a recommendation), they must be realistic and practical and must provide a pay-back which amply justifies the time and effort required to implement them. Auditors will need to understand the precise nature of what they have seen and how it works before their recommendations can meet these criteria.

SUMMARY

○   The audit team should introduce themselves to the management of the area, keeping the introduction relatively informal and tailoring it to the nature and purpose of the audit.

○   Investigation should begin directly after the introduction, with the audit team speaking with workers, not just managers.

○   Interviews use open questions designed to gather information, rather than specific yes/no questions.

○   Which people to interview and which topics or samples to examine are the choice of the auditor, not the auditee personnel.

○   Auditors must be absolutely sure of what they have seen before they report a problem or a recommendation, even if they are recognized technical experts.

○   Always verify via written or electronic records; do not accept verbal comments (there are exceptions to this rule, although they are rare).

○   Anything to be reported or recommended should be pointed out to the interviewee at the time to allow any misunderstandings to be clarified.

○   Take time to consider what is to be reported before actually running to the management with it.

○   Write up basic problems and recommendations before explaining final audit results to the auditee management.

○   Hold a feedback meeting to explain exactly what was found and what the results and implications are.

10

REPORTING AND DOCUMENTATION

❖

PURPOSE OF AUDIT REPORTS

Written reports are a ubiquitous feature of all quality audits. Although they can appear in a variety of forms, they all serve four main purposes, listed below in order of importance:

1. To act as a reminder to the auditee of what actions he or she needs to take.
2. To inform the client as to the results of the audit.
3. To act as part of the means of tracking resultant actions.
4. To provide evidence that the audit was conducted.

Note the last one. Although it is, in most cases, important to have some record showing what was audited and when and what the results were, in case of later enquiry, this should not be the primary or even one of the most important reasons for its creation. This means that we need to design our report formats to meet the above objectives, bearing in mind their priorities. One of the most important outcomes of this conclusion is that the reports need to be kept simple. Since most of the reasons for writing the report relate to the required actions that have arisen, then the report should be geared towards those actions, with anything else taking a subsidiary role.

Many certification bodies, for example, are now producing extremely simple and slim reports from each audit, sloughing off the cumbersome documents, several pages long, that used to be typical. The same is true for internal and supplier audits where the handwritten report is rarely seen today and the report is often generated simply through the completion of one or two standard forms.

THE VERBAL REPORT

Although we have already discussed the submission of a verbal report at the closing meeting, it is worth repeating some of the messages here.

Remember that the closing meeting is the place at which the auditors should inform those responsible for the area what has been found. The written report is not the place for this. Everything that appears in the written report must already be known and understood by those in the area. It is possible that the client may only know the results when reading the report, but the auditee management should certainly find it to be no surprise.

The verbal report should include everything that the auditors wish to say, including what was good, what was covered and comments on the audit process itself, as well as descriptions of each of the actions required. The written report may well repeat all of this but is actually likely to say less than was discussed at the closing meeting (it is amazing how many pages of text are occupied by transcribing 20 minutes of conversation). Remember that the written report should never include anything that has not already been discussed between the auditors and those responsible for the area.

CHOOSING THE WRITTEN WORDS

Since the findings that require action are the most important part of any written audit report, conventions have grown up which define how those findings should be written out. These have arisen to ensure the integrity of the audit process whilst maximizing the chances of timely action being taken.

NON-COMPLIANCES

The conventions say that non-compliance statements should be:

O   non-prescriptive
O   factual
O   complete
O   self-explanatory
O   traceable
O   verifiable
O   without criticism.

This means that auditors should avoid telling the head of the area what to do but should describe it in such a way that he or she fully understands what the situation is and is able to carry out any further investigation or action. The statement should also avoid pointing the finger of blame at any individual or suggesting that the required action is a result of poor performance.

So, for example, a simple statement such as:

> Supplier reviews should always be recorded on form Q37

is not appropriate since it tells the manager specifically what to do (perhaps Q37 is not the best means and the department head would prefer to use a database) and it does not fully describe the problem – is the auditor suggesting that they are not always being recorded on Q37, if so when did this happen and why is it a problem that they are not?

I have often seen auditors write non-compliance statements on a similar topic as:

> Supplier review procedures are not being followed.

This is about the worst type of statement that can be written since it tells the manager nothing. Although it will have been explained to the manager at the closing meeting, he or she may not be able to remember the details without a suitable memory-jogger. Simply describing that the procedures are not being followed does not serve the purpose.

An acceptable statement might be:

> Purchasing policy document P17, section 3, requires that annual performance reviews of major sub-contractors are conducted and recorded on a form Q37 for each one. A series of reviews was carried out during March 1999 but the details and results were entered into a database created by the Procurement Manager (accessible only from the hard drive of the Procurement Manager's desktop PC) and not onto the form.

This states what the requirements are, what has gone wrong, and provides enough information for the person concerned to go back and look for themselves. I have seen a number of experienced auditors use a little formula to help them remember how this should be written:

> Requirement – Failure – Evidence

Looking at my sample statement, we can see that the requirement was stated first, then details of what happened, including pointers to the evidence (the date of review and where the information can be found).

A good written statement includes every detail possible to enable the person taking subsequent action to fully remember and understand the circumstances. When explaining it at the closing meeting, though, the auditor will probably not mention every little detail. For example, it will make the issue sound cumbersome and pedantic if every document, item number and reference identification is mentioned, whereas this information will be invaluable in written form when carrying out subsequent investigations.

It is also important that the statement does not imply any criticism or point the finger of blame at an individual. For this reason it is a good idea to avoid putting people's names in non-compliance statements, unless the problem relates to specific training records viewed in which case it is probably necessary. In such circumstances, of course, errors in training records are rarely the fault of the individual so mentioning their name does not represent criticism.

Grammar and punctuation are not particularly important here if the space to write a non-compliance is limited (although see my comments at the end of this chapter), but detail and distilling the essence of the problem or opportunity are vital.

OBSERVATIONS

If the auditor wishes to report something that needs, or would benefit from, attention by the auditee management but does not represent a non-compliance, then similar rules apply. That is, the auditor needs to point out the facts, state why improvement is being recommended and provide enough information to enable the manager to act upon it later. Again, always avoid telling those responsible exactly how to run their operations, but rather point out where attention should be focused.

There are, though, some differences of emphasis. By definition, why action needs to be taken is less clear. If it is obvious that they are not following a rule then they should either start doing so or change the rules. If the auditor has not shown that rules have been broken, though, then they need a stronger justification of why they have to make changes. This means that the facts of the situation take a less important role and the reason why change is needed takes on a greater significance. Therefore observation or recommendation statements typically put most emphasis on what could be done differently to current practice and why this would be a good idea. A sensible observation or recommendation might be:

> It currently takes between eight and ten days to prepare and send out contract forms for new customers. Increased contract standardization and use of automation could dramatically reduce this time resulting in lower costs and increased customer satisfaction.

This does include some factual data in the report of the current cycle time. The major part of the statement, though, relates to an opportunity for change and even suggests some approaches to the improvement. Notice that there is no reference to any requirement; if there is no defined target for contract preparation then it is simply a question of looking to make things better.

In an audit aimed more at compliance, observations are usually only geared towards potential future non-compliances. In this case, an observation statement is likely to be less direct:

> It is recommended that the process for dealing with new customer contracts is reviewed since the current lengthy turn-round time could lead to errors which in turn could result in quality system non-compliances.

Again, though, sufficient detail here to make investigation easier would be more appropriate than the vague statement given above.

THE CORRECTIVE ACTION REQUEST SHEET

Although not the only way of recording non-compliances and recommendations, the use of some form of corrective action sheet is the most common means. A typical example is shown in Figure 10.1. This one is named 'Corrective Action Request' but other names are also employed, often accompanied by the abbreviations by which they are known:

O   Non-compliance note (NCN)
O   Non-compliance report (NCR – also often used for product rejects in engineering and manufacturing industries)
O   Quality audit report (QAR)
O   Audit findings record (AFR).

There are many other variations on the same theme. I do not have particularly strong views about the choice of name, although I do feel that a form containing the word non-compliance or similar only has limited potential use (we cannot use it to record observations, for example) and the term 'quality audit report' could be confused with the summary written report discussed later in this chapter.

The upper part of the form is a general header to explain the when, where and who of the finding. The first large box is the space for the auditor to record the findings, in the manner already described. The form shown includes a requirement for a responsible person (either the head of the area audited or the audit guide) to sign the statement to say that they agree the facts. This is not to ask whether or not they agree that it is a non-compliance, but simply whether the facts as stated are correct.

These are the only sections of the form that are necessarily completed during the audit itself. The rest of the report is for other people to fill in. The next box is for the head of the area to say what action will be taken to prevent the problem recurring, which of course should be signed to commit to ownership with a target completion date quoted. Interestingly, many organizations have spaces for recording two actions on the form, one for immediate correction of the non-compliance and the other to prevent recurrence through corrective action. Where there is only space to record one action then it is the longer term corrective action that interests us; in many cases going back and retrospectively fixing something, such as a missing signature, is rather pointless. There is then a comments space to make any notes after the action has been completed. This could simply be to confirm completion or to note any variations experienced when the action was actually taken. There are then spaces to confirm the effectiveness of the action (just because the action was taken doesn't mean that it actually had the desired effect) and to follow on the issue to a new CAR form if, for any reason, the action cannot be considered to be closed. Reasons for not closing out an action could include:

Raised by:		Date
Audit identification, company of area:		CAR No.
ISO 9001 ref:	N/C ☐ OBS ☐	
Details of problem: Related document(s):		
Signed: _____ (Auditor) _____ (Manager)		
Corrective action proposed: (to be completed by head of area) 		
Signed:	Target completion date:	
Action completed: date	Comments: 	
Action Reviewed: Date: Satisfactory? Y / N New CAR No.:	Signed: (Quality Manager)	
CAR Closed:	Date:	

FIGURE 10.1   Corrective action request form

○   it was not done;
○   it did not solve the problem;
○   it only partially solved the problem;
○   circumstances have changed which leave the issue unresolved but which make the proposed action no longer appropriate.

Under these circumstances a new CAR should be raised by the auditor or audit programme coordinator renewing the issue on a new sheet. This enables the issue to be kept alive whilst allowing for the fact that most of the original form has been filled in with no space for new actions to be proposed and reviewed.

The use of a form like this can be of benefit in subsequent actions and progress tracking. It allows the head of the audited area to look at one problem at a time and record what he or she intends to do on the sheet. It also allows the person tracking progress to keep those on which action is still due in an 'open' file, while the others can be filed away.

VARIATIONS

The exact layout and name of the form will vary according to the needs and preferences of the audit organization. For example, certification bodies may wish to add contract numbers or an audit administrator may find a specific audit reference number useful. There are, however, a number of variations on the form design which have direct bearing on the successful conduct of the audit:

○   For anyone other than third party assessors, the cross-reference to an ISO 9001 clause is not very useful. The audit is not usually conducted directly against the standard so the clause reference has only secondary relevance. It gives the auditor, who may not be expertly cognisant with the ISO 9001 contents structure, an extra thing to worry about that they are therefore likely to get wrong. Some quality coordinators like to analyse audit findings against ISO 9001 clauses but this is far less meaningful than analysis by business objective or root problem cause. Anyway it is likely to be wrong since the auditors will make mistakes and such analyses always look very similar with the same clauses regularly appearing.
○   The practice of asking somebody to sign to agree the facts of statements needs careful consideration. The problem is that people do not like to sign and, when asked to do so, may sometimes refuse. I have even seen internal audit forms which clearly offer heads of department the option to disagree with findings. If you have agreed things verbally and trust each other then there should be no need to sign. I accept that certification auditors will leave site shortly and need some evidence that the report has been agreed and understood, but it should always be emphasized that the signature really only applies to seeing and understanding rather than any form of agreement. I have heard some quality managers say that

they like a signature to signify ownership of the problem, but this is just as well served by a signature under the proposed action. If audit managers still like to have a signature here, then auditors will have to remember that they are likely to have to justify their findings twice: once when first explaining them and once when asking for a signature.

NO-ACTION FORMS

Where the audit programme includes both non-compliances and observations, with a clear distinction between them in terms of what action is required, it is common for a separate form to be used. In such cases the format described above is reserved for non-compliances where corrective action is obligatory, with a new design used for observations and recommendations.

These new designs are typically no-action forms where there is no facility to record or track actions resulting from a finding. An example might be as shown in Figure 10.2. This has similar heading information to the corrective action request form seen earlier but only has the section of the form for recording the nature of the problem, and nothing else. Forms are sometimes created in this fashion because ensuing action is optional and thus it is felt that recording of what happens as a result has less meaning.

The problem with this approach is that it positively encourages observations and suggestions to be ignored. If there is no place on the form to write a response then it is a reasonable conclusion that no response is required and many managers will simply note the interesting comment and then do nothing with it. In practice I find that the system works much better where exactly the same form is used both for non-compliances and for less rigid requirements. A simple check box will allow the difference to be clearly distinguished. Managers will then be required to make a response to every finding, even if their answer to a recommendation is: 'After consideration, it is judged that this would cost more to implement than the projected savings over the next twelve months.' At least then there has been serious thought given to the issue, rather than having it just placed in a dead filing tray and ignored.

If, for operational or policy reasons, an organization wishes to have audit finding forms whose only purpose is to record observations, suggestions and others for which action need not necessarily be taken, it is a good idea to still have a place for the head of the area audited to record his or her response.

SUMMARY REPORTS

In the earlier chapter on preparation, I mentioned the creation of checklists and explained how they can be used as formal documents which remain part of audit

OBSERVATION FORM	
Audit description:	Date:
Audit team:	
Details of observation:	
Signed: (auditor)	

FIGURE 10.2   Observation form

records. Some organizations like to use these formal records of what was looked at and others like to make them simpler, keeping them just as auditor notes. The advantage of creating full checklists and retaining them after the audit is that these, together with the corrective action request forms or similar, can represent everything that is needed to record the audit.

This system is often used for internal audits but can be just as valid for audits where detailed records are especially essential, such as third party assessments. As long as there is sufficient header information in the checklists and enough space for the auditor to write down anything that needs to be recorded, then nothing else should be needed.

ISO 10011, though, suggests the creation of a summary report. For this reason, and probably because there is a vague feeling amongst many of us that we ought to write a proper written report of any important activity, many audit regimes also incorporate a separate document which is intended to provide a general description and summary of what has occurred.

The first and most obvious way of dealing with this requirement is simply to ask the audit team leader to prepare a full written report following the audit. The usual rules for structuring and preparing a report would then be followed and the report circulated to all interested parties. There is nothing wrong with this if it is desired and it does represent the best opportunity to have a full and detailed report from an enthusiastic lead auditor. It does have two disadvantages, though:

O   It can make life difficult for the audit team leader who has to go through the sometimes onerous task of planning and creating a report from scratch.

O   If there is no format and contents list specified, it can result in meaningless short reports in which the auditor simply writes a single sentence stating that the audit was conducted.

An alternative approach which helps to overcome these drawbacks is to define a standard format which predetermines what the report will look like. This makes it easier for the author to decide what to write about and avoids the agonies of deciding upon the contents page. It also can eliminate minimalistic reports, especially if the defined procedures insist that all titles in the standard layout must have attendant words.

There is a big choice as to how the standard format can appear. It is sometimes given as a set of paper forms or can equally be a word processor template or simply a sample report. It can vary from a single sheet to a weighty volume running to 20 pages or more. However it is organized, the objective is to provide a medium for the team leader to record:

O   the details of what the audit was and what it was for;

O   any formal records or decisions (such as recommendation to award a certificate);

○   points to bring to the audit programme manager's attention which cannot be recorded elsewhere.

If a summary report is chosen to be part of the audit reporting system, then it is no longer necessary to include formal checklists as an element of the report, unless, of course, there is a liking for them in the organization.

My own preference is to use checklists and action requests to make up the audit report, with fixed ways (such as separate, optional, forms) of recording special features such as recommendation to award a certificate or to amend the audit programme in some fashion. I do recognize, though, that written summaries can be useful. For example, I often meet consultants and other people conducting similar services who are desperate for some convenient and recognized way of passing messages back to the administration. Simple summary sheets of the sort that they might use can be of some benefit to auditors, too.

SOME POINTS TO REMEMBER

○   The report should not mention anything which was not raised at the verbal feedback session or closing meeting – it smacks of underhandedness.

○   The report should be limited to those things which will be directly interesting to both the head of the area audited and the audit programme coordinator; anything else will not be read and will reduce the chance of the interesting parts being noticed.

○   Bulk will be off-putting and will also discourage reading, so avoid title pages, contents lists, etc.

○   Standard clauses and wording also get in the way and will rarely be read, especially after the first time – if these are needed they should be communicated elsewhere, such as in a memo or letter before the start of the audit.

○   Do not write the findings out again in the summary report if they have already been written onto corrective action forms; this is a waste of time and space.

○   Make sure that the audit programme coordinator or the administrative team actually reads the report, so that messages from the audit team are actually dealt with, and the report is not simply something to be ticked off as complete.

○   Ensure that the audit report and associated papers are only sent to those who have a real need to see them. They should be sent to those who need to take or monitor action but not those who might use them as a reason for criticism or meaningless comparison between areas.

ALTERNATIVE FORMATS

The basic method of reporting as I have described above, using a flexible mixture of checklists, corrective action forms and summary reports, is a common approach. It is the way that I teach during audit courses since it will often be encountered by the auditors, can easily be adjusted to fit a variety of needs and is simple both to describe and to understand. There are, however, other approaches to the subject. Although the basic objective of the reporting format remains the same, the objective can be met in different ways. Some of these are described below.

THE FULLY AUTHORED REPORT

This is a conventional written business report. There are some audit regimes, typically for supplier audits which are often less systematic than other types, which define no standard formats or templates for the written report, including all findings requiring action. As a result, the audit team leader is required to create a full report of what was looked at, background details, findings and conclusions from scratch. Exactly what is covered by the report, and how, is left to the discretion of the audit team leader. Although some commonality between reports from different team leaders may emerge, human nature dictates that auditors will prefer their own styles and occasionally deliberately vary the format from those of others to emphasize their individuality.

Advantages are:

O the report can say as much or as little as the occasion demands, structured in any way appropriate;
O it can satisfy those who see standard forms as signs of excessive bureaucracy.

Disadvantages are:

O it requires more effort to write a report on a blank sheet of paper than on a pre-defined form;
O such reports take a while to produce and therefore will often appear some time after the audit is complete;
O without formal guidance, important elements could be omitted or the report could be over-burdened with unnecessary items;
O lack of standardization could make the report less easy to read (in that we will not know where to look for the information that we seek);
O there is nowhere to continue the report via recording what action is taken and the final sign-off;
O recording information which might have been in checklists requires reference to detailed notes which is both time-consuming and prone to error.

On balance this is not recommended, since the disadvantages above greatly out-weigh the advantages. The exception to this could be where audits are so rare that defining a standard format makes no sense; an example of this is the consultancy audit which is carried out once, with a specific objective in mind. Consultancy audits will typically use this report format rather than one of the more standard-ized versions.

THE TEMPLATE-BASED FULL REPORT

A more structured method than simply asking the audit team leader to go away and write a report is to provide a template for that report. The template could be in paper form or, more commonly these days, a word processor over-writeable document or macro. This makes constructing the report easier and removes many of the disadvantages. It still requires some effort, though, and will need transcrip-tion of previous notes and separate recording of actions. If the full written report is a preferred approach, however, using a template is much better than allowing freestyle authoring.

It is a good idea to define the template in such a way that it is clear to audit team leaders which parts have to be included and whether or not they must be format-ted in the way shown, and which are optional and may be written in or left out as circumstances dictate.

SINGLE FORMS

A reporting method used by those wishing to be seen to use as little paper as possible is the device of a single form to cover everything. These are usually vari-ations on the theme of the checklist form shown in Figure 8.1 (p. 158). The docu-ment has the facility to record the headline details of the audit (when, where, what, etc.), what was asked, what was seen and the results. This may need a redesign to include more space for results to be recorded than in my checklist example, but it is essentially the same. Sometimes the reverse side of the paper is used to record actions taken by the auditee management and sign-off by quality management.

The advantage of this approach is, as mentioned, that there is only one piece of paper involved which gives the impression of reducing bureaucracy. In practice, though, similar volumes of paper are used since the same amount of information still needs to be written down. There is the added disadvantage that the restricted space necessarily devoted to each written element can make the auditor's life dif-ficult and cause the final result to look messy. It also usually requires a separate system to be created to track actions and final verification of completion. Some auditors like the system, though, since they can manage the entire job with only one style of form.

I have seen this format used for internal audits but rarely for other types. It tends to be too informal for third party audits and too inflexible for the range of features found in supplier assessments. Even for internal audits it can suffice for compliance reports but may be inadequate for detailed descriptions of suggested improvements.

DEFINED HEADER PLUS FREESTYLE FINDINGS

A report format used by one of the certification bodies and becoming more popular in other areas is to have a single sheet for recording the audit essentials followed by a set of free-format sheets to record findings and recommendations. In this type of report the front sheet covers all of the necessary background information such as audit scope, date, team membership, location, purpose, identification and coverage. The findings sheets are then little more than lined paper which allow the auditors to record their findings as simply or as comprehensively as they wish.

This reporting style has the advantage that it still appears to be form-filling, so it does not require the effort of structuring a report, but still allows plenty of scope for the findings to be written just as the team leader requires on this occasion. It also allows the auditors to record what was looked at as background information to the finding, in addition to the basic objective evidence requirements, if they so wish. It also uses only as much paper as is needed for the results to be recorded, unlike the use of one-per-problem corrective action forms which use a whole sheet for simple recommendations even if no subsequent action is taken.

I do not teach this method in my courses since some see the approach as minimalistic and trainee auditors usually require, at first, something more highly structured. For mature auditors, though, it is a simple yet highly flexible approach and I have found it very easy to use on the few occasions that I have been exposed to it. Its only disadvantage is that, like other methods that employ the minimum of space, there is no in-built corrective action recording and tracking mechanism. Certification bodies that use it typically rely on separate action plans, prepared and followed up by the audited organization.

REPORT CIRCULATION AND STORAGE

At the beginning of this chapter I stated that the purpose of the report was to record findings so that action can be taken. This means that only those who are directly concerned with that action need to see it. I would suggest that the report only needs to go to the representative of the area or organization audited and the audit programme coordinator (and one to the client too, if this is someone different to the other two), for the following reasons:

○   The audit team should not need their own copies since they will do little with them until re-audit or the next visit, at which time they can obtain the coordinator's copy.

○   Responsibility for taking action should rest at a single point; sending copies to multiple recipients may confuse this.

○   Senior auditee managers who see audit reports are tempted to jump on the wrong things, such as counting the number of non-compliances or picking on a single finding and using it as an excuse for a witch hunt.

I believe that this last point is most important. Senior managers in the audited organization should never see audit reports, with the exception perhaps of the manager directly in charge of the area audited who may be responsible for taking corrective action. The specific audit findings are there for action to be taken by the process owners and not for comparison between departments or for performance measurement; they are not meant for that and serve that function very badly. If senior managers in the audited organization are interested in the results of audits then the quality manager should prepare an analysis of results and what they mean for circulation and discussion, summarizing the individual findings and drawing out points more appropriate for top level attention.

The final, official copy of any audit report, together with full results of findings, reviews and sign-offs, should reside with the audit programme coordinator. This is true whether the coordinator is not part of the audited organization, as in second and third party audits, or performs a directly related quality functional role, such as quality manager, for internal audit reports. The heads of the audited areas are likely to keep basic records for their own reference but there is no need for any further copies to be kept. It should be pointed out that certification bodies do not want copies of internal or customer audit reports; they would be swamped with paper if they tried to do that.

REPORT WRITING SKILLS

Some of the report formats described above require free-form text to be written, either within a broader structure or as completely unrestricted reportage. To create these well requires a skill which may not be natural to all of us. Although a full treatise on how to write reports could fill another book, it is worth mentioning a few points here. Both when deciding how to define our reports and when writing them, we need to remind ourselves of the purpose, to ensure that effective and timely action is taken. This means that the report should make it easy for those concerned to identify what the problem is and give them as much information as they need to carry out their investigations and improvements.

We have already discussed how to write the actual findings statements to achieve this, but there are also some general writing tips that should be borne in mind:

O   Make the findings and recommendations stand out from the general background data. These are what the managers want to read and they will lose interest if they are difficult to pick out from amongst the boring bits.

O   Ensure that the typing and spelling are correct; your credibility is reduced (and hence your findings taken less seriously) if you make basic mistakes – do not rely on word processor spell checkers which cannot detect all errors and anyway often have inherent flaws (my English dictionary says that civilization and organization are both spelt with a 'z' but my word processor thinks that only US English uses that spelling).

O   Take the same care with grammar and word meanings; if you are not sure then use a simpler word or shorter sentence construction (both of these are good ideas anyway). Even punctuation errors can prevent your findings from being directly acted upon, so learn the rules and avoid making it complicated.

O   Do not fill the report with words which add nothing but simply increase bulk. The auditee may become fed up with it and give up before he or she has reached the important parts.

O   Be very careful about the use of humour, it can be misunderstood and may detract from the serious points in the report. It is probably best to leave the jokes and witty observations until the next time that you see the auditee in person.

SUMMARY

O   An audit report has a number of purposes, the principal one being to remind the auditee what action has to be taken.

O   The verbal report, at the closing meeting, allows the fullest opportunity for explanation.

O   Non-compliance statements should be factual, specific, non-prescriptive, traceable and verifiable.

O   Observation and recommendation statements have similar rules but are usually written in a softer style.

O   Corrective action request (CAR) forms or similar designs are often used to record findings, but other means can be employed.

O   Observation and recommendation statements should be written in such a way that they require a positive response.

O   Summary reports with more written detail can be used if required but are not strictly necessary if the basic details are recorded elsewhere.

O   The report itself is not intended for wide circulation – a summary analysis should be prepared by the audit coordinator or quality manager if wider distribution is required.

O   Good report writing skills are necessary if anything more than form-filling is required as part of the reporting process.

11

AUDIT MANAGEMENT AND FOLLOW-UP

❖

THE AUDIT PROGRAMME COORDINATOR

In this book I have often referred to somebody called 'the audit programme coordinator'. This is, perhaps, a clumsy title but it usefully covers the roles that could be occupied by a number of different people, depending upon the nature of the organization conducting the audits.

Internal audit programmes are often coordinated, in conventional organizations, by the quality manager. Today, though, many companies that adopt ISO 9001 disciplines are not based around traditional manufacturing structures and therefore do not have personnel dedicated to quality control and quality assurance. In such cases the audit management role could be fulfilled by anybody who is willing to take on the responsibility. Even where there is a quality manager, or equivalent position, the audit programme can stand apart from the usual inspection and quality assurance activities and could still be controlled by another person. Similarly, the audit programme coordinator does not have to be the same person that manages the other ISO 9001 activities such as certification body liaison, document control and quality performance analysis. There are sometimes good arguments why it should be the same person, but it does not need to be if other choices are preferred. For example, in small organizations where the control of the quality management system rests with somebody with an already difficult job, the burden could be shared more widely by allocating audit coordination to somebody else as a self-contained responsibility.

Whoever occupies the role, internal audit programme coordination is not a full-time occupation. I suppose it is conceivable that a very large organization could have somebody who could be kept fully occupied just planning, controlling, analysing and following up audits but I have never encountered it.

For third party certification companies, audit coordination is a critical and central role. This could be an individual but is more likely to be a team for certifiers of any size. It is certainly a full-time role and represents the ability to keep track of the certification scope and status of all companies registered under their banner. They will have to remind the auditee and the assessor of the due dates, confirm the frequency and duration of audits, maintain records, evaluate acceptability and timeliness of responses, determine the implications of changes and queries, deal with breaches of contract and the inevitable hiccups, issue certificates, ensure authorizations are obtained as required, maintain assessor diaries and any other administrative and technical tasks required to support the assessors in the field.

It should be remembered that third party assessors will spend all of their time carrying out audits at client companies and so will not be able, themselves, to keep track of all administrative tasks. They are not even present in a single office and able to regularly speak on the telephone. They need, therefore, a capable and efficient coordination team to enable the individual assessments to run smoothly. Somebody also has to plan their time to make most efficient use of the assessment resource, which is both the main fee earner and operational capacity of the certifier. Assessors employed as sub-contractors can be more independent but this brings its own difficulties in terms of ensuring compliance to rules and culture, loyalty, image and tying them down to dates. There are also debates as to whether sub-contract assessors need more or less management effort than full-time employees (for example they look after their own tax, insurance and overheads but, on the other hand, are far less willing to do a little extra without being paid for it).

The coordination role in a third party certification body has to cover both administrative and technical responsibilities. The administrative role includes aspects such as planning and scheduling, record keeping, resourcing, certificate issue and so on. The technical role covers such things as deciding upon corrective action acceptability, agreeing scope wording, adjudicating on assessor uncertainties, judging assessor competence (i.e. is the assessor capable of auditing this particular type of organization) and adjudicating appeals. Some of these can be done by the assessor 'in their spare time' but much of it will need to be done at the office. Some certifiers will clearly split administrative and technical roles between different groups of people but smaller ones may combine them in the same team.

Audit coordination for second party audits is usually a simpler affair. The overall technical and administrative management can, and is, typically fulfilled by the assessment team themselves, perhaps with a little assistance from one or more members of the procurement function.

SCHEDULING

We have already discussed scheduling and how it should work in Chapter 7. This is definitely a task that needs to be centrally managed; divided responsibility is likely to lead to confusion and error. It has to combine the twin objectives of making good use of the available audit resource and ensuring that all audits are done adequately at the correct time.

For most audit regimes ensuring availability of resources is not a huge problem. If we have a number of trained auditors it is simply a case of agreeing when they will make themselves available. It is trickier, though, for certification bodies who need to plan for all audits to be done on time whilst ensuring 80–90 per cent utilization of assessment staff. If the planning is done badly and assessors end up with bands of time when they are not auditing, that time earns no income and can never be regained, yet the assessor costs money in salary and overheads. Sub-contract assessors, too, need strict scheduling since they are unlikely to be available at very short notice but will demand compensation (or will refuse further work) if given bookings at long notice which are subsequently cancelled or changed nearer the time. Enough flexibility must be built into the programme, though, to allow for late inevitable changes or to permit some client adjustments and offer reasonable lead times for new prospective clients. Scheduling under these circumstances is a major, continuous process which cannot be left to the assessors alone or performed by somebody who sees it as a sideline of secondary importance.

INDIVIDUAL AUDIT PLANNING

When each audit comes due, the person responsible for administration needs to:

○　　confirm how many are to be in the audit team and how long the audit should take;

○　　inform both the audit team and the auditee representative of the proposed agenda, including start and finish times (for most audits, apart from internal audits in small organizations, this is normally in writing);

○　　make all documentation available to the audit team, including definitions of scope and objectives for the audit, as well as the previous audit report and any relevant quality system documentation needed;

○　　collect all audit report and supporting documentation and file it correctly;

○　　enter details of required actions into the tracking system to ensure that they are followed up at the appropriate time;

○　　arrange dates for re-audit, if appropriate, with both auditee and audit team;

○　　diary forward the next scheduled audit.

There are also basic tasks which would need to be carried out for any meeting. These could be carried out by the audit team themselves or the administration coordinator, as appropriate to the organization's needs:

O   Obtaining the name and contact details of the auditee representative.
O   Providing instructions on what to do when they arrive (e.g. sign in at the north gate, or go to the second floor, or meet the area representative in conference room 7).
O   Book travel arrangements such as flights, rail tickets or car hire.
O   Ensure that adequate arrangements are made for meals and refreshments (e.g. the audit site may have no canteen or other catering facilities so auditors will need to make alternative provision for food).
O   Confirm that enough office facilities will be provided (a quiet area to write up notes and reports, photocopying, etc.).

The coordinator also acts as the central point for pre- and post-audit questions, clarification of arrangements, granting of certificates and approvals.

Perhaps the most important administration task is keeping track of which audits have been carried out, and filing the reports in such a way that they can be easily retrieved for subsequent use or inspection.

Since there are so many small details to remember here, it is a good idea for an audit programme administrator to be provided with checklists for each step to ensure that nothing is forgotten.

ACTION TRACKING

IDENTIFICATION OF ACTION

When the audit team reports their findings at the closing meeting, they will ask those responsible to identify what action is to be taken. This may be possible in some cases but often some investigation will be needed before the best course of action can be decided upon. When this happens, the audit team will usually take copies of the forms recording the findings and ask the head of the area audited to return the originals to the audit programme coordinator, after having filled in the proposed action and target completion date. A time limit is usually set for return of the forms – a week for internal audits, slightly longer for external audits.

CONFIRMATION OF ACTION

In order for the whole process to really work, it is not enough simply to identify a problem and have a manager promise to fix it. There also needs to be a system which monitors the progress of action, ensures that it has been taken when and how promised, and that it actually did the job.

The first thing that is needed, then, is a way of keeping track of which actions are outstanding and their current status. They could be in one of the following states:

○   Raised as an audit finding but with no identification yet from the auditee management as to how it will be dealt with.
○   A corrective action proposed with target timescales but not yet due for completion.
○   Completion time due but no action yet reported or verified.
○   Action reported as complete but not yet verified.
○   Action verified and closed.

The audit programme coordinator should have a procedure in place to help identify quickly the stage of each audit finding, with the opportunity to chase them up as they are due to move on to the next phase. The use of individual corrective action forms can be one easy way to achieve this since they can be moved from one file, or section of a file, to another as the action progresses. Other systems can involve diaries, electronic schedulers, purpose-designed databases or simply a form upon which the progress is written at each stage. This tracking system is key to the whole audit programme since, without it, the findings so carefully winkled out by auditors will not be acted upon.

Note that it should be the coordinator who keeps track of actions, not the auditor. Auditors are employed to conduct the examination phase of an audit, either as often as possible to make most efficient use of their time or, for example, with most internal auditors, as an occasional duty away from their main role. In either case, to try to monitor the progress of actions would, for the auditor, be a distraction. Full-time auditors would have to devote time to it which could otherwise be spent in 'productive' audits and part-time auditors would find it an irksome distraction or probably even forget about it.

Somebody will also need to check that the action proposed by the auditee is reasonable. Whether through subterfuge, sloth or simple human nature, it will often be tempting to minimize the action required, thus also minimizing the amount of effort needed. Or it could simply be that the action proposed is based upon some misunderstanding or will clearly not serve the purpose. It is, of course, up to the head of the area or organization audited what action should be taken, but somebody with authority should be able to review what is intended and decide whether it is good enough. If the audit programme coordinator is also the quality system manager, or is otherwise technically responsible for reviewing actions, then it could be they who perform this task. If the coordinator's role is primarily administrative, however, then the action will need to be submitted to the auditor, or some other suitably qualified person, to perform the review. Note that the reviewer must be somebody with sufficient 'clout' in the organization to ensure that their views are respected and that they are able to have an action changed if it is not suitable.

FOLLOW-UP REVIEW OR AUDIT

When the coordinator is informed that the action is complete (which is likely to have to be chased up as part of the monitoring and tracking process) it is not sufficient simply to tick off the action in the tracking system. It must first be verified that the action has actually been taken in an appropriate manner. Again, this must be done by somebody with the technical ability and organizational authority to make their voice heard.

Often it is possible to decide upon whether the action is complete and appropriate from the information that is supplied on the corrective action sheet and any accompanying, supporting data. This approach can be taken if the action involves only amendment of procedural documentation, or is minor in nature. If the issue is more severe, or is complex in nature and cannot be verified from documentation, such as protection of materials or tidying up files, then it may be necessary to ask for a re-audit. Certification bodies have fixed rules that major non-compliances require a re-audit and minor ones do not. Other audit systems can afford to be more flexible and it can be left up to the programme coordinator to decide whether or not a re-audit is required. As re-audits can be disruptive, and unpopular with auditees, it may be a good idea to define guidelines as to when a re-audit is and is not required, allowing some discretion on the part of the coordinator to provide reasonable flexibility.

The purpose of a re-audit is only to confirm that the required actions have been completed and that they were effective. A re-audit does not usually look at new topics; this would then be a new audit. It is conducted in a similar way to the original audit: it requires preparation and verbal introductions and feedback; auditors ask general questions about the topic under investigation and compare the answers to what they would expect to be happening.

If the re-audit discovers that all actions have been completed satisfactorily, then the findings from the previous audit are simply signed off. If not, then it is usual for a new corrective action request to be raised to record that there is further action outstanding. It should be pointed out that the fact that the action has not been completed may not simply be a result of negligence or sloth. Sometimes legitimate factors have prevented the action being taken, or investigation has revealed that the proposed action would not have been effective and the search for the most appropriate alternative action is not yet complete.

Where there is something at stake, such as contract approval or certification, then the audit team needs to make a decision if the action is not fully complete. They should ask whether the organization or area has done enough to bring a degree of control back to the issue, with good prospects for further improvement in the future, or whether the situation is little better than seen at the original audit. Written guidelines for auditors on how to respond to this situation would be a good idea, but remember not to make them so rigid as to remove any possibility of credit for action which has been mostly, if not fully, effective.

It must be especially remembered that re-audit may not always be necessary. It is time-consuming, expensive and disruptive so if the action can be verified via documentation or is minor enough to wait until the next scheduled audit then there should be no need to re-audit.

Note that re-audit does not need to be conducted by the same auditor or audit team that conducted the original audit. It is usually a good idea if this can be achieved, but practicalities may mean that another person or team has to be chosen; in particular internal re-audits are conducted, as often as not, by the quality manager or audit programme coordinator.

VERIFICATION OF EFFECTIVENESS

When actions from prior audits are being checked or re-audited, it is often not enough simply to check whether or not the promised tasks and corrections have been completed. Auditors and audit coordinators also must confirm that they achieved the intended result. For example, a manager may promise to remind staff of the correct procedures as a result of an audit finding. While you can confirm that the reminder was issued, a large question remains (especially with actions of this nature) whether staff truly are now aware. This can only be confirmed by re-audit of the people involved to identify how aware they are.

It is most important that the procedures used for the audit process cover confirmation that the action has not only been taken but has been effective. The flexibility of review by the coordinator, re-audit or checking at the next scheduled audit remains, as long as the effectiveness is checked at some point in the audit cycle.

NON-COMPLIANCE ARBITRATION

Although it should not happen if everybody takes a reasonable approach and the auditors investigate properly before suggesting anything, there may be occasions where auditors raise a non-compliance, observation, suggestion or recommendation with which the auditee management do not agree. If they convince the auditors that they were mistaken or the suggestion would not work, then there is no further problem. If, however, the auditors insist that it is a point which requires action and the management insist that it is not, then we have an impasse. If two people decide to take up opposing positions it can become increasingly difficult for them, as the argument progresses, to back down and accept the other's point of view. If this happens there must be an escalation route, a method of referring the issue to someone else who can arbitrate and make an appropriate decision.

In certification audits, this arbitrator is typically the technical coordinator, or a senior manager, of the certification body. If the management of the certified organization feel that they have been unfairly treated by the auditor who has insisted upon something with which they not only disagree but which they feel will cause them actual harm by acting upon, then they should have someone to whom they can appeal. This person needs to be identified in documented procedures and communicated to the client as part of the contractual arrangements. In extreme cases, where the organization is still not satisfied with the response from this arbitration, there is a right of appeal to the accreditation body which grants the certifiers their authority. This procedure should only be used in extremis, however, since it destroys the relationship. Organizations may also find that the accreditation body may decline to comment upon individual circumstances in many cases and only judge upon whether the certifiers have acted in a professional and appropriate manner.

Auditees being examined by representatives of their customers can refer contentious issues to senior managers within the customer's organization but again must recognize that complaining about an auditor's judgement could damage relationships. They will, in any case, have to accept the decision of the most senior customer manager who will take an interest in the issue, since there is no higher authority in this case.

Of course, managers who remain dissatisfied with audit findings after all appeal avenues have been exhausted do have one further sanction. They could decide to forget the whole thing. It is possible to reach the conclusion that this customer is not worth doing business with (although one should carefully balance the inconvenience of doing what the auditor asks against the possible loss of business). Similarly those seeking certification could opt not to seek a certificate or decide to pick a different certification body.

Managers involved in internal audits also need a route to escalate the issue. If they feel that the auditor has made an error of judgement or is being unnecessarily pedantic, then they must be able to ask somebody else to strike the action from the system. A typical escalation route here is via the quality manager/audit programme coordinator upwards to one or more senior managers who will make the final choice. As before, exactly who should be involved and how the progression works should be the subject of documented procedures.

It is worth bearing in mind that the arbitration and escalation procedures in all audits exist for the benefit of auditors as well as auditees. Auditors faced with a strong manager who refuses to accept a finding often need some backup to help reinforce their position, especially in the case of internal audits where the auditee manager may have an apparently more influential position in the organization than the auditor. Choosing auditors of the right stature and calibre can help to resolve this, but ensuring that they can be supported by the most senior people in the company will resolve any impasses in those rare and extreme occasions where they occur.

BUSINESS-WIDE ISSUES

Another arbitration function that the coordinator may need to fulfil in an internal audit programme is to raise points which cannot be addressed by the auditee management. This may often happen if the auditor finds something that needs to be actioned but is outside the scope of authority of the head of the area audited. The coordinator should then ensure that ownership is given to the appropriate person, either directly or via senior management as appropriate to the organization.

This can also apply, in a slightly different form, to supplier audits. In some cases issues may arise from the audit of a supplier that are not the responsibility of the supplier organization but need to be addressed by the auditor's management (the customer). In such cases the audit team should raise the point with the audit programme coordinator who can then take it up with the appropriate person.

RESOURCE MANAGEMENT

Planning and use of audit resources (i.e. the auditors that are at your disposal) have a different emphasis, depending upon whether the auditors fulfil the role full time or have other jobs and only carry out audits occasionally. I have, therefore, dealt with the two areas separately.

FULL-TIME AUDITORS

I have already indicated that any organization employing full-time auditors will need to make most effective use of the time available whilst allowing flexibility for programme changes and time for the auditor to pursue continuing professional development and carry out some basic administrative tasks.

Certainly good use of the auditor's time is a key objective. As with any other professionals that sell their time, such as consultants, lawyers, etc., an essential planning activity is to decide the number of bookable hours or days per year that is required to make the job commercially viable. For example, let us look at the example of a certification assessor who costs his employer £36 000 per year (including overheads, car, expenses, support costs and so on) and whose time is charged to clients at £500 per day. Of course, not all of that £500 is available to cover assessor costs, so let us assume that £200 is for the auditor. A simple sum shows us that each assessor needs to spend 180 days per year carrying out paid audits. Allowing for company and public holidays, there are about 225 useful working days per year, which leaves almost a day per week for administration, training and emergencies. Since this does not look unreasonable, then we can consider that 180 days would be acceptable for a target minimum utilization.

This schedule needs to be carefully managed. If enthusiastic audit programme coordinators book every day of an auditor's free time they are likely to run into trouble if there is a change of schedule, sickness or the need to fit in unpredicted audits (such as re-audits to review major non-compliances). The biggest implication is in the planning horizon. Booking up auditors' time six months in advance is probably impractical and will result in problems. If the re-audit timescale, or the lead time promised new customers, is six weeks then auditors will need some spare slots six weeks hence.

It is going too far, though, to try to allow for short-term sickness. I was once in discussion with a Middle East client, who expressed concern about my ability, as a one man business, to meet my commitments in the event of sickness. It was an unfair question that no organization could have satisfactorily answered since no matter how many staff are employed, it is impossible to meet a commitment to a client or department when the appointed auditor calls in sick on the morning of the audit. Since this is the case, there is no point in even trying to accommodate it.

The other resource issue where full-time auditors are employed is the question of how many auditors to employ and their range of experience. A simple sum is to predict the number of days auditing required for the coming period and divide that by the target utilization rate for each auditor. This should then result in the number of auditors that need to be employed. It is not as simple as that, though. This calculation takes no account of possible sickness, significant changes in the number of audits required (such as a burst of new certification clients as a result of a marketing drive), peaks and troughs in workload or the fact that auditors are expected to have some experience of the specific organization or area that they are examining. If you only have a few audits which require a particular specialization then you need to take account of this somehow.

Some audit organizations cope with this by using extra auditors on an ad hoc basis. These can be freelance consultants for a certification body or other trained personnel who will step in when asked to assist a full-time internal or supplier audit function. Including the use of outsiders can be particularly useful where some audits require special skills, experience or qualifications but where these are too few to make it worth a full-time auditor pursuing the necessary development and training. This appoach has great flexibility advantages but can result in auditors who are less familiar with the processes than the full-time team. If this approach is not taken (some organizations feel uncomfortable with the use of sub-contract workers) then other approaches designed to cope with the demands of the overall programme could be:

○   to make the utilization target low enough to cope with workload peaks and unexpected changes;
○   to create some coordination jobs in the auditing organization whose occupants are chosen to also be able to carry out audits as and when required;
○   to limit the scope of work to reduce the variation of skills needed;
○   to strictly limit the number of audits that will be conducted.

This issue also has implications for resource planning in terms of how many auditors will be recruited and the skills mix that will be expected from them, as well as development requirements for existing auditors. Some form of skills matrix, showing the list of skills needed and how many auditors possess each, can be a useful tool to help with resource planning.

Note that where the frequent use of teams of more than one auditor exists, this makes planning and coordination more difficult and thus will probably reduce the overall possible utilization rate of audit staff.

PART-TIME AUDITORS

Resource planning where the auditors have other roles and only carry out audits occasionally is simpler. Making use of their time and balancing usage against flexibility is not an issue; audits not carried out on the planned date do not usually mean lost time but can simply be rescheduled with no loss of resource.

The main area for consideration here is to pick a suitable number of active auditors to make up the total available resource. Choosing the number should take the following factors into account:

O   There must be enough auditors to enable the audits to be completed without over-burdening any of them.

O   Each auditor should be able to spend enough time auditing per year to keep their skills up to date.

O   Some sickness and wastage will occur, as well as the common problem of auditors complaining that they are too busy with their full-time jobs, so some fat will be needed to allow for this – although temporary resource shortages are not as big a problem here as they might be with full-time auditors since rescheduling is always an option.

O   Just as with full-time staff, the part-time audit team will need to contain the right balance of skills to cover the schedule – there remains the problem of how to cope with this if one skill set is only needed rarely, and again the use of some outside resource may be appropriate here.

O   The available set needs to be large enough for internal audits to ensure that independence is guaranteed and that nobody audits areas of their own responsibility.

AUDIT ANALYSIS AND REPORTING

The prime purpose of audits is to identify actions which should be carried out by management to correct problems or implement improvements. It should never be forgotten that this low level objective is what audits are for, especially when carrying out analyses of results or preparing reports for senior management.

In particular, the position should be avoided where senior managers are given the opportunity to count non-compliances. Where audit findings are reported by giving the quantity of corrective action requests raised, and managers allowed to make judgements based on this, the value of the process is immediately reduced. If we judge audit performance based on numbers of findings, the following disadvantages arise:

○   We know that we will be criticized if the numbers appear high, therefore we will try to minimize the numbers by keeping things from auditors and by arguing with them about the points that they do uncover. For internal audits where we are looking for maximum communication to identify improvements this can be counter-productive and it could even be the areas which have the most actions to take that are doing the most to achieve corporate objectives.

○   The numbers are meaningless anyway since even if we categorize our findings we still cannot tell within each category how severe the problem is – 'none of the staff have ever been trained in how to do their jobs' and 'there are no records of any of the training that the staff have received' would both represent certification major non-compliances but one is obviously a bigger problem than the other, yet both are counted as 'one' if we report numbers.

○   Even ignoring the above drawbacks, there is still the question of what we do about number counts – if one department has received seven action requests, the second six and the third five, what further action does this prompt us to take?

Similarly, reporting numbers of non-compliances against the requirement reference of ISO 9001 is relatively meaningless. Certification assessors are probably expected to do so since they are auditing directly against requirements of the standard but even then one wonders what use it is, other than to assist the audit team to identify whether or not so many individual problems have been found in one aspect of the business that the raising of a major non-compliance is warranted. For other auditors, who are auditing against specific requirements rather than the standard, this form of analysis is meaningless (and anyway most auditors will make errors in assigning the reference which makes the analysis even worse).

In fact the best type of analysis is to concentrate on final results rather than the outcome of the examination phase of the audit. In order to let everyone know how successful and useful the audits have been we should only report the final consequences once actions are complete, which could include such outomes as:

○   an improvement to a process resulting in reduced costs, timescales, etc.;
○   new or continued ISO 9001 certification;
○   new or continued approval by a customer;
○   an activity or process which we have had to introduce in order to maintain certification or customer approval.

The fourth of these represents a negative result, whereas the others are positive (good) outcomes.

The only other issues worth reporting to senior management are those which cannot be resolved and need high level attention. Even here, though, these are probably better left to the escalation process and only to be formally reported as part of a general analysis when they have been resolved one way or the other.

MANAGEMENT REVIEW

Management review is careful consideration by senior management of the organization of recent quality performance, actions that are needed as a result and how future developments are likely to impact quality and customer service. It has a number of purposes within a quality management system, one of which is to look at the internal audit programme.

It should not be the job of the review to compare audit results, count non-compliances or level any criticism. On the other hand, it can usefully:

O   decide whether the overall approach is doing the job and how it could be improved;

O   consider what benefits have been produced by the programme since the last review (which can, if nothing else, help to sell the audit regime internally);

O   suggest further business activities or elements which could usefully be looked at by internal audits;

O   see how the lessons learnt can be put to wider use;

O   indicate continued high level support for the programme.

The audit programme coordinator is the best person to implement any actions arising from the review, with commitment and support from senior management.

EXTERNAL AUDIT MANAGEMENT REVIEW

Although we normally think of management review as being related to internal audits as part of an ISO 9001 system, a regular audit management review is also a very good idea for external programmes. These will not usually look at the actions that have been taken as a result of audits as they were carried out in, and produced the benefits for, other organizations. They can be useful, though, to consider how the programme is conducted and what improvements could be made as well as what lessons have been learnt and how these can be applied to improve future audits. Future resource planning could also be discussed here to provide top level commitment to future resource needs.

SUMMARY

O   The audit programme coordinator is the person who controls the whole audit regime for any organization.

○   The coordinator is likely to be the quality manager for internal audits, the procurement manager for supplier audits, and can be split between a number of people in a certification body.

○   A schedule needs to cover everything that has to be examined.

○   The schedule should be specific enough to allow reasonable planning but flexible enough to allow for changes and the reluctance to set dates too far in the future.

○   Some coordination support for individual audits is needed in terms of agreeing times, arrangements and travel.

○   Action tracking is a key coordination activity, keeping abreast of progress.

○   The audit team may assist the coordinator with technical evaluation of actions.

○   Best use should be made of resources, particularly the efficient utilization of full-time audit staff.

○   Some technical arbitration of actions is required when auditors and auditees cannot agree or when action cannot be taken by auditees.

○   Careful analysis of what the findings are and what they mean is necessary to make the best use of audit results.

○   Management review should not look at individual audit results but should look for improvements to audit effectiveness, both for internal and external audit programmes.

12
TECHNIQUES

❖

THE NEED FOR AUDIT TECHNIQUES

In every job that we do we need to make sure that we understand the tools of the trade and learn the techniques which will make it successful. Auditing is no different. There are various things that we can do, building upon the basics that we have already discussed, which can make the difference between a good audit and a mediocre one. Much of what is often discussed as good audit technique should come almost automatically to those who are experienced and do it all the time – just as established lorry drivers know without thinking how to manoeuvre and reverse their vehicles, even though new trainees have to study the way do it at length and initially find it very difficult. Those who are new to the role, or who only act as auditors occasionally, will probably need to remind themselves of how to obtain the best from the activity each time that they are asked to join an audit team or conduct their own investigation.

I should emphasize, though, that auditing is not a game. We are not learning techniques so that we can trick interviewees into revealing secrets, or phrasing things in such a way that we can get one over on the people in charge of the system that we are examining. The techniques are about learning to do things well.

In some respects, auditing is a 'hard' skill. That is to say, it follows a set of rules and we could flow-chart the process showing one step following after another. Thus on training courses I often display a slide showing a chart similar to that shown in Figure 12.1.

I also tell trainees (who are often nervous about having to pass an examination or continuous assessment) that they probably already possess the basic skills and all that auditing requires is a knowledge of the framework used. This is all true; most of the personal skills required are simply common sense. As with any other business practice, however, we can always work on our personal skills

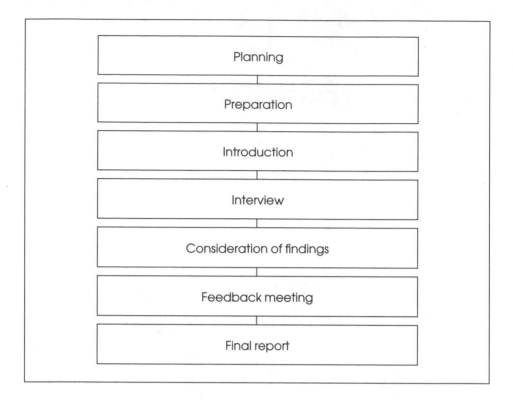

FIGURE 12.1   Audit steps

to enhance them and increase our performance in the role. The personal skills needed by auditors do not represent any particularly advanced level of behavioural change. They are usually a simple application of tools and approaches that are taught in a variety of other disciplines where interface and personal effectiveness skills matter (people management, project management, presentations skills, holding meetings and interviewing, to name but a few).

It follows that although auditing is carried out against a firm set of rules, there are a number of 'soft' skills that are needed to make it work well. I have tried to pick out a number of themes that teams in all types of audit need to think about and describe them in enough detail for new auditors to gain an understanding of what they have to take into account. I cannot, though, pretend to have covered every detail of the topics indicated by this chapter's headings. Most of the subjects have been the topic of books or training courses in their own right and there is certainly not room here to explore them to their fullest extent. What I have tried to do is distil the essence of each one to remind readers of what they must take account of during all stages of the audit.

TIME MANAGEMENT

A problem, these days, is that we never seem to have enough time to do anything. Despite a multitude of labour-saving technology both at home and at work, we still feel that we are rushing around to do as much as we can, and becoming over-stressed by the things that we cannot. We are told that this is a modern phenomenon; I am probably not qualified to judge but it does seem that we lead a more hectic life than is portrayed by idyllic pictures of the past.

We are, then, all used to having to manage our time to make the most of it. The more hectic we become, the more that time has to be managed well. This is certainly being recognized in industry: as long ago as 1980 my employer at the time decided to send every office worker on a time management course to enable them to make better use of the limited hours in a week and so that everybody had a common approach. This worked quite well and resulted in far fewer annoying distractions and niggles in a day than we had previously experienced.

Auditors, too, need to carefully plan and use their time. Audits are usually of limited duration, either fixed by the timings that have been agreed with the auditees, or by availability of the audit team, or both. This means that the entire scope of the audit has to be covered within deadlines and there is no time to waste.

The most important point, then, is simply to be aware of the passage of time. There is much to examine so the audit team need to be prepared to plough through it without spending longer than they need to. Once you have covered everything that you need to under one topic, it is time to move on, not to stay and look at more because the interviewees are being cooperative or there is so much that is interesting to see. And there will certainly be interesting things to see. I am always interested to see how much things cost or sell for and could easily be distracted by exploring that topic, which usually has nothing to do with the audit, if I did not stay alert for potential stealers of my time.

TIME-WASTING

Everyone new to the subject is always warned of deliberate time-wasting. This is certainly something that every external auditor will encounter at some point, although it is less of a phenomenon with internal auditing. Auditees who have something at stake, such as an ISO 9001 certificate or a customer contract, recognize that auditing is very much a negative activity: the more auditors look at the more 'bad' things they will find. Thus it is in the auditee's interest to minimize what auditors do actually get to look at. The amount and nature of time-wasting that results ranges from those who permit a wastage of time to those who deliberately make it happen.

Permitting time to be lost without any sense of urgency can include:

○   answering telephone calls or dealing with visitors in depth and detail, without mentioning that there is an audit in progress and asking the caller to call back later;

○   stopping to discuss something with people in the corridor;

○   checking for messages every time that they return to their desk;

○   insisting upon taking breaks in the canteen or cafeteria rather than taking drinks at the workplace (where it is permitted);

○   not having things ready such as documentation, loan safety clothing for the auditor's use, security passes and so on;

○   not preparing transport arrangements in advance;

○   not having a quiet area already set aside for the auditors to study documentation, hold audit team discussions or write up notes;

○   allowing the auditor to hold forth on his or her favourite topic.

Worse, though, are deliberate efforts to use up the audit time on non-audit activities. These can include:

○   taking the 'pretty route' (the long way round) from one place to another;

○   constantly offering excessive quantities of hot drinks;

○   deliberately asking potential interviewees to take their time in arriving;

○   giving the standard company background slide presentation or showing the latest promotional video (sometimes this might be genuinely thought of as being of interest to the audit team, although it is hoped that this would have been covered at early information gathering stages and would not be part of the examination phase);

○   talking a lot, during both meetings and interviews, including enthusing about new or intended business initiatives;

○   pretending not to be able to find files or computer records until the last minute;

○   questioning everything that the auditor says;

○   insisting upon showing the auditor things in greater detail than they have been asked for;

○   encouraging the auditor to hold forth on his or her favourite topic.

Good auditors are aware of these tactics. They are less likely to be used on internal auditors but even they may experience the unintentional wastage of time. As I have said, simply being aware of the passage of time can solve many of these problems, as can careful planning and preparation. Naturally garrulous auditors should watch out for those who allow or even encourage them to talk about their pet subject; it is tempting to do because it seems as if people are interested – they are not; they are simply pleased that you are talking about something other than the possible faults in their systems.

REPEATING A FINDING

Some sources of wasted time can be created by the auditors themselves. For example, many new or inexperienced auditors are often pleased that they have actually found something worth recommending to the auditee management. They are so pleased with it, in fact, that they keep finding it again and again:

Auditor: 'I see this form here isn't countersigned by the head of department.'
Auditee: 'Oh yes, you're right. I think we've fallen out of the habit of doing that.'
Auditor: 'Ah, well it says you should in the procedure, so I'll be including that in my report. Look, this one's the same.'
Auditee: 'Yes, as I told you, you'll find most of the recent ones are like that.'
Auditor: 'And here's another one.'
Auditee: 'Yes, I know.'
Auditor: 'And another one!'
Auditee: *Deep sigh*

In such cases auditors may be delighted to keep being able to point out that there is a problem but they are wasting time, and upsetting the auditee into the bargain, if they keep pointing out the same thing once they have found it. Each problem can only be reported once and when an auditor has decided that it truly is a problem, he or she does not need to keep finding fresh examples. Remember that it is not the auditor's job to find out exactly how many things are wrong in the area, simply to give the management concerned a pointer to which areas require investigation and corrective action.

FAILING TO FINISH

Failing to cover everything within the audit scope is not a good idea since it tends to disrupt the system. In extreme cases, such as initial certification assessments, it can be disastrous since assessors cannot really recommend certification if they have not looked at all key aspects, yet the arrangements probably prevent them coming back later to finish off. This is why good planning, preparation and time management are essential.

Failing to finish is a little less of a problem for internal audits where another audit can always be arranged and there is nothing directly at stake. In fact I often tell internal audit trainees that if they run into this problem then it is better to investigate one area well and identify real improvements than skimp or try to extend the audit duration and upset other plans. Really, though, it is better to plan and manage so that the problem does not arise in the first place.

CONDUCT OF MEETINGS

We have already dealt with the details of how to conduct opening and closing meetings in Chapter 9. The requirements explained there are based upon the assumption that standard good meetings practice is also adopted as appropriate.

In fact this is a good thing to bear in mind – these are actually business meetings, not presentations or lectures. We must understand, therefore, that those present at the meeting will expect to ask questions, debate issues, explore possibilities and identify courses of action just as they would at any other business meeting. Auditors must not see the meeting as simply an opportunity for them to hold court, but accept that those present will actually speak and wish to discuss any points raised.

The usual rules for running good meetings apply. This is a large subject but the following points are pertinent:

O   Start on time – the audit team leader must arrange to be there on time and not wait for late arrivals (although a good compromise if someone like the CEO is late is to begin by dealing with the minor issues and formalities).

O   Do not allow anyone to waste time by boring the meeting to death about their pet subject when it is not contributing to the purpose of the meeting.

O   Try to ensure that everyone in the room understands what is agreed; take note if somebody feels uncomfortable but has not actually said so.

O   Use a checklist or written agendas to ensure that every intended item is covered.

O   Keep detailed explanations or discussions for a separate meeting or for written reports. (I once witnessed an auditor and auditee have a lengthy discussion of the technicalities of static electricity precautions which took up much of the available time but was of little interest to anyone other than the two experts.)

O   Give attendees an idea, in advance, of how long the meeting will last and manage the progress to try to see that it does not substantially overrun (but allow enough time and avoid the temptation of many auditors, especially external teams, to shorten the meeting to allow them to start the journey home sooner, leaving the auditees shell-shocked after a barrage of non-compliance reports).

QUESTIONING

The most important thing to remember about auditor's questions is that those used at the start of interviews must be general, open questions. These are intended to start the interviewee talking to gain the maximum of information. Later questions, when you are seeking more specific information, can look for yes or no answers but if you use them at the early stages then you will gain little more than a basic understanding of compliance with procedure documents. You will then not identify if there are things being done other than those in the documents or if there are problem areas that need further investigation.

Good questions which lead to long answers and the widest set of data will arise naturally from a strong sense of curiosity. If the auditor is genuinely interested in how the processes work and wants to find out more then the whole interview will go smoothly. Any auditor worthy of the name should either be really interested in what is being studied or be able to fire that interest in themselves as part of the audit process. Certainly those who are simply going through the motions and asking standard questions for the sake of it, rather than because they are interested in the answers, should ask themselves whether the role is right for them. The skill in auditing is to use natural curiosity and eagerness to find out how other people do things (yes, there is an inevitable element of nosiness associated with this), to explore the issues that are relevant without allowing digression down avenues of self-indulgence. My own weakness is to be interested in the relationships between the organization that I am auditing and others with whom I have had contact over the years. If I find one that is a supplier to the auditee then I am most inquisitive about their perceived level of performance and the amount of business that is transacted. In many cases, though, this has little do with the purpose of the audit and I have to steel myself to direct my curiosity towards more relevant topics.

If, however, an auditor can make the interview more of a good chat than an interrogation this will be far more effective than any set of pre-prepared questions, however good they might be. It also makes the interviewee more at ease and more likely to provide information.

A few other specific points are worth making. I have given some sample auditor questions below to illustrate these:

1. *'I wonder if you could tell me what training you need for this job, where that training is recorded, how you re-evaluate training needs and what other departments directly interface with you?'*
   This is actually several questions and the likely result is that the interviewee will immediately become confused. Even if you ask just two questions together, you are only likely to receive an answer to one of them, usually the easiest one.

2. *'Do you have a special way of doing this?'*
   Although it is intended to elicit information, this question is closed and could be answered with a simple 'yes', which would cause an embarrassment and reduce communication since it would be obvious that either the auditor or auditee is being obstructive.

3. *'Are you really telling me that you haven't even had any basic report writing training?'*
   Never use a question to make a criticism, even an indirect or subtle one. Although we often suggest that the word 'why' is a great way of identifying potential improvements, this does need to be used with care since it can sound like a criticism: 'Why haven't you done it?'

If you do ever finding yourself making one of these mistakes, mentally give yourself a slap on the wrist and follow it up with another question, designed to gain the information that you were after or correct any false impressions that you may have given.

LISTENING

Good questioning skills are all very well, but they are only useful if combined with excellent listening ability. After all, a question is only of use if we listen to the answer and it provides us with the information that we need. Most of us have heard of the saying that is attributed to an old Chinese proverb: we have one mouth and two ears and we should use them in proportion.

Auditors should certainly be prepared to listen more than they talk. In fact if talkative interviewees are encountered then the auditor may elect to say almost nothing, only seeking clarification occasionally and asking them to move on to a new point if they begin to waffle or talk about something outside the auditor's area of current interest. You should avoid the danger of assuming that your questions are all-important. Badly done, an audit can become a series of clever questions to which you never hear the answers because you are too busy thinking about the next question while the previous one is being answered.

I mentioned above that the best questioning comes out of an interest in the subject and a desire to know more. The same applies to listening. Those who are thought of as being good listeners are those who show an interest in what is being said. It should be noted that such people are rarely silent sitters who simply sit there and let us talk at them. Indeed, we tend to gain the impression that those who sit there unresponsively have not heard a word that we have said. In fact most good listeners participate actively in the conversation by giving constant feedback signals to show that they have received the message.

We can equate this to a computer communications link. When computers 'speak' they do not rely on one sending and the other sitting quietly and hoping that the information is received accurately. There is a constant handshaking between the two where the sending computer paragraphs its conversation by explaining that each packet is now complete and it is ready to send another. The receiving machine continually sends messages back saying whether or not it believes it understood the last packet. Then at the end of the communication the receiving computer sends a checksum which the other computer can compare against its own summary calculation of what it sent, thus making sure that they have confirmed understanding.

People can also do this. It is quite possible for an individual to reflect little pieces of the message back as they are being spoken to. This acknowledges the other person's input, enforces careful attention since we have to pick out the key pieces of the message and repeat them and reinforces the message in our minds (I find that I am much more likely to remember a telephone number, for example, if

I say it out loud than just read or hear it). If we can also summarize at the end of a conversation that will double the effect: 'So if I understand you correctly, how it works is . . .'

If our summary is good then it again reinforces the message in our memory and lets the other person know that we really were listening, so that they are likely to be pleased at our interest and attention and tell us more. If it is a poor summary then it lets the other person know and they are able to put us right.

This active listening can also be of great help on those occasions when we are tired or listening to something with which we are very familiar, as it helps us to concentrate. A final warning, though, is not to be tempted to go too far with it. An acquaintance of mine continually makes little 'mmm, mmm' noises as one speaks to her. It is her unconscious method of active listening but is so frequent that it is off-putting and damages, rather than improves, communication.

NON-VERBAL COMMUNICATION

I have to put something about this here. Every audit training course I have ever seen and any major text on the subject that I have read all have some explanation of the importance of body language. Auditors should carefully watch the body posture and facial signals of their interviewees, the accepted wisdom goes, to identify if there is anything that they are trying to hide or if there is any issue which makes them feel uncomfortable. Such signs, we are told, could even let us know whether or not a person is telling us lies.

As far as I can tell from my understanding of the subject, body language is real and its analysis can be relatively scientific. That is, there are signs that we give that tell how we are feeling and thinking. The problem for most of us, however, is that the technique relies on probabilities and signal clusters. If we see a single sign that means one particular thing then we only have a tiny probability that the person we are speaking to is exhibiting the behaviour that the sign indicates. It is only when we see a cluster (i.e. several) of those signs together that we begin to have a good probability of interpreting the signs correctly. Even at its most effective, the technique only provides us with probabilities, not certainties, which must be carefully understood by anybody wishing to use it during an audit. The difficulty level is increased by the fact that some signs can mean more than one thing and only become meaningful when seen in the context of a related sign cluster.

This means that auditors wishing to include body language interpretation as part of their interview approach must become expert at knowing and spotting each sign and what it means. They then have to practise adroitly watching for those signs and interpreting them without the subjects knowing about it (if they know what we are doing then this in itself will change their behaviour). This must be managed whilst simultaneously asking good questions, being an active listener, taking notes, acting upon internal alarm bells, remembering what we have understood about the processes and plans so far and referring to our checklist.

As a result I recommend that body language needs to be studied with a view to becoming an expert before it can be interpreted in an audit. If you are not an expert, then I would suggest that you ignore any little snippets that you may have picked up on the subject as they can be dangerous. For example, I once watched a popular training video on the subject where it was suggested that touching one's nose indicates untruth. In fact it could just mean that I have an itchy nose but the interview could take a turn for the worse if the auditor mistakenly assumes that I am lying as a result of my rubbing it two or three times.

I should add that today's world is increasingly coming to resemble the global village that we hear so much about, so that many of us work in multi-racial and multi-cultural environments. As each culture has its own variations on body language signals then understanding how to interpret the signs correctly becomes even more difficult.

I am not saying that auditors should ignore the basic intuitive feelings that they encounter. We all can feel whether somebody is angry, unnaturally subdued and so on from overall impressions. These are natural human communication skills and certainly can be taken into account during an interview. Individual signs and strict interpretation of them, though, should be left to experts.

OBSERVATION

Traditionally, audit training and instruction concentrated on the interview, with attendant examination of documentation, files, records and examples. My own courses originally opened with an explanation of these two elements as the foundation pillars of any quality audit. In fact, though, using one's eyes to look around has often been a part of quality auditing in engineering and manufacturing environments. It is also becoming more important in the moves towards looking at improvement, plans and actions rather than simple compliance with a documented procedure and instruction manual.

Auditors should always take the time and trouble to look around them during the examination phase, and possibly during the preparation phase too if there is a chance to visit the area (such as during a certification initial visit). As mentioned, this is already accepted practice in manufacturing areas where a group of materials seen on the line or in storage can be investigated for identification, inspection and test status, protection and handling and so on. These opportunities are also used to look for measurement instruments which need to be investigated, practices which could damage the product and suitable records for non-conforming product or free-issue items belonging to the customer. A similar approach can be taken in warehouses and other storage locations where auditors can look for identification, protection, shelf life, product condition and matching stock records.

It is not necessary to wait, however, until something directly relating to ISO 9001 requirements or that we remember from reading procedure documents hits the eye. Auditors should also be looking around and asking about anything interesting or unusual that occurs to them. Questions like 'What is that man doing over there?' or 'What does that machine do?' are entirely valid and may start a line of enquiry that would never have been uncovered simply by conducting the standard interview.

A good approach is also to ask about places that you have not been taken to. External auditors may find that this leads to them occasionally being shown the inside of broom cupboards and empty rooms, but it can produce results. As a consultant I once ignored a cabin on the edge of a dump-truck sales yard; if I thought of it at all I suppose I believed it to be where the fitters made their tea or changed their clothes – the assessor did think to ask and found that it was a storage space for tools, many of which should have been tested and calibrated but had not been because nobody had asked about them. Even internal auditors can ask to see into certain rooms or buildings; they are likely to already know what is in there but they can verify their knowledge and may occasionally be surprised at what has been tucked in there out of the way, or what activities have been moved in there as an overspill from the usual location.

This can even be done in offices. I like to look around and see what is written on the spines of files on shelves or desks. It is amazing how many people have files labelled 'quality' somewhere close by. I always ask what is in them; sometimes it is nothing interesting but on other occasions they have contained records of improvement meetings or action plans which have yielded plenty of topics for further digging. I once found a completely new undocumented activity which was poorly understood by everyone expect the one person dealing with it, simply by asking why the interviewee had a box file on her desk with the name of one of the company's major customers on it.

Do not be dismayed if often when you ask to see something it is a waste of time (cupboards full of safety hats or drawers containing nothing but old trade magazines), because every now and then it will produce something that is worth the persistence. Remember not to pull open doors, cupboards and drawers yourself but always ask those to whom they belong if they would mind your looking inside. And never ask people about their desk drawers, unless they tell you specifically that they keep something important there, because they will only contain personal things such as car keys, lunch, newspapers and such like. The interviewee could be embarrassed by your seeing some highly personal articles such as medicines, pay slips, disciplinary letters and so on.

ANALYSIS

We have already dealt with analysis of the audit programme by the coordinator and how this may be reported within the audited or auditing organization. Some analysis is done, however, by the audit team before the audit programme co-ordinator ever comes to hear of the findings. This is carried out after the examination phase is complete and before the closing meeting.

Basic analysis involves simply deciding what is to be said to the auditees and how to categorize the findings. There are a few other things that the auditors may also wish to consider before the verbal reporting session:

○ If there are a number of actions required relating to a specific topic or an individual section, then the team may wish to identify this and mention them as being related when discussing the findings with the auditee management.

○ Some actions to be taken may only impact the department, project or process looked at, whereas others may affect the wider organization; this must be considered by the audit team since it will, in turn, affect how action is initiated.

○ The team must think about whether the issue is going to be difficult for the head of the area or organization to address. If so, then it would be a good idea to have some idea of how it can be tackled before raising it. Certification assessors should, strictly speaking, not do this but can mention how they have seen it addressed elsewhere.

AUDIT COLLATERAL

Although it does not, strictly speaking, affect the techniques used in an audit, the collateral provided by the audit programme coordination function has a great impact on the methods used within quality audits. This collateral is usually documentation of one form or another. Auditors must, of course, be provided with the forms that they should complete and the appropriate report templates, where they exist, but they may also require the following:

○ Defined procedures on how to plan and conduct the audit, run meetings, raise findings, write reports and follow up actions
○ Checklists for meetings and audit coverage
○ Rules for recommendations (supplier approval, certification, etc.)
○ Codes of practice
○ Rules for retention of records other than those embodied in the reports
○ Answers to frequently asked questions
○ Information sheets for auditees
○ Complaint and arbitration rules
○ Business sector interoperation guides
○ Standards, rules and regulations
○ Guidelines on what to do when things go wrong.

In Chapter 7 we discussed the fact that collateral needs to be collected by the planner for use by the audit team. Before this can happen the collateral must be created by the audit programme management. This can be a sizeable task and its scale should not be underestimated. In practice, much of the collateral will be generated as the audit system matures and created as the appropriate experience is gained or the need identified.

SUMMARY

○   Every business activity has associated methods and techniques which lead to success; the same is true of quality auditing.

○   Auditing is not a game, though, and requires us to think carefully about the needs of the business.

○   Many of the skills needed for auditing are the same as used elsewhere in business, put into a standard audit framework.

○   Audit teams must be aware of using their time well, and avoid time-wasting by themselves or the auditees.

○   Constantly referring to a problem found is unproductive.

○   Time should be managed to cover the proposed scope within the given period, but sometimes you have to recognize that you have run out of time and report on what you have covered.

○   Open questions that are easy to understand are the auditor's most powerful tool.

○   Listen to the answers to your questions, employing active listening techniques where you can.

○   Other than at the intuitive level, taking account of body language signs without expert knowledge can be dangerous.

○   Much information can be gathered by simply looking around and asking questions about what you see.

○   Auditors must be sure of what they intend to say, and why before going to the closing meeting.

○   Audit teams should be provided with a range of materials and collateral to aid their work and to ensure consistency of approach and interpretation.

13

PRODUCT AND PROCESS AUDITS

❖

MANAGEMENT, PRODUCT AND PROCESS AUDITS

When the concept of quality auditing was first introduced it was almost universally described as management auditing. Certainly it grew from the idea of general operational auditing which, although it had its origins in financial auditing and often leaned heavily towards financial elements of the business, was aimed at examining how the business was managed.

Today the majority of quality audits are based on this principle. They are thought of as looking at how work is planned, controlled and verified, without actually looking at the work itself. Thus most training courses make two particular points:

○   Quality audits are not about checking the work itself, since this is *inspection*, which is different.

○   Standing and watching somebody do their work is not productive because it only examines the technicalities of the job itself, does not look at any management aspects, takes a lot of time, produces dubious results since the personnel involved know they are being watched and will behave accordingly, and may be impossible to do effectively since independent auditors are unlikely to have enough technical understanding to appreciate every little detail (this is not always true, but there are certainly a large number of cases where it applies).

There is much talk today, though, of process auditing. The problem with this is understanding what it means. For many, it is only about looking at an activity instead of a function, or performing conventional audits in process-based organizations. It thus remains essentially a management audit. A true process audit looks at how the process itself works, rather than the management surrounding it. This

241

is different to how most quality audits operate, so requires a different set of techniques. Similarly, product audits examine the product structure in detail and also require their own sets of rules and skills.

It is interesting to note that ISO 9001:2000 does not specifically require product and process audits to be regularly programmed, but does expect that management review will consider whether there is a need for any such audits to be carried out. I suspect that many organizations will decide to ignore this in the same way as they ignored the identification of the need for statistical techniques in previous versions, but it is now a requirement. This means that we will see the growth of these types of audit, even if they are not universally employed.

To avoid having to keep using the cumbersome phrase 'process or product audits', I shall discuss below how we conduct process audits, with a section at the end of the chapter describing what is different for a product audit.

WHY CONDUCT PROCESS AUDITS?

Process audits are conducted to confirm that any process is being operated in ways which represent technical best practice, are efficient, are capable of supplying conforming products or services and take account of any risks and pitfalls. Although much of this is aimed at meeting basic customer satisfaction and thus may be part of any audit programme, in practice process audits are typically carried out to identify improvements or squeeze a little more out of quality performance. With this in mind, it is unlikely that process audits will ever become a standard practice in third party certification assessments. Internal auditors may perform such audits as part of improvement drives or fault reduction programmes; customer auditors may carry them out if the supplied product or service is critical and cannot be verified adequately at later stages or is simply an area for potential cooperative improvement.

PLANNING THE PROCESS AUDIT

Scheduling is unlikely to be on a routine basis, for reasons already discussed. Another factor is that process audits will often represent a thorough analysis of a process and potential improvements. Since a process audit is less of a sampling exercise than a management audit, conducting them again in the near future on the same process will probably reveal nothing new. Thus process audits are likely to be instigated as a result of identification of a need. This could be for one of the following reasons:

O   A new process has been created (e.g. for a new customer contract, or when a new piece of capital equipment is acquired).

○   There have been major changes to an existing process.
○   Other processes which directly interface to the one in question have been newly introduced or subject to major change.
○   There are concerns about the effectiveness of the process (e.g. it seems to have resulted in excessive scrap or customer complaints).

This is why ISO 9001 now suggests that the need for process audits may be identified at management review.

THE PROCESS AUDITOR

Once you have identified that a process audit is to be carried out, you need to appoint the investigation team. As with any other type of audit, the team can be just one person or several, depending upon the size, nature and scope of the task in hand. However large the team is, each auditor needs to be selected with care. They should, of course, be suitably trained and experienced in the technique of carrying out audits. Unlike most other audits, though, process auditors need to have a detailed technical understanding of what they are investigating. This is because they will be expected to specifically analyse each process step and determine whether it is the best approach to managing that process; this is impossible if they do not understand what the process step does or its place in the scheme as a whole.

This may mean that the ideal of auditor independence will have to be put aside in some organizations to allow an adequately detailed process audit to take place. The need to have auditors able to make specific recommendations in relation to the technicalities of a process has other implications, too. It implies that the auditor must have enough credibility and confidence to be able to perform detailed analyses with the cooperation of personnel involved and ensure that the analyses and resultant recommendations are taken seriously. If the process audit is to be carried out internally, for example (the most common form of process audit since they are aimed at improvement rather than compliance), then the usual approach of simply asking for volunteers from amongst all levels of staff and training each one to be an internal auditor may not be enough; process auditors will have to be carefully selected for their technical and interpersonal skills.

PREPARATION

Once you have found the right auditor(s), the next step is to understand the scope of the audit. Most importantly, you should define the system boundaries for the process. Although there might be a general agreement as to what the process is, auditing can be made unnecessarily difficult if you do not appreciate, for purposes of this audit at least, exactly where the process begins and ends, and which ancillary operations are considered to lie within the process and which lie outside its limits.

Then the preparation for the audit itself can begin. In principle, this is the same for any other audit, in that its purpose is to ensure that we fully understand what goes on. The main difference, though, is that the process audit requires a detailed technical map of exactly how the process works. A common way of achieving this is to create a process or system diagram. At its simplest level this is simply a flow chart of the steps involved. To conduct a true process audit, though, requires more sophistication than simply creating a flow chart.

When I perform a process audit, I typically start by producing a system diagram similar to the one in Figure 13.1. This shows a key manufacturing process for a cable factory where I used to work. It shows the very first process in cable manufacture where a number of steel wires are wound together to form a strong core (more flexible than a solid steel core yet still very strong) and a copper tape is then folded over the wires into a circle, with the seam electrically welded to create a continuous tube (a thin layer of copper is all that is needed for high frequency transmission owing to something called 'the skin effect'). Once I have the basic diagram, I then re-draw it to fill in the details and make it more comprehensive, including sub-elements of each step and noting intermediate measurements, addition of materials such as lubricants and so on. Once I am happy with the complete map, I then add to it further details, depending upon what I am particularly looking for during the audit. These could include every measurement point (including the use of go/no-go gauges); energy injection, usage and wastage; tolerance ranges (dimensions, times, etc.); durations; material and product consumption and wastage points; places where there is human intervention or decision; or material inputs and outputs as shown on the example below. It may be possible to use the diagram to analyse every aspect of the process under consideration, but in practice this will probably make it unwieldy. If there are several objectives for the audit then it may be best to use a number of different system diagrams, each defining a different aspect.

Another useful part of preparation is to gain some general familiarization with the process itself. If the audit is internal then there should not be a problem since it is probably well known and understood already. If the auditor is not someone who regularly works or interfaces with the process (such as a customer auditor or external consultant) then the auditor needs to gain a general 'feel' for it before the start of the audit itself. A good way of doing this is to go and look at it. This means visiting the area where the process takes place (the shop floor, the kitchen, the workshop, the sales counter, the print room, etc.) or even going out with an operative if it is a mobile service. In fact it is an excellent idea to do this before the desktop preparation if at all possible. Spend enough time in the area to see the whole process operate at least once, if you can. This will help to make sense of any analyses that the rest of the preparation involves.

The next step is to collect as much data as possible about the functioning of the process. This will include performance reports, quality reports, financial data, productivity figures, scrap rates, productivity calculations, consumption analyses,

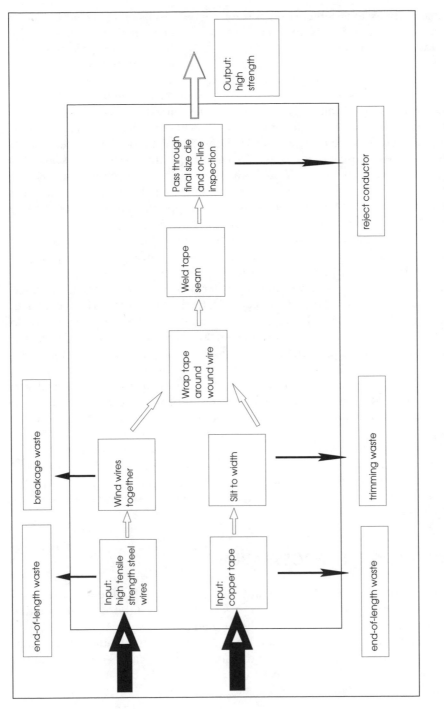

FIGURE 13.1   Process system diagram: making inner cable conductor

regulatory submissions, target comparisons, survey results or any other source of data that is available. This is not a simple task. It is unlikely that the data will be ready and waiting in one place simply for you to pick up a file or view on screen. It will take careful and tenacious rooting to dig out what information exists. You will be surprised exactly how much there is once you start to look.

This raises an interesting point, that the organization as a whole must be aware that the process audit is taking place, who is conducting it and why. If people suspect that it is a witch-hunt or that there is some sort of certification at stake here, they are unlikely to be helpful. Financial information, in particular, is often hard to winkle out unless those looking after it are certain that the auditor is authorized to see it and nothing to their disadvantage will result from it. If not managed properly this can be a problem even for internal auditors, let alone the difficulties that a customer auditor may face. If there is any doubt, agreement of a code of practice acceptable to all parties to the audit can be a great help.

From this data, the audit team can begin to add numbers to the diagrams that have been prepared to help indicate exactly where the strong and weak points of the process lie and what efficiencies are seen. These numbers can also be compared with targets and objectives and any other performance aims (e.g. accepted industry performance levels). As far as possible, the numbers should be reconciled. For example, the total mass of material input to a process should equate exactly to the mass of material output from a process (including waste, residue and scrap). If the numbers do not add up then there is obviously some data missing or incorrect; this will lead the auditors to further investigation during the audit examination itself. Finally, the preparation should involve the creation of a standard checklist in the same way that a management auditor would prepare. This is generated from looking at the steps in the process, plus the controls and interfaces that surround it and any associated documented control systems. The questions should, as always, not be a script but a reminder of any specific points that need to be addressed by the auditor, produced by looking through each step of the process and considering what things common sense would tell us should be explored.

Armed with this comprehensive set of information and questions, the examination can begin.

CONDUCTING THE PROCESS AUDIT

The usual introduction needs to be made. Since there is little difference between introductions and opening meetings in process audits and those in other audits we do not particularly need to discuss them again here.

The audit then includes some interviewing, just as with a management audit. After all, this is the only way of discovering information which is not contained in any documented data. The majority of the audit, though, consists of examining the actual operation of the process in detail.

If the process is one that can be stopped and restarted at will (for example strip down and reassembly of an engine, or any manual construction activity) then this makes the audit much simpler. The auditor can ask the operator to stop and explain what is going on, measurements and readings can be taken and it may even be possible to repeat the process step, perhaps even altering the process conditions slightly to see what happens. This is lengthy and time-consuming but can provide enormous amounts of information. Unfortunately, though, this is not possible with most processes:

O   A continuous production line cannot be stopped because it will disrupt output and may, depending upon the process, create scrap or defective product.

O   A process in which the customer is directly involved cannot be stopped since it will mean that the customer has not been properly served (for example any front end retail process).

O   Time-critical processes cannot be stopped (for example heat treatment or injection moulding).

There is also a danger if the process is continually stopped and started at the auditor's request that it becomes more like a demonstration than a true audit. This defeats the object since the auditor only sees what the operator wants him or her to see.

Even if it is not possible, or desirable in the particular circumstances, to stop a process and allow full examination before moving on to the next stage, the auditor should study the process stage by stage. In a continuous process, for example like the cable central conductor manufacture described earlier in this chapter, the first step in the process can be studied and its variations watched until it is fully understood and sufficient data has been gathered before moving on.

The auditor then continues this way through the whole process, gathering detailed information about the controls, measurements, consumption and error rates from each step. Where there are different paths for a process (if this happens, do this, otherwise do that) then each needs to be followed to its conclusion. If the process has multiple decision or action points, then the audit team may decide to select only certain paths to keep the audit to a practical size and degree of complexity.

The other aspect to conducting a process audit is data gathering. Although we have already discussed this as part of preparation, it forms an element of the actual investigation as well. The missing numbers from the system diagrams created earlier (failure rates, yield, dimensions, consumption, etc.) should be identified during the investigation. This can be done from recorded data available from the process management team itself or, if not available, may have to be taken as measurements during the audit. In extreme cases, where data is not measured and is not available, the auditors may have to take the measurements themselves, or at least arrange for them to be taken.

Thus the boundaries between audit preparation and audit investigation are blurred in this case and some of the same activities will be carried out in both. Another result of this varied means of investigation is that audit timing cannot be easily predicted or controlled. Audits may even have to be halted while measurements are awaited or until process conditions move on to the state that you wish to investigate. It also means that, unlike most management audits, you cannot restrict your investigation to a limited number of people; you may well have to visit, or seek the services of, another department that holds or can collect the data that you require.

CONCLUSIONS AND FINDINGS

Ultimately the audit team will have fully investigated the process, understand what goes on at every step and how it interfaces with other steps, how well the process operates, what the measurements and ranges are and where failures can and do occur. All of this will require further study, consideration and analysis before any conclusions can be drawn. This will typically mean some time away from the audit itself and careful thought, which could include a realization that not enough information is available and a demand for further investigation.

The implications of this are that you cannot follow the conventional rules of pointing out problems to auditees then and there, since you will probably not know they are problems until later, and of holding a feedback meeting very soon after completion of the investigation. There should still be a feedback meeting, but it may have to be several days after the audit has been completed (which may itself have taken some considerable time).

The analysis of findings should determine whether there is anything in the process which:

O   results in incompatibility between steps or interfaces;
O   causes delay;
O   uses incorrect, insufficient or faulty equipment;
O   is not being managed according to definitions of best practice;
O   is producing lower yields or higher failure rates than desired;
O   is inadequately measured and monitored;
O   creates waste or effluent;
O   contains unnecessary steps;
O   has excessive variation;
O   contains anything else that the auditor feels could be done better.

Each of these should then result in something which the auditor recommends should be changed or improved.

Some of these findings may well represent direct non-compliances against defined rules and practices. For example, if an electronic instrument on a production line is found to be not working, then this is not compliant with the process design. If an operator is failing to take readings at correct intervals, thus making appropriate adjustments impossible, this is not compliant with process operation requirements. These findings should be reported as any other audit non-compliance. That is, a corrective action form needs to be completed, the immediate problem must be fixed and suitable corrective action taken (investigation, action to prevent recurrence and monitoring of effectiveness).

Just as we found happens on many internal management audits, and almost as often with customer audits, many of the findings do not represent a failure to comply, but are things identified by the audit team as opportunities for improvement in customer service, yield, effectiveness or efficiency. The difference with a true process audit, though, is that the findings are being made by a recognized technical expert and thus carry much greater weight than observations made in any other audit.

Owing to the level of detail explored during the investigation, and the particular technical understanding of the auditors, it is also likely that findings will be much more specific than in a management audit. A typical management audit observation might be:

> It is suggested that the number of approval signatures required for F72 authorization is reduced from its current level of five since the process is currently slow and cumbersome.

Whereas a process audit recommendation might be:

> A 5 metre extension to the pressurised section of extrusion cooling trough, with a consistent extension to the non-pressurised section, would result in a potential 12 per cent increase in throughput speed for extrusion machine number 1. This would result in this machine alone being able to cope with production demands in all but the heaviest peaks, thus allowing extruder number 2 to be stood down in normal factory conditions and only brought into use when required, resulting in considerable energy savings and reduction of requirements for direct and indirect labour.

Or

> An on-line break monitor at the feed drum would enable breaks to be detected before the end disappears into the machine, enabling a splice to be quickly made and run on, rather than having to rewind the machine at each break.

The first of the two would still require further investigation and justification, such as the cost of making the extension and the pay-back period, but it is a much more weighty observation which cannot be dismissed lightly, as sometimes happens with management audit observations.

There is, of course, some overlap. The second of the two process audit observations could have been made by management auditors if they happened to see a break occur during the audit and thought about it, and if they knew that on-line break detection was possible. The point is, though, that management auditors will only identify such opportunities if chance enables the right circumstances to appear and the auditors happen to think about it at the time. Process auditors will seek out the circumstances and will know that they happen and will be familiar with technical approaches to the problem.

Since the above examples all relate to manufacturing industry, it is worth looking at a service example. Consider a parts sales desk or any other over-the-counter sales operation. If you are visiting a unit where the practice is for each sales person to go to the store room to collect the items requested by the customer, then this will cause delays by the people constantly walking backwards and forwards between the counter and the stores, and could result in nobody being at the counter when a customer comes in since they are all searching the stock shelves. Both process and management auditors may recommend that the system is changed to have some staff collecting stock while others deal with the customer at the counter. The difference is that management auditors might not notice that this happens and may not even look at the counter side of operations since they are more concerned with off-line interviews and examining records. Process auditors will carefully analyse every step and watch it happen; the possibility of all staff being away from the counter at the same time will be an obvious conclusion from looking at process variations and 'what-ifs'.

REPORTING AND ACTION

As we have already mentioned, there certainly should be a feedback session where the audit team explain the findings in detail to the people responsible for the process. This happens for the same reason as we hold a closing meeting in a management audit. As always, it should be held before the written report is circulated. It may, though, be necessary to prepare an outline report before holding the meeting. This is for two reasons:

1.   There needs to be a great deal of analysis and consideration before the findings can be reported and it will be difficult to report this analysis (or even remember what it contains) unless it has been written down.
2.   Usually a process audit has less reliance on corrective action forms – these may be used for strict non-compliances but many findings will require detailed explanation, justification and supporting information which cannot be noted on a simple form, thus a full written report is more appropriate.

The closing meeting will be held, in principle, along the same lines as a meeting for a management audit, but it is expected that there will be less gentle acceptance of the auditor's findings with vague promises to 'look into it' and a more technical discussion with outline agreement on the way forward arising as a direct result of the meeting. These actions can then be added to the report which will then be finalized and distributed.

As always, the final responsibility for any action rests with the people in charge of the process being audited. In this case, though, the audit team may also take a direct involvement in helping to complete any resultant actions. After all, they are seen as the technical experts and they have spent much effort in getting to grips with the detailed issues, perhaps now understanding some aspects better than the people working with the process (remember that the people responsible for operating a process are not always those who best understand its technical design aspects).

Process auditors, then, are often asked to form part of, or even to lead, the action team which puts the recommendations in place. This can be sensible for internal auditors or for external consultants, and can even be managed by customer auditors for those organizations who like to take an active role in helping their suppliers to improve. It cannot work with third party assessors or other independent auditors, which is another reason why this type of audit is rarely performed for certification reasons.

ACTION PLANNING

Action planning to address audit findings should follow the same model as with any other similar activity, that is actions should be allocated to a single person or team who has responsibility for making it happen, and timescales should be provided for completion. For large or complex action plans, some form of project management disciplines will need to be applied. And, of course, we should remember the plan-do-check-act philosophy. That is, when we have carefully planned an action and put it in place, we must monitor to see that it has been effective and act to correct any discrepancies. This may involve some form of re-audit to see that the changes have had the desired effect on the process (for example has splitting the counter sales force into stores and counter teams really improved service, or have we now made ourselves inflexible and made the jobs less interesting? If so we will need to make adjustments to make the new system work better).

PRODUCT AUDITS

Product audits are similar in general approach to process audits, except that they look at the physical output of a process rather than the operations of a process itself. They are thus only applicable to those organizations that produce physical products (there may be some debate about this since some service organizations conduct what they call product audits – these may actually be product audits if they are auditing physical items upon which they have conducted some transformation for their customers but are more usually process or customer satisfaction audits).

A product audit involves stripping the product down to its component parts and looking at each item in detail, including its dimensions, characteristics, performance and fit, in the same way that a process is stripped down to its component steps. The product as a whole is also looked at and its performance examined, including the interface between its physical parts and its various functions. Normally a number of product samples are chosen to work on to look for variation and its implications (note: the audit does not involve submitting the product samples to production test again, or even probably to type test).

As with a process audit, much of the audit involves data gathering in terms of yield, failure rates, output, field performance, reliability, variation, test data and so on. Some of this can be obtained in advance and some will be acquired during the examination of the products themselves.

Product audits can only be carried out by auditors who have a full technical understanding of how the product is made, how it works and how it is used by customers. In all other respects the general requirements for product audits are very similar to those for process audits. That is, they are highly detailed and technical, with the findings usually related more to product or process design improvements than to compliance with any management standards or procedures.

SUMMARY

O   Process and product audits have some things in common with management audits, but there are also variations.

O   They require audit teams with precise technical understanding of what they are examining.

O   Process audits involve detailed technical examination of the actual process.

O   Product audits usually involve a product strip-down.

O   Feedback and reporting may have to wait until the data gained during the audit is analysed.

O   Process and product auditors often play an active part in the subsequent actions to address issues raised.

PART THREE

THE FUTURE

❖

14

QUALITY SYSTEMS AND AUDITING – IMPLICATIONS FOR THE FUTURE

❖

QUALITY SYSTEMS – THE FUTURE

The only thing that we can be certain of in the future is that the way in which quality systems are defined and implemented will change. Modern business finds that it has to run as fast as it can just to keep up with the competition, so its support functions and initiatives have to develop and grow to keep up.

There are a number of possibilities that occur to me when trying to foresee what will happen to the management of quality. It is likely that for the first decade or two of the twenty-first century the development of quality systems will be inextricably linked to the future of the ISO 9000 family. ISO 9001 certification is so widespread that it is the first thing that anybody thinks of when the word 'quality' is mentioned and there are some people who are unaware that any other quality programmes exist. Beyond this, who knows? The position in the second decade of the twenty-first century is a decent forward horizon for our speculation.

QUALITY SYSTEMS – GENERAL

It is impossible to believe that the idea of a planned, controlled and coordinated approach to the management of quality will fall out of favour. No matter how much some people dislike ISO 9001, everybody recognizes that a consistent approach, taking care to cure and prevent errors, is important. Whilst there will always be some individuals and organizations who believe their own approach is best, the majority will follow accepted good practice and adopt recognized quality management systems. Of course, even those who follow their own direction will still have a quality system, it may just not be as formal as others or based upon any recognized standard.

So, if quality systems are here to stay, then so are formal definitions of how a system should perform. Even where there is no official recognition of a standard programme, people will seek one to satisfy their need for structure. As a result the most popular consultancy TQM programmes are those based upon a defined, standard approach.

We can conclude, then, that quality management systems and standards which define them will be here for some time. This is not to say that the standard will always be ISO 9001, or even that any future standard will have similar requirements. Investors in People, for example, is a recognized UK standard for employee awareness and development, an integral part of any quality system, which requires no documentation other than a business plan and thus differs substantially from the conventional quality approach.

ISO 9000 CERTIFICATION

I am often asked whether the next major step in enforcement of quality certification will take place: for governments or other regulatory agencies to insist upon it as a prerequisite to conducting business (in the same way that incorporated companies have to be formally registered and have their accounts audited). Whilst none of us can predict with absolute certainty what individual national administrations might do, I think that this is extremely unlikely. It is filled with too many practical and commercial problems. The 'push' for adopting ISO 9001 will always come from those organizations who see it as being a good thing and see advantages in encouraging their suppliers to take it up, just as it has always done.

The next big question for many people concerned with the subject is whether or not ISO 9001, and in particular independent quality management certification, is here to stay. After all, other management initiatives and styles reported as being the answer to good practice have been welcomed on a wide scale but have quickly fallen into decline. Strategic planning is one example, where the Boston Consulting Group model of star–cash cow–dog–doubt is now taught as being a way that companies *used* to look at things. Another more recent example is business process reengineering, which fell from grace almost as quickly as it rose to stardom (the quick rise was due to a few real successes gained using the associated tools, but it crumbled owing to the lack of real intellectual foundation to the models involved). On the other hand, the more closely related philosophy of total quality management has shown surprising longevity. Although most programmes are no longer known by that name, the basic tools and philosophies are still being widely employed in every type of industry and agency. In some ways ISO 9000 has a better chance of sticking around than TQM because it is a fixed standard with a huge industry created to support it, and international agreement on exactly how it should be maintained.

ISO 9001 certification is only popular because of the certificate and logo that come with it. If the need for an independent certificate, or the apparent business credibility that goes with it, becomes unpopular then ISO 9001 will also fall from grace. Already organizations that do not see independent certification as being of great benefit or feel that they have grown beyond it are seeking alternative frameworks upon which to base their programmes. But there is such a large international industry based around certification it is hard to see how it can suddenly become unpopular.

Taking all of this into account, my guess is that the future of ISO 9000 and its associated standards will develop in one of two ways. Either the world will become bored with it and registrations will be dropped, until it gradually fades and disappears like other management fashions, or it will grow to the point where it becomes 'normal'. In fact, in the UK, this latter has almost occurred already, and in most industry sectors it is expected that if your company has more than a few people and is more than 2 or 3 years old then you should have an ISO 9001 certificate. Indeed it is so 'normal' that some very small companies (employing only one or two full-time staff) seek a certificate simply to avoid having to explain why it does not really apply to them. If I had to make a wager, I would say that quality management standards certification is here to stay for at least the horizon that we are considering. The only difference we will see is that it will gradually become less of a talking point and more ordinary, just like the conventional annual financial audit of accounts.

ISO 9001 STANDARD

If quality systems certification is here to stay then it follows that the ISO 9001 standard also has a future. After all, there must be something to certify against.

There is, of course, a possibility that ISO 9001 will be replaced by something else. There are, already, other well known and popular systems such as the European Business Excellence Model, the Malcolm Baldridge Quality Award or the Dubai Quality Award. These are awards given to a strictly limited number of organizations per year and most businesses adopting them do so for the direct commercial benefits of improved performance rather than the hope of the badge on the wall. If certification were to lose its popularity, though, then these models may certainly replace ISO 9001 since they are seen as more sophisticated.

What is more likely, I suspect, is that certification will remain but that ISO 9001 will move closer to the requirements of standards such as the Business Excellence Model. We can already see a hint of this in ISO 9001:2000 and it foretells greater convergence in the future. Hence we can probably expect to see results-oriented measures creeping into the ISO 9000 family in future updates, moving towards a more comprehensive approach than we are used to today. The difficulty with this could be its validity as a universal certification model because the implication is that poor results could jeopardize granting of the certificate. This is a total departure from the current philosophy and may be a step too far for industry to take.

INTEGRATED SYSTEMS

I have already mentioned that the idea of integrated management systems, with integrated certification, is a popular talking point amongst quality professionals (less so in environmental and health and safety circles, interestingly). The explanations of the reasons behind the developments of ISO 9001:2000 as given in the forewords to the drafts also include a strong commitment to a commonality of approach with ISO 14001 (the environmental management system certification standard). It has also been stated by the standards committees that it is hoped that organizations will be able to create company-wide systems where common elements (e.g. document control, training planning and recording, measurement equipment control) are only dealt with once and not duplicated.

Certainly this avoidance of duplication will be a strong theme for the near future. If we create completely separate procedures for quality and the environment, this is a clear acknowledgement that we see them as something apart from the main business, done only to achieve a certificate. If we adopt them as the way we do business, then we should not have entirely independent approaches to any one topic. The way that we control our measuring equipment, for example, should be the way that we want to control measuring equipment, not any other way, or described differently when talking to different assessors. Integration should also occur with any initiatives that we already have in place:

○   Internal operational audit departments should be able to coordinate with internal quality audit coordination to avoid duplication of effort.

○   Finance department analysis should not duplicate quality cost reporting by the quality manager.

○   Health and safety management should have integrated elements, similar to those shared between quality and environmental systems.

○   Policy, mission and goal statements on a variety of topics could be combined to give a single vision of the company's philosophy and approach.

○   IT strategies can relate directly to management system needs.

○   Supply chain management can emphasize smooth inter-organizational system interfaces.

What is less clear, however, is how the systems can be audited in an integrated way. Regimes that I have seen where an internal audit team is sent to evaluate both quality and environmental aspects of a whole department in a single audit have not given either subject the attention that they deserve. They require people with the skills, knowledge and experience of auditing for the appropriate objectives. Environmental auditing, in particular, requires sufficient knowledge of ecosystem issues and is even less about procedural compliance than modern quality auditing should be. It even requires a different mind-set. The common elements, as described above, need only be audited once but the operational aspects must be examined separately. The only way that I can see a combined audit working well is if the team comprises experts who investigate their own areas, in which case it becomes two (or more) audits conducted simultaneously, rather than a single audit. This will then only make sense for some types of external audit, such as supplier assessments, when we wish to have the entire thing over in a short period of time. It will become even less possible to conduct integrated audits with the same people as further systems, such as health and safety, fall under the common umbrella.

THE FUTURE OF QUALITY AUDITING

Exactly what will happen to quality auditing in the future will depend upon which type of auditing we are thinking about. For this reason I have dealt with the three main categories separately below.

THIRD PARTY ASSESSMENT

Third party assessment will remain as long as certification remains. If organizations continue to seek a certificate from a recognized body then this will always require a third party audit. I cannot see the system ever moving away from independent bodies to grant the certificate, going back to the bad old days where customers and others without complete impartiality conducted the examinations.

It is also unlikely that we will move away from allowing independent, profit-making companies to grant certificates. The alternative would be to move towards only permitting government agencies to carry out assessments, which is a step away from the current trend towards increased market liberalization. This liberal trend is accompanied by increased regulation of services, to ensure that market players in key positions play their role fairly and honestly. As a result we are likely to see greater international cooperation and regulation concerning the role of accreditation services, certification body operation and auditor qualification. We have already seen many moves in this direction and will surely see a greater level of integration as time passes.

One possible move might be to make it illegal to offer unaccredited certification, at least in those countries that have their own accreditation agency. This is more likely than insistence upon certification for all companies and would be easier to implement. It would also be a popular move with existing accredited bodies and with many quality professionals.

Third party techniques

Throughout this book I have emphasized the fact that certification assessors should only be looking for compliance. Any attempt at advice and consultancy on their part would be to diminish the process. Taking this viewpoint, there is little development of assessment techniques that can take place in the future. As long as the auditors understand in detail the requirements of the certification standard and how they are to be applied to the particular industry then there is little else to ask for. Perhaps the only change that we could expect would be developments to improve consistency of interpretation between different certification companies and different auditors.

The new emphasis of ISO 9001:2000, however, does change this slightly. Now that we are looking at continuous improvement and action plans leading towards achievement of objectives, this takes us away from the old idea of direct compliance against specifications and procedure documents. We will, then, begin to see assessors who start to make greater judgements about whether objectives fit policies, actions and procedures relate to objectives and whether improvement actions have been correctly targeted. If this is to develop adequately it will require more attention to both auditor training and competence and the amount of time and effort that assessors devote to their investigations. If management come to feel that the strategy and achievement of their organization is being questioned by someone who barely understands what they are doing and has spent no more than six hours or so trying to cover everything, they are unlikely to look favourably on the whole process. It may be that assessors have to become more focused on particular types of organization that they are qualified to assess. It is possible that they will also have to increase the duration of their audits, or concentrate only on specific aspects at each one, hoping to cover the whole gamut over the space of several visits. It is hard to see how this can be managed whilst certifying that the entire quality system appears to be operational, without increasing audit duration and frequency.

I have not yet seen any evidence of this line of thinking from certification companies. Indeed most assessors probably feel that they are already equipped to fulfil this role; the new approach, to them, is only making full use of their existing talents. How this works in practice, though, is yet to be seen and certification bodies will have to handle the development of auditing sensitively and professionally to avoid discrediting the entire ISO 9001 certification business.

SUPPLIER AUDITING

There are two main paths that are most likely for second party audits, both of which see a continuing integration with ISO 9001 and similar standards.

First, we should see that as the certification standard becomes more rigorous in terms of improvement, objectives and customer satisfaction, audits that customers perform on their suppliers will reduce in extent and scale. If we believe that independent certification is proving the capability of the supplier in general, then we will only need to conduct a technical examination of its operations. Although I do not see this type of audit disappearing as a result of increased standards coverage, they will certainly become smaller and fewer.

On the other hand, there are currently large numbers of organizations, especially medium and small enterprises, which do not carry out any formal evaluation of their suppliers at all. Many of these go no further than sending out a basic questionnaire simply to keep the external assessor happy. As the consciousness of good quality management increases and we see how important the entire supply chain is to our own customer, then we are all likely to pay more attention to how our suppliers perform. This is likely to result in more organizations commencing to audit their suppliers in some fashion. The modern phenomenon of the virtual organization, and the continued growth of outsourcing, will enhance this trend as our suppliers become increasingly tied up with the way that we serve our customers. In such circumstances, ensuring that our suppliers are 'on the ball' will be more important than ever.

Thus we may see a reduction in number and scope of audits from larger customers but an increase from smaller ones. Since there are many more small companies out there than big ones, this does make me fear that we could be in for an explosion of audits. We will need to watch out for this since receiving audits is time-consuming and disruptive to work flow. Organizations will need to be encouraged to audit only those suppliers who are critical to their business and to limit those audits to the elements that really cannot be verified in any other fashion. Technical product requirements, for example, could be verified by evidence from some other external certification schemes, such as product marking, or by type approval of initial and regular samples.

The actual techniques of supplier audits are unlikely to alter significantly. They already are highly specific and prescriptive, which is just the way that they will serve customers best in the future. There is little chance that they will begin to grow more detached and objective since that role is already being performed by third party certification and no company likes to duplicate effort. The only reason that supplier auditing may move towards looking generally at outline system establishment and maintenance is if some unforeseen future event or development causes the demise of independent quality certification.

INTERNAL AUDITING

The future development of internal auditing is, perhaps, the most interesting of all three. The first thing to observe is that internal quality auditing is here to stay. It has been recognized as a primary tool for identifying development, progress and compliance within an organization. Many managers use it today as a way of identifying whether new initiatives really have taken hold, rather than just being talked about, regardless of whether it has anything to do with ISO 9001 or other certification regimes.

My own prediction is that, even if quality management certification were to gradually become unfashionable, the foothold that internal auditing has gained in industry will not be lost. Those responsible for the success of their business are recognizing its value and will continue to employ it as a management tool.

This is not to say that some organizations would not drop it. We are all aware that some internal audit programmes are conducted at a token level with no intention to make the best of them or to do anything other than enough to keep an ISO 9001 certificate. Those responsible for running such programmes will have no hesitation about stopping the audits if nobody is insisting upon them. However, the drop-out rate would not be 100 per cent and a very large proportion of oganizations would automatically continue the discipline as an essential part of running the business.

The clear appreciation of the benefits of internal auditing mean that its development and growth are also pretty much assured. Many organizations already are looking for tools and techniques which will increase the benefits from their internal audit programme and this is likely to continue. I hope that one or two things mentioned in this book may assist with that process. The fact that ISO 9001 now is taking a wider business perspective than basic proceduralization of processes will also reinforce this trend. Internal quality auditors will be expected to have a discussion with managers about the achievement of objectives and not just ask operators if they have filled in the correct form. The standard, then, will force changes and improvements in the way that internal audits are conducted.

Internal audit techniques

We have already discussed, at various points in the book, how internal auditing is often prompted, in the first place, by ISO 9001 certification but is very different in flavour to the certification assessment. The growing recognition of this, plus the new emphasis in ISO 9001:2000 will highlight and enhance this difference. Internal auditors will become more like internal consultants, looking for progress of the business towards strategic and tactical goals, maintaining some element of ISO 9001 compliance examination but reducing its emphasis from the high level often still seen today.

The gradual departure of internal audit emphasis from simply being a reduced version of the external assessment to a tool in its own right may well produce other changes. It is possible that standards, literature and training events for internal auditors will grow to the point where they clearly represent a different branch of the specialization to certification assessment. I certainly hope that the accepted practice of allowing those who have attended an external auditing course to carry out internal audits will cease; it gives entirely the wrong message and does not produce good internal audit teams.

The development of the emphasis and techniques of internal audits will undoubtedly require some development in the selection of those who perform them. The status of such people will grow and they will be chosen from amongst the brightest and best. It will become something that is seen as a firm career enhancer; a role that many aspire to and all hope to be able to occupy for at least some part of their climb up the corporate ladder.

I do not believe, though, that the future path for internal auditors lies in full-time, professional teams. It is likely that the nature of the beast will still require that the role is fulfilled on a part-time basis by employees who have other jobs, supplemented in some cases by members of the quality management function or by expert outsiders.

AUDITOR SKILLS DEVELOPMENT

Much of the way that auditor skills will require to develop is dependent upon the way that the audit programmes themselves grow, but there will be some common elements.

The prime driver of personal skills development for all audit types is likely to be the development of the ISO 9001 standard and its family. We are now seeing the first real move away from basic procedural compliance towards objectives, target setting and action programmes. Assessing these will require a different approach to the old style of auditing which concentrated highly on procedural documentation. This should come as a welcome relief to the younger generation of auditors who can quickly become tired of checking version numbers of manuals and whether forms have been dated, wondering how this really assesses business performance.

The fact that it does require a different approach, however, means that the auditors themselves will need to change. Training and company development programmes will need to breed auditors who are willing to, and capable of, carefully considering a programme of action and discussing with auditees how this can achieve overall goals. It will require a more cooperative approach than has often been used in the past. In many cases this will require more training than simply explaining to auditors what the standard requires, but also a refocusing of their basic methodology.

Certification assessors can only take this so far, of course. They may become involved in discussions of forward programmes to the extent that they become involved in decision making or providing personal input. In order for independent certification to work they will have to maintain their impartiality and independence. This could well be a difficult tightrope to walk as investigation involves improvement and correction of key business issues yet must stay slightly aloof. This is made worse by the desire of many certification assessors to 'add value' to the audit, as I have already mentioned. The danger is that companies will become disillusioned with the certification regime if assessors become too involved. If we effectively have to revisit our strategy meetings or programme reviews every time the assessor visits it may be a burden too much to bear, especially as companies already are expressing doubts about the heavy cost of increased audits and certification with the abundance of management initiatives being proposed. Assessors will have to be able to investigate deeply enough to confirm suitability of internal developments without overstepping the mark. Although this might sound simply to be an extension of what they already do, the reservations I have already expressed earlier in the book about assessability of some ISO 9001:2000 requirements will make the balance more difficult to attain. This will be even more difficult to manage well if future enhancements of ISO 9001 move even further towards business strategy and results analysis.

First and second party auditors, on the other hand, will not face this dilemma. As the standard, and its attendant audit requirements, moves closer to the core business issues at the heart of management, rather than being seen as on the periphery, audit teams can move their approach at the same speed, taking on a deeper role as quality standard requirements become indistinguishable from all aspects of good business practice and performance.

One of the main implications for this will be in the selection, training and development of auditors. To examine and support business strategy and results at all levels, auditors will have to become like internal consultants. This means that only the best and most respected employees will be able to occupy the roles, either for internal or supplier audits. Although most organizations do not currently pick idiots to be auditors, neither do they necessarily choose their stars. This will have to change if auditing is to be at the heart of an increasingly important quality management initiative.

Of course, all of this may simply be too much. We could find that organizations are just not willing to create and support an internal audit programme with this strategic philosophy. In that case they may be even less eager to develop a strong consultancy team to assist their suppliers. If the audit system does not develop strongly, however, then neither will the development of quality management systems; they are inextricably linked. If we try to stretch the boundaries of one without pulling the other along with it, then the system will snap, and the formal systems approach that we have seen for the last twenty years or more will fall out of favour.

AUTOMATION

Increased automation and computerization of business processes seems to be a phenomenon that is here to stay. Growing utilization of IT systems to manage the organization fits well with quality management concepts. ISO 9001 and similar models encourage consistency, reliability and the adoption of reliable methods. Information systems can achieve all of these; computer programs always produce the same output for the same input and force people to run their processes in standard ways. In fact I am always surprised by how little ISO 9001 implementation initiatives take account of information systems and how rarely IT managers see ISO 9001 as an ally. I see them as entirely compatible and complementary.

The problem with this concept is that, whilst computer solutions may make quality systems more reliable, auditing processes based on IT resources is far more difficult than auditing those founded on paper systems. Despite the prevalence of computers in all aspects of our daily lives, there remain many people whose eyes glaze over at their mention. Since auditors are drawn from the general population, there are many of them who are also uncomfortable with the use of IT and find it difficult to even use the language that information technology employs. Even those who have learnt to swim in the IT sea find it difficult to assess computer-based systems where the organization or area examined uses platforms or applications unfamiliar to the auditor. Whereas we can all grab a paper file and easily understand its structure and contents, we usually have to ask the auditee to bring up individual records for us on the screen, one by one, thereby limiting and slowing the whole audit process.

Futurists tell us that we will shortly see a departure from all computing being carried out by a powerful, large and easily interfaced desktop personal computer. The vision is that our daily lives will be augmented by a host of individual devices which inter-communicate but each perform individual tasks. These may be built into standard home and office items such as desk, refrigerators and even in our shoes! They will communicate with each other and perform several background tasks automatically, interfacing with us only when we are required to make some form of input. If this is so then it will become increasingly difficult to audit what is happening since the processes will be invisible to human beings.

At the moment our usual approach to heavy automation of processes is to perform a perfunctory check of the human interface aspects, understanding that often these will be more reliable than manual systems owing to the strictures of the computer programs in use. As the systems become more pervasive, more integrated and require less human interaction, we will not even be able to perform this basic level of examination. If we are not careful, quality auditing could be marginalized as it becomes only interested in secondary elements such as employee awareness and communication or infrequent processes such as the setting of corporate direction.

There are two ways that occur to me in which auditors can address this issue. The first is to pay significant attention to how IT systems are designed, selected, installed and implemented in an organization. If we know that those processes are suitable, then it should follow that the operation of the final IT processes are also suitable. In fact this should be happening now and, as I have said, I find it hard to understand why so many assessors pay it such little attention. Certainly all auditors should already be including an assessment of how major IT systems are managed in their programmes. As the use of such systems increases and burrows deeper into the fundamental business processes, so should the auditor's investigation, reducing the study of the final activities accordingly where they are heavily automated.

The second is more radical but may represent a possible future off-shoot of the quality audit process. If the processes of a business are heavily dependent upon IT, yet the purpose of a quality audit is to prove the capability of a business process, then perhaps the audit should concentrate on proving the adequacy of the IT system. This could involve, as one option, a rigorous manual reliability evaluation of a program (applying a wide range of input combinations to confirm that the outputs remain sensible) within the context of its application to the particular business. In fact, though, this should be carried out by the organization or area adopting the software in conjunction with the software developers and is probably not an appropriate task for audit teams. An alternative way of confirming process capability may be to try the system using a dedicated IT audit system. It is not clear how such an approach could work in practice but it conjures a vision of the auditor sitting at a terminal and running an audit program which itself carries out a compliance and effectiveness verification of the operational program. There are no signs of any developments of this type at the moment but the idea may not be so far-fetched as it sounds. If, however, we are looking at the first decade or two of the twenty-first century then this sort of approach is probably beyond our reach.

In the foreseeable future, then, we will have to cope with assessing the heavy use of computer systems using traditional audit techniques. This must force managers of audit programmes of all types to establish tools and methods for studying computer control of processes. Auditors will then have to be coached in the use and interpretation of those methods, including an encouragement to spend time using them in direct proportion to their use within the examined quality management system.

SUMMARY

O   Business and industry is changing fast; audit techniques will have to develop equally quickly to stay relevant.

O   The adoption of formal quality management systems is well accepted and it is unlikely that opinions on this will change in the foreseeable future.

O   As long as ISO 9001 stays appropriate to business needs and is realistically interpreted it will continue to be the most popular model for quality management systems.

O   Independent ISO 9001 certification is probably also here to stay, as long as it also develops to meet business needs without trying to overstep its limitations.

O   The ISO 9001 standard itself is likely to move further away from basic documentation and verification requirements and more towards business development and improvements as we progress through further releases.

O   If independent certification remains popular then we will see increasing integration and overlap between various systems such as quality, environment, health and safety and employee development.

○ Auditing in general is probably well enough established to survive even if independent certification does not, although the third party assessor's role is, obviously, inextricably linked with the continued popularity of quality systems registration.

○ Audit techniques will have to grow in line with changes in emphasis in quality systems.

○ Businesses are already making heavy use of computer systems; auditors should be paying attention to how these are selected, tailored, commissioned, installed and maintained.

○ Increased automation will result in greater attention being paid to how IT systems are used and the possible rise of entirely new audit approaches.

INDEX

❖

Genba Kanri

The Disciplines of Real Leadership in the Workplace

Edward Handyside

Is manufacturing your business? Does the idea of cutting operating costs by 30% appeal to you? Would you like to know how the search for improvements in quality and productivity can be embedded into everyday routine?

Genba Kanri companies are the most productive and cost-effective in the world, according to the author of this remarkable book. Drawing on his experience with Nissan UK, Edward Handyside explains that, though the name is Japanese, in fact Genba Kanri is derived from older, Western traditions long neglected in their countries of origin. He shows how, by connecting 'people' concerns with the operational aspects of manufacturing, GK disciplines:

• make it easy to change production methods and systems
• replace 'management by remote control' with real leadership out on the shop floor
• help to promote and sustain continuous improvement
• reinforce the key role played by the first-line supervisor
• introduce 'the standard operation' (Japan's best kept manufacturing secret).

Handyside looks at the management practices required to enable GK disciplines to function, and in the process finds little place for some of Western management's favourites – among them suggestion schemes, re-engineering, hourly pay systems and self-managed work teams.

Find out what Genba Kanri could be doing for your company by reading this persuasive and practical book.

Gower

A Practical Guide to Business Process Re-Engineering

Mike Robson and Philip Ullah

Most managers will by now have some understanding of Business Process Re-Engineering and the immense benefits it is capable of bringing. Here at last is a detailed guide to realizing those benefits.

The authors begin with a warning to think carefully about whether the BPR approach is suitable for your particular organization. They go on to show how it can be planned and implemented in a systematic way. With the aid of examples and illustrations they take the reader through the various stages involved, introducing both the principles and the techniques that apply. Finally they explain how to ensure sustained improvement by managing the changes achieved.

Anyone responsible for improving business effectiveness will find the book a worthwhile investment.

Gower

Strategic Supply Chain Alignment

Best Practice in Supply Chain Management

Edited by John Gattorna

Supply chain performance will be a key indicator of overall corporate success into the next century. This book, edited by logistics and supply chain expert John Gattorna, and with international contributions, presents unpublished material on next generation thinking about the management of the supply chain. Based on the recently developed strategic alignment model it shows how external market dynamics, the company's strategic response, and internal capability must be aligned if competitive advantage is to be achieved.

Supply chain management is a strategic challenge demanding top level management attention. This book tackles the subject at that strategic level to help companies reposition their supply chains successfully. The book then offers the vital link between strategy setting and implementation, providing comprehensive coverage of the main areas of execution, and making it an essential compendium on all aspects of the subject. With case studies from major organizations from around the world, it is a 'must' read for anyone wishing to be at the forefront of international supply chain management thinking.

Strategic Supply Chain Alignment brings together for the first time the world's leading logistics professionals, management consultants and academics to offer their insights and experiences on the latest supply chain management techniques. This collection of previously unpublished material offers the reader a unique opportunity to identify the hot issues, discover emerging strategies and uncover key industry and market perspectives.

Gower